D0315870

Local childhoods, global issues

This book is part of the series *Childhood* published by The Policy Press in association with The Open University. The four books in the series are:

Understanding childhood: a cross-disciplinary approach (edited by Mary Jane Kehily)

ISBN 978-1-447-30580-4 (paperback)

ISBN 978-1-447-30927-7 (ebook)

Children and young people's cultural worlds (edited by Sara Bragg and Mary Jane Kehily)

ISBN 978-1-447-30582-8 (paperback)

ISBN 978-1-447-30925-3 (ebook)

Childhoods in context (edited by Alison Clark)

ISBN 978-1-447-30581-1 (paperback)

ISBN 978-1-447-30924-6 (ebook)

Local childhoods, global issues (edited by Heather Montgomery)

ISBN 978-1-447-30583-5 (paperback)

ISBN 978-1-447-30926-0 (ebook)

This publication forms part of the Open University module E212 Childhood. Details of this and other Open University modules can be obtained from the Student Registration and Enquiry Service, The Open University, PO Box 197, Milton Keynes, MK7 6BJ, United Kingdom (Tel. +44 (0845 300 60 90, email general-enquiries @open.ac.uk).

www.open.ac.uk

Local childhoods, global issues

Edited by Heather Montgomery

Published by
The Policy Press
University of Bristol
Fourth Floor, Beacon House
Queen's Road, Clifton
Bristol BS8 1QU
United Kingdom
www.policypress.co.uk

in association with
The Open University
Walton Hall
Milton Keynes MK7 6AA
United Kingdom

First published 2003. Second edition published 2013

Copyright © 2013 The Open University

All rights reserved. No part of this publication may be reproduced, stored in a retrieval system, transmitted or utilised in any form or by any means, electronic, mechanical, photocopying, recording or otherwise, without written permission from the publisher or a licence from the Copyright Licensing Agency Ltd. Details of such licences (for reprographic reproduction) may be obtained from the Copyright Licensing Agency Ltd, Saffron House, 6–10 Kirby Street, London, EC1N 8TS (www.cla.co.uk).

Edited and designed by The Open University.

Typeset by The Open University.

Printed in the United Kingdom by Bell & Bain Ltd, Glasgow.

British Library Cataloguing in Publication Data:
A catalogue record for this book is available from the British Library.

Library of Congress Cataloging-in-Publication Data

A catalog record for this book has been requested

ISBN 978-1-447-30583-5 (paperback)

ISBN 978-1-447-30926-0 (ebook)

2.1

Contents

Series preface

The books in this series provide an introduction to the study of childhood. They provide a cross-disciplinary and international perspective which develops theoretical knowledge about children and young people, both in the UK and overseas. They are core texts for the Open University module E212 *Childhood*. The series is designed for students working with or for children and young people, in a wide range of settings, and for those who have more general interests in the interdisciplinary field of childhood and youth studies.

The series aims to provide students with:

- the necessary concepts, theories, knowledge and skills base to understand the lives of children and young people

- relevant skills of critical analysis

- critical reflection on and analysis of practices affecting children and young people

- an understanding of the links between children's experiences on a global and local level

- an understanding of the analytical, research and conceptual skills needed to link theory, practice and experience.

The readings which accompany each chapter have been chosen to exemplify key points made in the chapters, often by exploring related data, or experiences and practices involving children in different parts of the world. The readings also represent an additional 'voice' or viewpoint on key themes or issues raised in the chapter.

The books include:

- **activities** to stimulate further understanding or analysis of the material

- **illustrations** to support the teaching material

- **summaries** of key teaching points at appropriate places in the chapter.

The other books in this series are:

Kehily, M. J. (ed) (2013) *Understanding Childhood: A Cross-disciplinary Approach*, Bristol, Policy Press/Milton Keynes, The Open University.

Bragg, S. and Kehily, M. J. (eds) (2013) *Children and Young People's Cultural Worlds*, Bristol, Policy Press/Milton Keynes, The Open University.

Clark, A. (ed) (2013) *Childhoods in Context*, Bristol, Policy Press/Milton Keynes, The Open University.

Professor Mary Jane Kehily

Series Editor

Contributors

Mary Jane Kehily

Mary Jane Kehily is Professor of Childhood and Youth Studies at The Open University, UK. She has a background in cultural studies and education, and research interests in gender and sexuality, narrative and identity and popular culture. She has published widely on these themes.

Heather Montgomery

Heather Montgomery is a Reader in the Anthropology of Childhood at The Open University, UK. She has carried out research with young sex workers in Thailand and written extensively on issues of children's rights, global childhoods and representations of childhood.

Catherine Panter-Brick

Catherine Panter-Brick is Professor of Anthropology, Health, and Global Affairs at Yale University. Her research in global health addresses issues of poverty, disease, malnutrition, social marginalisation, and armed conflict. Her work on youth has included research with street children, refugees, famine-stricken households, and war-affected communities in areas of conflict and humanitarian emergencies. She was awarded the Lucy Mair Medal by the Royal Anthropology Institute of Great Britain and Ireland; an award to honour excellence in the application of anthropology to the relief of poverty and distress, and to the active recognition of human dignity.

Martyn Hammersley

Martyn Hammersley is Professor of Education and Social Research at The Open University. His early research was in the sociology of education. Later work has been concerned with the methodological issues surrounding social and educational enquiry. These include objectivity, partisanship and bias, and the role of research in relation to policymaking and practice. More recently he has investigated ethical issues in social research and how the news media represent social science research findings.

Samantha Punch

Samantha Punch is a Senior Lecturer in Sociology at the School of Applied Social Science, the University of Stirling. She has conducted research on sibling relationships and birth order; rural childhoods in Bolivia; youth transitions and migration in Latin America; rural livelihoods in China, Vietnam and India; Scottish young people's problems; and children's food practices in residential care in Scotland.

Introduction

In the contemporary world children are a source of interest and concern as never before. From the wealthiest children of North America, Europe and Japan to the poorest children in the countries of sub-Saharan Africa and Asia, children's lives are of critical interest to the media, to governments and to international agencies – as well as to their own parents. This book examines why issues around childhood are so central to modern world politics and what particular areas of child welfare cause greatest concern. It also discusses the variety of children's experiences throughout the world, acknowledging the great differences between children and childhoods in different contexts. Gender, age, place in the birth order, ethnicity and religious background will all have impacts on children's experiences of childhood and warn us against over-generalisation. Despite these differences, however, there are similarities – and possible points of comparison – between different childhoods, and certain ways of understanding these links, so that, for example, the theme of inequality, at a global, national and familial level, features strongly in many such accounts.

In order to keep these distinctions and differences in mind, this book uses the terms 'minority' and 'majority' worlds throughout rather than the more old-fashioned 'developed' and 'developing' world. Using these terms reminds us that the majority of the world's population live in countries that are economically poor and have younger populations. Resources and wealth tend to be concentrated in a minority of countries in Europe, North America and Australasia which have ageing populations. Over 20 per cent of the population in minority-world countries are aged over 60 and just 17 per cent are under 14. This contrasts starkly with the majority of the world where, in parts of Africa and Asia, only 8 per cent are over 60 while 31 per cent are under 14. Thinking about the world in terms of minority/majority countries therefore invites a consideration of global inequality and the imbalance in power relations between these two worlds. This is reflected not only economically but also demographically in the gap between the ageing, white, minority world and the younger, non-white, majority world.

The rise of children's rights forms an important background to this book. Since the United Nations Convention on the Rights of the Child (UNCRC) came into force in 1989, children have become a significant area of concern for national and international agencies. Organisations such as UNICEF have argued that children's interests must be respected and promoted, and that they should get 'the first call' in the allocation of resources. Due to the almost universal ratification of the UNCRC, governments are now legally obliged to protect children's rights to the best of their ability. Yet, despite the good intentions, the prospects for many children in the world continue to be bleak. Around 7 million children under the age of five die every year, 600,000 million live in poverty, 129 million are underweight and 121 million are not in school. Many of their deaths are preventable and would not occur if families had access to adequate medical care, proper water supplies and sanitation. There are many thousands of child soldiers in the world, and many more children are forced out of their homes by poverty, war and social upheaval. Even in the wealthy minority-world countries, such as the USA or the UK, significant numbers of children live in poverty or suffer from racism and social exclusion.

In many ways, therefore, the plight of children in the world seems grim. The above statistics certainly make for depressing reading. However, there are some positive indicators and, as this book examines, children's own resources and coping strategies mean that few children are passive victims of fate, helplessly awaiting rescue by benevolent adults. Children's reactions to adversities and their agency in coping with them are central to this book, and children's voices feature prominently in many chapters. All the authors have had extensive experience of conducting first-hand research with children, interviewing them about their lives and listening to them tell their stories.

The concept of well-being is woven throughout these chapters. Well-being is concerned not just with children's physical health, but also with their emotional and psychological health. It encompasses children's ability to make friends, to participate fully in the social life of their community, to fulfil their potential and abilities, to access services and to realise the possibility of changing their own lives. Focusing on well-being allows the authors to look at the difficulties that children face even when they are wealthy and living in stable societies. Affluence can cause its own pressures and threats to well-being, just as effectively as hunger or ill-health.

Chapter 1, 'Interventions and ideologies', starts the book by examining how and why adults have intervened in children's lives. It looks at various policy interventions, starting with a historical perspective on 'child saving' before examining childhood and social policy in the late twentieth and early twenty-first centuries. It focuses on the ideologies behind various interventions, looking at the shift from individual philanthropy, to the rise of the welfare state, and through to the adoption of a children's rights agenda in the late twentieth century. It also analyses the changing relationships between families, children and the state, and the impact that these changes have had on children's lives.

The next three chapters look at the problems of poverty, ill-health and violence, which face children in all parts of the contemporary world. Although presented as separate topics, each chapter emphasises the ways in which these problems are interconnected. Chapter 2, 'Children, poverty and social inequality', starts by defining what is meant by poverty, focusing in particular on the differences between absolute and relative definitions of poverty. It then looks at the causes and impacts of poverty, in both the minority and the majority world, placing particular emphasis on social inequality and its impact in families, within countries and between countries. Chapter 3, 'Achieving health for children', discusses some of the major health issues for children, and the steps taken on their behalf to achieve good health and improve their well-being. It looks at critical issues of child nutrition – from food shortages in the majority world, to obesity in the minority world – and is equally concerned with physical and mental health. It ends by looking at some of the global and local success stories in improving children's health. Chapter 4, 'Children and violence', examines the many forms of violence that children encounter in their daily lives. It starts by problematising the concept of violence and the many ways in which the word is now used, before looking at the impacts of violence on children's lives. It turns then to different sites of violence: the home and domestic violence, as well as children's violence towards themselves in the form of self-harm; in schools, in particular the impacts of bullying and knife crime; and in armed conflict.

The chapters in this book show that children in both the minority and the majority worlds face a number of adversities and risks, and that adults have intervened in many different ways to ameliorate the negative impacts of some of these risks. Chapter 5, 'Resilience and well-being', looks at children's own reactions to these adversities. Children are not always vulnerable or passive victims even when faced with the most difficult circumstances, and sometimes they seem to thrive despite all the odds stacked against them. This chapter explores what resilience means and how the concept might be used to protect children, concentrating on the key mechanisms of resilience identified in both psychological and sociological research. The second half of the chapter takes a critical perspective on the concept of well-being, exploring why both well-being and resilience are contested – and somewhat slippery – ideas, and why they are so difficult to utilise in practice.

The final chapter of the book, Chapter 6, 'Research on childhood issues as social problems', reflects on the problems of using research on childhood issues in practice. Most researchers hope that, in studying topics such as poverty, ill-health or violence (or indeed resilience and well-being), their work will lead to practical interventions that improve children's lives. However, the relationship between research, social problems, policymaking and practice is not a simple one. What is, and what is not, treated as a high-priority social problem is a product of social, cultural and political processes, in which research can play a variety of roles. Much the same is true of the development of policies to deal with such problems. The chapter concludes this book by describing the various ways in which social research contributes to the identification and treatment of childhood problems, and discusses some of the considerations that must be taken into account when evaluating research findings and their implications for social problems and policy interventions. Finally, it sets out the different roles that researchers play in relation to children, and the contemporary shift from research 'on' children to that 'with', or even 'by', them.

To summarise, this book:

- looks at children's lives holistically; by drawing on the concept of well-being, the book examines children's welfare in its broadest possible way – covering all aspects of children's physical, emotional and psychological health and well-being
- emphasises diversity as well as similarity; it acknowledges that all childhoods are culturally and historically specific, and must be understood within their own social contexts, but that there are similarities between certain aspects of children's experiences which can be usefully compared and analysed
- analyses power relations; the book views children's experiences as occurring within unequal power relationships inside families, between regions, within countries or internationally
- critically examines children's rights; children's rights are taken as an essential basis for understanding contemporary childhoods and in formulating interventions to improve children's lives.

Many people helped in the preparation of this book and I would like to thank the following people at The Open University: Sara Bragg, Alison Clark, Grace Clifton, Martyn Hammersley and Mary Kellett who read drafts of various chapters and always provided timely and useful comments; and Maria Francis-Pitfield, Liz Camp and Lara Knight who handled so much of the administrative side. Mary Jane Kehily was the chair of the module this book is associated with and was a great source of inspiration and leadership, while David Messer, Head of the Centre for Childhood, Development and Learning, provided gentle guidance, sustained support and wise advice before, during and after the writing of this book. Professor Chris Philo (University of Glasgow), in his role as external assessor, was consistently prompt and helpful in his comments on chapters and gave very generously of his time. To all these people, I am very grateful.

Heather Montgomery,

The Open University, 2013

Chapter 1

Interventions and ideologies

Heather Montgomery

Contents

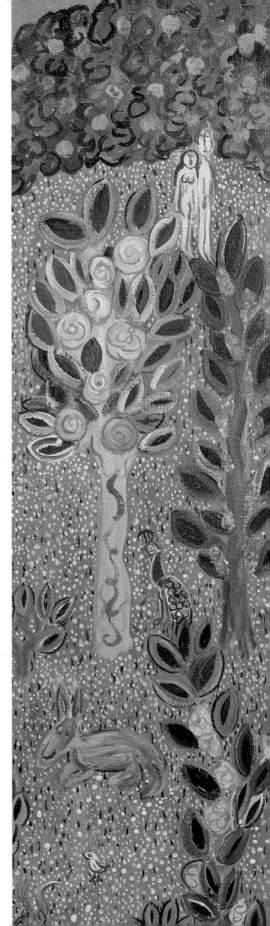

In this chapter, you will:

- learn about different ways of intervening in children's lives
- consider the link between how children are conceptualised and the policies put in place to improve their lives
- examine interventions in children's lives based on ideas of charitable rescue
- consider the different forms of welfare states in contemporary societies
- critically discuss children's rights.

1 Introduction

This book focuses on the various adversities facing children in the contemporary world. Before poverty, ill-health and violence are each considered in the following three chapters, this chapter will examine the various ways in which adults have intervened in children's lives and the ideologies behind such interventions. The term 'ideology' is a complex one but is used here to mean the system of ideas that form the basis of social, economic or political policy. Although the word is often used in a pejorative sense, implying dogmatic adherence to a certain world view or set of policies, it is used here simply to mean the philosophical basis on which interventions are based and to emphasise that all interventions have some ideological basis, even if they claim to be above politics.

Adults have, of course, always intervened in children's lives; at a very basic level by feeding them and keeping them safe, as well as more broadly through different forms of child-rearing, education and discipline, all of which can be seen as forms of intervention designed to help children grow up to be fully socialised adults. Parenting practices are not the focus of this chapter, however, even though they are critically important to individual children. Instead, this chapter will examine some examples of how social institutions such as charities, governments and NGOs have intervened in children's lives. It will look at three types of intervention and the rationale behind them: those based on individual charitable work; those based on ideas about social welfare and usually implemented by the state; and those which support children's rights and conceptualise children as active participants in society. Each form of intervention is multi-dimensional and they are not mutually exclusive, but each implies an ideology which says something about the perception of childhood and the responsibilities that adults have towards children.

2 Why intervene in children's lives?

Both adults and children are vulnerable to a range of adversities but many feel that children *as a group* should have special claims to protection and intervention in order to protect them from harm. There are many reasons for this – at a very simple level young children are highly dependent and most in need of resources. Young children cannot fend for themselves and adults have a moral duty to step in and protect those most at risk. Even older children are relatively powerless to act for themselves – and often legally prevented from doing so – and consequently adults must act to defend their best interests. Another argument for intervening in children's lives rests on their future potential and the idea that supporting children is an investment for the future. Investment implies a return and, using this reasoning, children are singled out for special protective measures because they are the productive adults of the future. More generally, they are the way in which society will replicate itself and therefore necessary for its continued existence. It might also be argued that intervening in children's, rather than adults', lives is an 'easy' option; because they are innocent and bear no culpability for their situation, helping children raises no difficult questions about accountability or personal responsibility.

2.1 Fulfilling children's potential: investing in the early years

In many countries in the majority world there remains inadequate investment in children's welfare. Millions of children continue to live in poverty, suffer and die from preventable diseases, and grow up illiterate. Not only is this an individual tragedy for them and their families, but it is also a waste of future resources and a loss for the society because these children will not grow up to contribute to the economy. Investing in children's earliest years, keeping children alive through vaccination programmes, or ensuring access to clean water, health care and education have been seen as some of the most effective forms of intervention, as well as an investment for the future. When governments have not been able to do this, international NGOs (non-governmental organisations) such as Save the Children or UNICEF (United Nations Children's Fund) have stepped in.

Figure 1   An early childhood intervention programme, funded by UNICEF in the town of Kisantu, Democratic Republic of Congo

UNICEF has focused a great deal of attention on early childhood development programmes, arguing strongly that these should be seen as a future investment in children themselves, and in the future economic and social prosperity of the country:

> The rights of children and the cause of human development are unassailable reasons for investing in early childhood. The neurosciences provide another rationale that's hard to refute as

they demonstrate the influences of the first three years on the rest of a child's life.

In addition, there are also compelling economic arguments: increased productivity over a lifetime and a better standard of living when the child becomes an adult, later cost-savings in remedial education and health care and rehabilitation services and higher earnings for parents and caregivers who are freer to enter the labour force.

And there are social reasons as well: Intervening in the very earliest years helps reduce the social and economic disparities and gender inequalities that divide a society and contributes to including those traditionally excluded.

And political reasons: A country's position in the global economy depends on the competencies of its people and those competencies are set early in life – before the child is three years old.

(UNICEF, 2001, pp. 12–13)

Intervention in early childhood is grounded in ideas about fulfilling individual and social potential, producing productive citizens and fostering a sense of social solidarity at both national and international levels, as well as in children's rights. Although children are at their most vulnerable in the early years, intervening then is based not only on pity but also on economic and political ideologies that see children as an investment for the future.

2.2   Children or families?

Children are not a homogeneous group, of course, but differentiated by age, gender, ethnicity or religion. All these factors affect how children will experience, and react to, adversity. But they also affect how interventions are planned and executed. What might be beneficial for certain groups of children may have different and unthought-of implications for others. In some cases protecting children may come at the expense of their families and wider community. An example here is that of the *Kindertransport*, the granting of asylum and visas to German Jewish children before the Second World War, which enabled them to escape to the safety of the UK. Very few countries were willing to admit Jewish adults, but the British Jewish Refugee Committee petitioned Parliament to allow large numbers of Jewish children between the ages of 5 and 17 into Britain. Because they were children, they were singled out as weak, vulnerable and in need of special protection, although their parents were at just as great a risk. Over 10,000 children came to Britain without their parents in 1938 and 1939 and were singled out for protection for many of the reasons mentioned above. In many instances, however, their parents did not survive the Holocaust and while the *Kindertransport* saved these children's lives, it is impossible to ignore the anti-Semitic prejudice of this policy which differentiated between Jewish people on account of their age and viewed only the youngest members as vulnerable and worthy of rescue.

Figure 2   Young members of the *Kindertransport*. These children arrived in March 1939 aboard the US liner *Manhattan*, as part of a group of 88 German-Jewish children who were resettled in the UK. What happened to their parents is not known

---

Activity 1   The siege of Sarajevo
Allow about 15 minutes

Between 1992 and 1994, the Bosnian city of Sarajevo was at the centre of a civil war in the former Yugoslavia. Its inhabitants were being besieged by Serbian forces and death was a daily reality for many in the city. A blockade was also in force, making food scarce. Under the circumstances a charity called the Children's Embassy organised an evacuation of children from Sarajevo. Throughout this period, a young woman called Elma Softić kept a diary. In the following extract she records her thoughts about the evacuation of the children from the city. Read the extract and make notes on the issues you think it raises about singling out children to be saved.

18 May 1992

Today, under the auspices of the Children's Embassy, a convoy of children left Sarajevo for Split. The Children's Embassy called on everyone who has any sort of means of transport (except for bicycles, motorcycles, and horse-drawn vehicles) to participate in the transport of the children. The column was about ten kilometres long. Television cameras filmed the sorrow and grief of the scene. It was dreadful to see the trucks under whose tarpaulins were crammed the children and their tearful mothers. The life of Sarajevo is leaving. The children and their mothers are leaving. Sarajevo is not merely bleeding to death – it is dying of old age. The young men are being killed, the young women are leaving along with their children. The strength, creativity and intelligence of this city are leaving.

I don't know what to think about this. Keeping the children in Sarajevo means condemning them to possible death or to certain suffering – starvation is doubtless knocking on the doors of the families of Sarajevo. But by escorting them out, we are condemning to death the future of this city, the city that exists now and that its citizens love. What is more important: the life of the individual or of the group? I have always believed that a thriving and promising society is impossible without healthy, courageous, strong, and self-confident individuals. However, is the life of each one of these young people more important than the survival of the community? There was a time when I would have said yes without hesitation, but now I am no longer sure.

(Softić, 1995, p. 31)

Comment

There are no right or wrong answers here. Clearly, it is a deeply emotive issue. For some children, removal from the city was indeed in their best interests, and maybe individual families were more concerned about the life of their child than they were with abstract issues about the survival of the city. Others might argue that evacuating a few thousand vulnerable children does nothing to address the situation of the rest of the people, or tackle the geopolitical problems that caused the conflict in the first place. This short extract shows how problematic the idea of rescuing children is in reality and how difficult the decisions are that have to be made by parents and communities in the face of crisis.

Summary of Section 2

Children are seen as a special priority because they are perceived to be vulnerable, helpless and at risk.

Children can be seen as representing an investment in the future. Intervening in their lives early on is based on the assumption that they will grow up to be productive, useful citizens.

Intervening in individual children's lives can have unintended consequences for other family members and the wider community.

All interventions in children's lives are based on ideological concerns about the nature of childhood and how children should be treated.

3 Rescuing the innocent

Child rescue or child-saving has a long history and is based on the view that children are dependent, weak and powerless victims in need of adult help and protection. When this cannot be provided by their parents, it is up to other adults to step in. Charities set up specifically to look after poor and vulnerable children have existed for a long time, and this section will look at the early work and impact of two of the most famous, Barnardo's and Save the Children. It is important to note that both have changed radically since their inception and much of their work today is focused on policy change rather than child rescue. The word 'charity' is also used to refer specifically to the nineteenth- and early twentieth-century incarnations of groups who relied on private, voluntary donations (i.e. not from the government), which they spent on groups of children in need of support and rescue.

3.1 Charitable interventions in children's lives in Victorian England

The nineteenth century was the era when ideas about childhood, and particularly about children's innate innocence, became most clearly articulated. Children deserved charity because they were born innocent and it was up to adults to do everything they could to shelter them from the realities of the adult world, and protect their specialness and vulnerability. Although this ideal was far more attainable for the middle classes than for the poor, the Victorian 'cult of the child' had, as its ideal, an understanding that childhood should be a special, protected space where innocence could flourish. Previous work among poor children had been based on missionary evangelisation, but now child welfare reformers in London and other cities turned to rescue work. While there were competing ideologies at the time about the role and status of children, one prominent view was that children could be saved from adult corruption by the right intervention and that rather than preaching to parents to repent of their sins, it would be better for reformers to rescue children from the environment in which sin occurred. Charitable work, according to this view, meant minimising the malign influence of parents, and intervening directly in children's lives to remove them from their families and to redeem them as useful members of society. It was thought that children could be removed from the environment which had corrupted them and, having been inculcated with a work ethic, middle-class values and proper social training, they could become model members of the respectable working classes who knew their place, accepted the social hierarchy and provided for themselves and their families through hard work.

One of Victorian England's most famous social reformers and champions of poor children was Dr Thomas Barnardo (1845–1905). In 1866 he was on the verge of becoming a missionary in China, but a visit to the East End of London showed him a hitherto unimagined level of squalor and misery that existed among children in England. He wrote in his autobiography:

> There on the open roof, lay a confused group of boys, all asleep. I counted eleven … The rags that most of them wore were mere apologies for clothes … I realized the terrible fact that they were absolutely homeless and destitute, and were almost certainly but samples of many others; it seemed as though the hand of God Himself had suddenly pulled aside the curtain which concealed

from my view the untold miseries of forlorn child-life upon the
streets of London.

(Quoted in Walvin, 1982, p. 154)

Figure 3   'Street urchins' taken in by Dr Barnardo around 1875

In response to their plight, and as an expression of his Christian duty,
Barnardo founded homes for these children away from their families
where they could be purged of the stain of poverty and turned into
useful citizens. Eventually he encouraged the mass emigration of poor
children (even those with living families) to the British colonies of
Australia and Canada where they could be placed once and for all away
from their parents.

With hindsight, the outcomes of many of Barnardo's interventions were
not as benign as intended and may not have improved children's lives in
the way he had hoped, as will be further discussed in the reading below.
However, it is important to remember the social constraints under

which he worked and what he was attempting to do. His was a humanitarian response to individual children with basic needs for shelter. He was less interested in the wider implications of why so many children should have been destitute in a city as wealthy as London.

Activity 2   Reading A
Allow about 30 minutes

Turn now to the first reading associated with this chapter, 'Sweet childhood lost' by Shurlee Swain, which looks at the ideology of the child rescue movement in Victorian London. Read through it and then comment on:

- what Victorian reformers perceived as the 'best interest of the child'
- the political and social ideology that lay behind this perception.

Comment

Victorian philanthropists were working in an era which promoted the 'cult of the child' – a notion based on the ideology of childhood innocence, specialness and helplessness. Interventions were designed to reinforce and protect this ideal but, as Swain argues, behind the expressed intentions to act in a child's best interest, these interventions almost always involved removing the child from the family, revealing the particular attitudes and assumptions that middle-class reformers made about poor, working-class families. Such families were seen as a potential source of moral and social contamination and removing children from their parents into the custody of a benevolent organisation was seen as the best way of looking after them. Swain argues that far from liberating children from poverty or ensuring that they enjoyed middle-class childhoods, these institutions were often restrictive and conservative, reinforcing a poor child's lowly place in society and ensuring that they worked hard in respectable but servile jobs which kept them in lifelong dependency on others. Furthermore, there is a sense that these children were never fully trusted – the circumstances of their birth and the stain of poverty was liable to come out if a very close eye was not kept on them.

Behind the benevolent intentions, Swain argues, the ideology was essentially repressive. Reformers were not saving children, they were actually teaching them to 'know their place'. She claims that the child rescue movement penalised and demonised poor parents and failed to take account of the wider structural inequalities which meant that poor families had no safety net, limited chances of earning decent wages and few opportunities for social mobility.

It could be argued that Swain, while pointing out the assumptions and unintended consequences of the actions of social reformers, is using today's standards to judge those such as Barnardo, who were interested in social action rather than wealth redistribution and social inequality. Although Barnardo's homes have since been criticised as a paternalistic attempt to decide children's best interests regardless of the wishes of their families or indeed the children themselves, they were not seen as such at the time. For other reformers, rescue campaigns of poor children coincided with political campaigns to improve children's lives. Lord Shaftesbury was the inspiration behind several Factory Acts which limited the hours children could work in factories, and the rise of universal, compulsory, free education by the 1880s belies the suggestion that Victorian philanthropists were interested only in charitable rescue work, detached from political intervention. However, Swain's article usefully points out how assumptions and unconscious beliefs influence policy towards children, and makes clear the links between ideological motivation and social policy.

3.2   International charity

Before the twentieth century, many Christian missionaries, backed by churches or other religious groups, had offered medical help, food and education to both children and adults overseas. However, in the UK ecumenical or non-religious based organisations offering aid to children, without this religious motivation, did not begin until after the Great War (1914–1918). One of the first to do so was the Save the Children Fund.

In the period between the cessation of fighting in 1918 and the signing of the Treaty of Versailles in 1919 (which brought a formal end to the war), France and Britain imposed a blockade on its defeated enemies to make them comply with the terms of the treaty. Food supplies became very scarce in Austria, Germany and Serbia and many children faced starvation. Their plight attracted the attention of Eglantyne Jebb, who in 1919 started the first overseas relief agency for children – the Save the Children Fund (SCF). Jebb estimated that up to 5 million children were starving in Eastern and Central Europe and resolved to set up a special fund to help them. She was greeted with a great deal of hostility at first because she was raising money for what were perceived as 'enemy children', of whom it was said "'These children had much better die"; "They will only grow up to fight us'" (quoted in Jebb, 1929, p. 5). Furthermore, others questioned her motives for doing this at a time when British children were also suffering from serious social problems. However, the basis of her work was that *all* children should be saved regardless of their ethnicity or where they lived. Jebb claimed in 1919 that 'the SCF pays no regard to politics, race or religion. A child is a child whether red or white, brown or black' (quoted in Wilson, 1967, p. 183).

Figure 4 Eglantyne Jebb (1876–1928), founder of Save the Children Fund

Save the Children Fund took as its basic premise that rescuing children from suffering should be seen as a humanitarian rather than a political issue. However, Jebb was astute enough to recognise the political causes of children's suffering. A committed pacifist, she was acutely aware that children were suffering as a direct result of what she saw as political intransigence by the victorious nations. Nevertheless, her argument was that children were the innocent victims of adult wars who should not be tainted by the guilt of their governments. Her message was 'All wars,

just or unjust, disastrous or victorious, are waged against the child'
(quoted in Buxton and Fuller, 1931, p. 82).

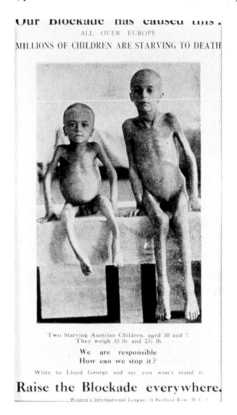

Figure 5   A leaflet showing pictures of starving Austrian children used by
Jebb to raise awareness of the effects of the Allied blockade of the defeated
nations in Europe in 1919

Despite the argument that saving children was apolitical, Jebb's
interventions were based on a particular ideology and ideas about the
nature of children, their role in society and the responsibilities of adults
towards them. Jebb's view of childhood rested on two assumptions:
firstly, the conventional idea that children were pure and uncorrupted
and, secondly, the idea – articulated so forcefully by the Romantic poets
– that protecting children could prove redemptive, not only to the
children themselves but also to the adults who saved them. Saving
children therefore was merely the first step towards saving humanity
itself. Jebb claimed:

> The sphere of its [SCF's] influence is illimitable. It certainly
> extends far beyond the bounds of the work of charitable relief, and

it may go far to sweep away that international distrust and jealousy which have done so much in the past to set man against man. We set out to save the lives of children, but if we remain true to this ideal, and do all that in us lies to further it, we may make a worthy contribution to the task of saving the soul of the world.

(Quoted in Buxton and Fuller, 1931, p. 48)

Alongside these two ideals lay a third: that children should be protected not out of charity but should be fed, clothed and sheltered as a *right*. Adults had a duty to protect and save all children wherever they were. A child in need in Austria was as worthy of help as a child in distress in the UK, regardless of the actions of his or her parents. It was a principle that, after much lobbying by Jebb, was enshrined in international law in 1924 when the League of Nations agreed The Declaration of Geneva – a five-point declaration which set out the special rights that children had because of their age and perceived vulnerabilities, and the responsibilities adults had in fulfilling those rights.

3.3 Contemporary rescue work

It would be tempting to believe that work to rescue innocent child victims, especially that which penalised parents for being poor, was a thing of the past and that modern welfare programmes are based on more nuanced understandings. Unfortunately, this is not always the case and the idea of rescuing innocent children let down by inherently inadequate parents, rather than an unjust social system, continues to resonate and retain its emotional power.

Activity 3 Reading B
Allow about 30 minutes

Turn now to the second reading at the end of this chapter, 'Crack babies' by Ana Teresa Ortiz and Laura Briggs, which looks at the moral panic over babies born addicted to crack cocaine in the USA in the late 1980s and 1990s. Read through it and then answer the following questions:

- How do ideologies of childhood innocence demonise poor parents in this instance?

- What do the authors claim these children are really being rescued from?

- Why do the authors claim that the 'extract-the-child' policy advocated here is inadequate?

Comment

In this highly polemical piece, the authors argue that the category of 'crack babies' was created as part of a moral panic which served to demonise poor, African American mothers. They acknowledge that many children born to mothers who used crack had poor outcomes, but argue that this was not necessarily caused by crack itself but by other factors, including alcohol, tobacco, the effects of living in poverty and general maternal ill-health. They claim that the emergence of crack babies as a medical problem allowed for a simplistic solution to a very complex social issue. Although these women had chaotic and difficult lives (many were homeless, alcohol users or in violent relationships), attributing all their babies' problems to crack allowed for mothers to be criminalised and children to be 'rescued' and saved through a massive input of white, middle-class parenting. By transforming the multiple problems of poverty and race discrimination into the simpler issues of irresponsible drug taking and child endangerment, the state was mandated to step in to protect these children without providing any sort of social care for the mothers or indeed any alternative except prison.

For some individual children, extracting them from poor, chaotic situations and placing them in materially better off homes may be beneficial. But the price for their parents, and for other children born in equal poverty, is very high. Rescuing a very few 'crack babies' does nothing to alleviate poverty or discrimination and indeed may even reinforce them. While on the surface it might appear that swooping in and taking malnourished, underweight babies to better homes offers them the best possible chance in life, the reality is much more complex. This reading further reinforces the point that there is no such thing as purely humanitarian intervention – all interventions are ideological and most have unforeseen consequences.

Summary of Section 3

The idea of rescuing children relies on the belief that children are particularly vulnerable and have no power to change their situation.

Conceptualising children as victims in need of charity can decontextualise the social, economic and political circumstances of their suffering.

> Despite her claims that children were above politics, Eglantyne
> Jebb's interventions in their lives were based on an ideological
> stance that viewed them as having rights.
>
> Ideologies of child victims needing rescue continue to resonate in
> the contemporary world.

4 Children and welfare states

By the mid-twentieth century shifts had taken place in the UK and
elsewhere concerning the respective relationships between children,
parents and the state. After the social upheavals and sacrifices made by
many during the Second World War, there was a broad consensus that
children (and their families) should no longer need to rely on charitable
donations given by individuals but should be able to depend on the
state to provide support to families raising children. Historian Asa
Briggs has defined a welfare state as 'a state in which organized power
is deliberately used (through politics and administration) in an effort to
modify the play of market forces in at least three directions' (Briggs,
1961, p. 228). Briggs identified these three directions as follows:

> guaranteeing individuals and families a minimum income
> irrespective of the market value of their work or their property; ...
> narrowing the extent of insecurity by enabling individuals and
> families to meet certain 'social contingencies' (for example,
> sickness, old age and unemployment) which lead otherwise to
> individual and family crises; ... ensuring that all citizens without
> distinction of status or class are offered the best standards
> available in relation to a certain agreed range of social services.
>
> (Briggs, 1961, p. 228)

Clearly this is an ideal rather than a blueprint of how services should be
organised and run, but it suggests the fundamental philosophy and
vision behind the welfare state in the UK.

One of the architects of the welfare state in the UK was William
Beveridge (1879–1963), an economist and Oxford don, whose *Report on
Social Insurance and Allied Services* (1942) – usually known as the
Beveridge Report – formed the basis of the post-war reforms. It was

the first attempt to introduce a system of universal welfare and his reforms included the creation of the National Health Service, the expansion of National Insurance and, later on, the development of child benefit payments. Although there had been attempts by previous governments to institute benefit payments (such as the National Insurance Act of 1911), the welfare state went much further. It set up a national system of benefits to provide 'social security' and protect all members of the population from 'cradle to the grave'. Beveridge's proposal was for a flat rate contribution for everyone and a flat rate benefit for everyone. Linking these benefits to National Insurance contributions was designed to avoid the stigma of handouts and to give people ownership of their benefits.

Figure 6   The architect of the UK's welfare state, William Henry Beveridge

The welfare state was envisaged as a means to ensure social cohesion and was based on an ideology of equality and justice; every person has the right to support from the state if they need it and the state should provide a security net for everyone. A good education or access to health care according to need became the right of everyone, not just those who could afford it. Nigel Parton has argued:

> Social insurance fundamentally transformed the mechanisms that integrated the citizen into the social order. Not only were

individuals to be protected from the evils of 'Want, Disease, Idleness, Ignorance and Squalor' (Beveridge, 1942), but they would be constituted as citizens bound into a system of solidarity and mutual inter-dependence. Social insurance was seen [by its architects such as Beveridge] as a scientific and statistical method of encouraging passive solidarity among its recipients. Everyone would contribute and everyone would benefit, although some would do so more than others. The overall rationale of welfarism was to make the liberal market society and the family more productive, stable and harmonious; and the role of government, while more complex and expansive, would be positive and beneficent.

(Parton, 2005, p. 132)

The Beveridge Report was implemented by the Labour government in 1945 and was overwhelmingly popular with the public (if not universally welcomed by doctors or by the Conservative opposition). However, it was highly ambitious and the economic conditions of the UK at the time meant that benefits were not always set at high enough levels to keep people out of absolute poverty. There was simply not enough money to meet all of the population's unmet needs in terms of health, education and housing. In practice, the lack of funding which hampered the introduction of the welfare state has haunted it ever since and it has consistently fallen short of the ideals set out by Beveridge. Family allowances, for instance, were never as generous as Beveridge had imagined. He had wanted them to cover the full costs of raising a child, but budget constraints, themselves a product of ideologically underpinned financial priorities, meant that this was never possible. Furthermore, Beveridge made certain assumptions about family make-up and economic provision which were not borne out in practice. For example, family allowances were only introduced for second and subsequent children. Beveridge believed that it was not necessary to pay for the first child since all men working full time would bring home enough wages to support their wife and first child relatively easily. This was often far from true. Furthermore, if the first child was born to a mother without a partner to support her, she could not claim child benefit from the state. On top of the social stigma, financial hardship made it extremely difficult for a single mother to raise a child on her own.

Figure 7   Great Britain, July 1948. A newborn baby is weighed at a Bristol clinic. This service was provided free on the National Health Service

Since its beginnings, the welfare state has transformed relations between children, family and the state, although the nature of this relationship has been heavily contested and shifts depending on economic climate and political culture. These changes demand a chapter in themselves but, as a broad generalisation, between 1945 and the 1970s there was a general political and social commitment to the basic institutions of the welfare state (such as the NHS and child welfare benefits) which led to a sustained fall in child poverty rates until the 1970s. This consensus started to break down in the 1970s when economic recession and political change led many people to challenge the welfare state's basic tenets. Margaret Thatcher famously declared that 'there is no such thing as society' and while there is some debate about whether this quote is taken out of context, it is clear that she envisaged a very different relationship between families and the state from the one she saw around her. She said:

> I think we have gone through a period when too many children
> and people have been given to understand 'I have a problem, it is

Figure 8   There over 700,000 children living without adult supervision in Russia, including these street children living by the Kursky train station in Moscow

chapter looks at different forms of child welfare in the former Soviet Union, which existed from 1922 to 1991. Much more so than the West, the Soviet Union was based on the premise that the state could and should intervene in all aspects of family life, and it was through the child that the transformation of society would occur. Welfare provision for Soviet citizens was universal and there was no private or charity provision, meaning that the state, in theory at least, provided everything for its citizens. When the Soviet Union collapsed in 1991, its welfare services were hard hit. A sudden switch to a capitalist system, with limited provision for the most vulnerable, meant that many, especially the poor, the elderly, the sick and the young, were profoundly affected.

Read through Reading C, 'The cycle of child displacement in the Russian north' by Elena Khlinovskaya Rockhill, and, as you do, make notes on the following:

- What is the relationship between families and the state?
- In what ways might this form of welfare benefit children and in what ways might it harm them?

Comment

This reading describes a country in a state of painful economic and social transition. The Soviet Union provided a safety net for many and without this, families struggle to cope. The state appears to be withdrawing in some ways – cutting kindergartens, schooling, welfare, etc. – but also acting in intrusive and coercive ways, pressuring women to give up babies into care and setting very opaque rules for how they can get them back. Mothers are not given any help to keep their babies or to improve their economic situation through training, childcare or access to jobs.

On the one hand the state is taking responsibility for vulnerable children. It is acknowledging that children should live in adequate conditions, be well housed, fed and clothed, and it undertakes to provide when parents, especially mothers, cannot. However, it is also clear that these homes are highly inadequate and do not provide children with the nurture they need.

This reading shows powerfully that state policies in the former Soviet Union and elsewhere can have devastating impacts on children, even when the state claims to act in their best interests, protecting them from neglectful parents. It also shows, like the previous reading, the difficulties faced by the economically and socially marginalised under a free market system, which stigmatises those who seek aid and blames them for their own poverty.

Summary of Section 4

The period after the Second World War saw the formation of the welfare state in the UK. It rejected the notion of charity and promised to look after its citizens from 'cradle to the grave'.

There are other models of welfare state, which place different emphases on individual responsibility and social equality.

The ability of governments to provide adequate resources to meet children's needs varies greatly. In some cases, outside agencies and organisations work in partnership with them to try to ensure children's well-being.

5 Children as rights-bearers

The first piece of children's rights legislation, the Geneva Declaration of the Rights of the Child, was passed by the League of Nations in 1924.

> ## Summary of Section 5
>
> The UNCRC represented a significant change in how children are understood and shifted the basis on which adults should intervene in their lives.
>
> Children's rights remain contested at an ideological level because they reflect a minority-world image of an autonomous child which does not exist universally.
>
> Despite its emphasis on participation, the UNCRC discusses only adult responsibilities towards the child. It does not discuss a child's responsibilities to adults, thereby reinforcing the image of the child as a helpless dependant.

6 Conclusion

Adult-led interventions to improve children's lives have a long history. This chapter has looked at some of the different ideologies behind these interventions, examining how each of these conceptualises the child and how they envisage adult/child relations. It is important to note that these are not mutually exclusive and that different agencies have a mixture of priorities and agendas in their work with children. Nor are the three categories discussed (rescuing the innocent, setting up welfare states or promoting children's rights) exhaustive – there are other ways of conceptualising children and intervening on their behalf. However, by foregrounding these three approaches, certain continuities can be observed, most noticeably the continuing power of ideas about rescuing needy children. While other interventions based on ideas of social cohesion or children's rights are more recent, they too are derived from particular histories and ideologies. Even the ostensibly most benign, charitable and seemingly ethically 'pure' interventions can be interpreted to possess problematic ideological underpinnings, and social control never seems far away from ideas of child welfare.

References

Beveridge, W. (1942) *Report on Social Insurance and Allied Services* (*Beveridge Report*) (CMD 6404), London, HMSO.

Briggs, A. (1961) 'The welfare state in historical perspective', *European Journal of Sociology*, vol. 2, no. 2, pp. 221–58.

Burman, E. (1996) 'Local, global or globalized? Child development and international child rights legislation', *Childhood: A Global Journal of Child Research*, vol. 3, no. 1, pp. 45–66.

Buxton, D. and Fuller, E. (1931) *The White Flame: The Story of the Save the Children Fund*, London, Longman.

Freeman, M. (1992) 'Introduction: rights, ideology and children', in Freeman, M. and Veerman, P. (eds) *The Ideologies of Children's Rights*, Dordrecht, Martinus Nijhoff.

Goodman, R. (1996) 'On introducing the UN Convention on the Rights of the Child into Japan', in Goodman, R. and Neary, I. (eds) *Case Studies on Human Rights in Japan*, Richmond, Japan Library, Curzon Press.

Jebb, E. (1929) *Save the Child! A Posthumous Essay*, London, Weardale Press.

Margaret Thatcher Foundation (1987) 'Margaret Thatcher interview for Woman's Own' [online], http://www.margaretthatcher.org/document/106689 (Accessed 31 July 2011).

Parton, N. (2005) 'Risk, advanced liberalism and child welfare: the need to rediscover uncertainty and ambiguity', in Hendrick, H. (ed) *Child Welfare and Social Policy*, Bristol, Policy Press.

Pupavac, V. (2001) 'Misanthropy without borders: the international children's rights regime', *Disasters*, vol. 25, no. 2, pp. 95–112.

Spicker, P. (2010) 'An introduction to social policy', Aberdeen, Robert Gordon University [online], http://www2.rgu.ac.uk/publicpolicy/introduction (Accessed 1 May 2011).

Softić, E. (1995) *Sarajevo Days, Sarajevo Nights*, Toronto, Key Porter Books.

UNICEF (2001) *The State of the World's Children*, New York, UNICEF.

Walvin, J. (1982) *A Child's World: A Social History of English Childhood 1800–1914*, London, Penguin Books.

Wilson, F. (1967) *Rebel Daughter of a Country House: The Life of Eglantyne Jebb, Founder of the Save the Children Fund*, London, Allen & Unwin.

Reading A
Sweet childhood lost

Shurlee Swain

Source: 'Sweet childhood lost: idealized images of childhood in the British child rescue literature', 2009, *The Journal of the History of Childhood and Youth*, vol. 2, no. 2, pp. 198–214.

The origins of the British child rescue movement can be found in the evangelical outreach to the inner cities, feared lost to Christianity in the wake of the rapid urbanization which accompanied the Industrial Revolution. It was first apparent in the Ragged Schools Union, founded under the patronage of Lord Ashley (later Earl Shaftesbury) in 1844, which sought to provide a basic education to poor children excluded from the existing system. The teachers attracted to the new schools, many of whom saw their involvement as a preparation for, or an alternative to, work in the foreign missions, were encouraged to provide more than a basic education to their students by visiting their homes and encouraging their families to embrace Christianity. The founders of the child rescue movement all had experience in such evangelical outreach, experience which led them to conclude that more was needed if children were indeed to be saved. Thomas Barnardo (18[45]–1905), founder of Dr. Barnardo's Homes (1868), had moved to London to prepare for the China Mission but claimed that his life goal was changed through an encounter with boys who had no home to go to and no parents to whom they could look for guidance and care. Thomas Bowman Stephenson (1838–1912), founder of the Wesleyan National Children's Homes (1869), cited a similar encounter with so-called street Arabs, while engaged in outdoor preaching, as the motivation behind what became his life's work. Edward de Montjoie Rudolf (1852–1933), founder of the Anglican Waifs and Strays Society (1881), began as a Sunday school teacher in Lambeth, where he observed children in desperate need for whom the church was failing to provide. Benjamin Waugh (1839–1908), founding secretary of the National Society for the Prevention of Cruelty to Children (1889), had displayed an affinity for children in his work as a Congregational minister. His writing on the subject of child neglect attracted the interest of the founders of the society who were quick to recruit him as its chief organizer.

These charismatic men were able to attract many writers, artists, and poets, both in Britain and in its former colonies, who incorporated child rescue themes into their work. Child rescue propaganda was highly effective. Donations flowed in to finance a third group of services for children ineligible, because of the presence of parents, for traditional orphanages, yet considered deserving of better than the workhouse. Each organization developed its own mix of reception facilities, supposedly family-like children's homes and villages, boarding-out and emigration schemes, training schools, and hospitals within the lifetime of the founders. While child rescue advocates appealed to the notion of an idealized childhood to which the children that they aimed to rescue had no access, their vision of the fate of the rescued had little in common with such romanticized notions. …

The stories, poems, and vignettes that filled the magazines issued by the key child rescue organizations consistently constituted the state of the neglected child as one of 'lack.' Innocent, pure, helpless, and unprotected, these were children who had 'never tasted joys of childhood.' 'Childhood,' Barnardo argued, was designed to be 'the divinest flower in God's garden,' but the children amongst whom child rescuers worked 'had no heaven-surrounded infancy.' 'Fair childhood' had been 'blighted on life's bleak shore.' They had been 'defrauded' or 'robbed' by the 'enemies of childhood,' who substituted 'sorrows' and 'wrongs' for the 'joys' which a 'real childhood' entailed. Rather than a life of freedom and innocence the street child was little more than 'a valuable slave … all the joy and health of his childhood … being sold.' Where the image of childhood lost or tainted was invoked, a series of other terms commonly followed. The children were depicted as waifs and outcasts, homeless, helpless, friendless and hopeless, destitute, hungry, ragged, degraded, wretched, miserable, and pitiable. …

Central to this literature was an emphasis on the urgency of rescue. It was a mission with both divine and earthly sanction.

> The children's angels are yearning o'er
>
> Fair childhood blighted on life's bleak shore,
>
> 'Mid earth's dark scenes and din.
>
> 'Nobody's Darlings!' Gather them in.

'In this living grave of sin and putrescence, where the blessed sunshine never shone,' Barnardo, in constructing a poignant tale of rescue, asked, 'who was there to see and help this blue-eyed little waif, alone and forsaken among it all?' The resolution in each case was the same. The child rescuer was at hand, wanting only the prayerful, and financial, assistance of the reader to immediately remove the danger. ...

Where American child rescuer Charles Loring Brace liked to depict the boys he rescued as the most evolutionarily advanced of individuals because they had survived the struggle for existence in the nation's harshest environments, his British equivalents were more concerned to combat fears of degeneracy. A change in environment, they sought to persuade their supporters, would, however, triumph over poor heredity. 'Ruskin has reminded us that the most turpid puddle can still reflect the blue heaven and the stars; and so the soul most ingeniously darkened and befouled by man can still reflect the light and love of God,' the Rev. W. J. Dawson informed readers of the National Children's Homes magazine, *Highways and Hedges*. The high-born babe who 'by some terrible mischance, inhale[d] only the impure atmosphere of vicious indigence among the brutal and miserable ... [would] prefer to pilfer rather than suffer the pangs of hunger,' while the lowly-born 'sheltered carefully from contact with the vicious and the mean' would in adulthood show not 'the faintest stain of infamous origin, or brand of ignoble birth.' All such children needed was 'a *good mother* and a decent *home*' as far away as possible 'from the influences and associations of their early life.'

Such philanthropic narratives, Lydia Murdoch has recently argued, served to demonize poor parents. There was never any critique of the society which allowed such conditions to exist. The fault was always seen as lying with parents who, through their behavior, exposed their children to homelessness, vagrancy, cruelty, and want. In such scenarios 'the child represented pure virtue, and the intervening philanthropist played the role of hero or judge.' (Murdoch, 2006, p. 17) The central purpose of such narratives, Murdoch believes, was to define the urban poor as unworthy of citizenship and thus to deflect their claims for inclusion in the nation. While that endeavor was, ultimately, doomed to failure, the impact on poor children was longer lasting. Detached from their parents, their natural protectors, their 'best interest' as defined by their self-appointed rescuers was a preparation for a dutiful and subservient adulthood, their place mediated by class and race. ...

... [I]t is important to look beyond the melodrama of the rescue to ascertain the new life to which the rescued children were destined. Despite repeated references to the equality of all children in the eyes of God, and hence of their equal access to the Christian promise of life after death, there are few instances in which the rescued child is depicted as being entitled to the accoutrements of a middle-class childhood while still on Earth. Notions of innocence and joy are all too often replaced with references to training and discipline as the child is transformed from victim to threat. Even the most angelic of children, readers were warned, could harbor evil within. 'Careful training is required both for body and soul,' for even the most 'loving and tender, simple and sweet' children 'had learnt much that was evil, nothing of self-control, while theft and untruth were looked upon as accomplishments.' The negative aspects of the street child's plight were at the core of all arguments for the necessity and efficacy of the training which the homes could provide. The children of 'careless and vicious parents' were 'infesting the streets,' in areas that functioned as 'manufactories of criminals' who were 'systematically trained in vice and infamy.' 'Depraved,' 'idle,' 'ignorant,' and 'ill-conditioned,' without 'moral reformation' they 'fester in the bosom of society.' 'Stunted,' 'wicked,' 'worthless,' and 'scorned,' they called out for rescue. …

Training was designed to 'fit' the children 'far better to do the work and withstand the temptations of their future life.' Success in the future demanded simple training in the 'habit of steady, useful industry, the ability to turn their hands readily to any useful calling, and the power to fit themselves for a decent life.' The children were 'expected to be clean, obedient, respectful, hard-working and to "keep their brains employed."' The value of such training overrode any doubts that the children were being equipped for jobs fast disappearing in the face of mechanization. 'The discipline of sitting quiet and working industriously is very necessary for them; indeed, it is oftimes the only discipline they have,' wrote one sister working in an Australian child rescue organization. …

Redemption came through labor, for boys 'a trade … [which] placed within his power a guardian in temptation's hour,' for girls, a life of domestic service, a fate clearly articulated in Barnardo's 'Song for Little Servants':

> Keep me strictly honest
>
> Steady and upright
>
> Thoughtful of my mistress
>
> In and out of sight.
>
> If her things are broken,

By my carelessness,

Let me mind 'tis better

Always to confess.

I must be good-tempered

Always neat and clean

Civil in my manners,

Never pert or mean.

Then my fellow-servants

Will respect my ways,

And I need not mind it,

If I get no praise.

… Child rescuers frequently constructed their work in opposition to the orphanages and institutions of the past which 'glorified the worker at the cost of the child' and made no efforts to reproduce true childhood. … By constituting inadequate parents as the enemy, however, child rescuers created a discursive environment in which removal could be justified as being in the best interest of the child. The 'children of the dangerous classes' were depicted as calling out for rescue from parents who were training them to 'habits of profligacy and crime.' As popular support for the child rescue movement grew, this discursive environment was replicated in legal reform articulating a status for children separate from their parents, establishing the conditions in which a child's rights to care and protection overrode parental rights to the child as property.

What this legislation and the bureaucratic structures which grew up around it all too often failed to do was to ensure that 'the best interests of the child' were also central to their post-rescue care. Nineteenth-century child rescuers used the notion of childhood lost to argue that it was in the best interests of the child to be removed from parents or guardians found wanting, but the future they offered the children they rescued was one that served to perpetuate the inequalities which, arguably, lay at the centre of their distress. Disempowered, cut off from their families and communities, and trained for a life of servitude, their childhoods were shaped primarily by labor, with love dependent on chance or good fortune. Nor did their rescue guarantee their safety from future harm. The magazines of the child rescue organizations delighted in reproducing stories of adult success, but later historical studies have clearly demonstrated that success was consistently overrated. More importantly, survivor narratives, whether in family histories, published autobiographies, or evidence before government enquiries, all testify to the vulnerability of the 'rescued' child and the prevalence of physical and sexual abuse in the cottages, foster, or adoptive homes in which they were placed. While the child rescue movement played a valuable role in articulating the rights of children to protection from neglect and abuse, its limited vision of what childhood could offer such children left a mixed legacy which continues to haunt child protection practice today.

Reference

Murdoch, L. (2006) *Imagined Orphans: Poor Families, Child Welfare and Contested Citizenship in London*, New Brunswick, NJ, Rutgers University Press.

Reading B
Crack babies

Ana Teresa Ortiz and Laura Briggs

Source: 'The culture of poverty, crack babies, and welfare cheats: the making of the "healthy white baby crisis"', 2003, *Social Text 76*, vol. 21, no. 3, pp. 39–57.

In the 1980s, pessimism about the culture of poor children turned into a concern about their biology. In 1989, crack babies were the news story of the year. Major newspapers ran huge, multipage features, and network news shows bombarded their audiences with regular images of women using crack cocaine during their pregnancies, characterizing their offspring as likely to be born early, to experience exceptionally high rates of perinatal mortality, to be born addicted and quivering, to experience a host of neurological, digestive, respiratory, and cardiac problems, and to be headed toward a childhood of learning difficulties, hyperactivity, and ultimately, delinquency and jail. The bitter irony is none of it was true. Crack has very little, if any, effect on pregnancies or fetuses. For decades, the legal and child welfare systems worked very hard to make women who used crack during pregnancy suffer. Between 1985 and 2000, more than two hundred women faced criminal prosecution for using cocaine and other drugs during pregnancy, and tens of thousands lost their children to foster care. In March 2001, medical researchers Deborah Frank and colleagues published a meta-analysis of research on the effects of prenatal cocaine exposure in the *Journal of the American Medical Association (JAMA)*. Their conclusions are literally incredible to most people: they found virtually no evidence that cocaine use during pregnancy had any negative effects on offspring. They wrote:

> After controlling for cofounders, there was no consistent negative association between prenatal cocaine exposure and physical growth, developmental test scores, or receptive or expressive language. Less optimal motor scores have been found up to age seven months but not thereafter, and may reflect heavy tobacco exposure. No independent cocaine effects have been shown on

standardized parent and teacher reports of child behavior scored
by accepted criteria.

(Frank, Augustyn, Knight, et al., 2001)

While there is debatable evidence for attention problems, that is it. In a
commentary on Frank et al. in the same issue of *JAMA*, Wendy
Chavkin suggested that all the 'hullabaloo' about crack babies had much
more to do with politics than it ever was about medical effects on
fetuses (Chavkin, 2001).

While this may ultimately prove to be quite true, it fails to account for
the extent to which everyone—medical researchers included—jumped
on the crack babies bandwagon. This was a moral panic of the first
order, taking in right, left, and center. Even cocaine-using pregnant
women were persuaded that jail was the best place for them. …

Neoconservative commentators were certainly among the most
vociferous. Douglas Besharov of the American Enterprise Institute
referred to the birth of a 'bio-underclass' whom Head Start [an early
years intervention programme in the US, designed to tackle child
poverty through early education] could not help, and syndicated
columnist Charles Krauthammer, in high eugenicist mode, referred to a
'generation of physically damaged cocaine babies whose biological
inferiority is stamped at birth,' who represented between 5 and 15
percent of all black children (Krauthammer, 1989). Yet even liberal
African American commentators like Derrick Z. Jackson of the *Boston
Globe* and William Raspberry of the *Washington Post* joined in, arguing
that high rates of black infant mortality were caused by crack, and that
efforts to decriminalize drugs should be opposed because of the effects
of cocaine on babies.

There is a haunting question about how the most vulnerable, most
impoverished people in the United States—pregnant women, often
prostitutes, sometimes using multiple drugs (prominently alcohol and
tobacco), often homeless, more often than not facing violence during
their pregnancies, frequently dealing with long-term ill health and often
mental illness as well—became a symbol of everything that was wrong
with the country. For all these reasons, the case often seemed plausible
that the children of 'crack mothers' were not doing well (they weren't,
but crack was a correlate, not a cause). The entire edifice of the moral
panic about crack babies rested on two statistics, both of which
ultimately proved to be wrong. The evidence for a growing 'epidemic'

of cocaine use, rooted in the newly available, cheap form of the drug, crack, was a slight increase in a daily and weekly usage statistic provided by the U.S. General Accounting Office. These statistics were notoriously unreliable because they relied on very small samples, and this one proved wrong: the percentage of the U.S. population using crack remained absolutely stable between 1988 and 1994. A second statistic showed a sharp rise in the mortality rate of African American infants in Washington, D.C., in the first half of 1989; officials later realized that a large number of these deaths had really occurred in 1988, and infant mortality rates had, in fact, stayed relatively stable. It is striking how few people acknowledged that the case for the crack 'epidemic' wreaking havoc in inner cities and blighting a generation of babies was extraordinarily shaky, despite the availability of countermanding evidence in the 1980s. Instead, crack babies were poster children for the War on Drugs and an allegory for debates about abortion, exhibit A for the mostly conservative policy makers and prosecutors who wanted to show why small-time drug users were a danger to the society as a whole and deserving of jail time (since what were being called boarder babies were putting an incredible strain on hospital finances, and the children were entitled to expensive special education classes at public expense), and why fetuses needed to be protected from dangerous mothers who, to paraphrase the columnist Krauthammer, would kill them if they were lucky.

This was also an intensely racializing moral panic. Although the typical user of both cocaine and crack was a young white male, by 1985, television and print media were portraying crack as a drug used by African Americans and, to a lesser extent, Latinos. From 1988 to 1990, the nightly news was engaged in a war against crack mothers—who were all but definitionally black. In that period, 55 percent of the women portrayed in network TV news stories about crack use were black; in later years, from 1991 to 1994, it was 84 percent. The newspapers were, if anything, worse.

At the precise moment when the Reagan and (first) Bush administrations had all but succeeded in disallowing race as a legitimate term of political grievance through their attacks on policies like affirmative action, and following on decades of deindustrialization and the flight of jobs from cities that disproportionately affected communities of color, race emerged sharply as a term in which to characterize pathology—indeed, a specifically biologized pathology. The terms of this discourse explained away a multitude of things caused by

Reagan-era economic policies, such as homelessness and increasing infant mortality rates, especially among African Americans. The crack baby crisis invited people not to think about the economic causes that led communities of color, and urban youth of whatever race, to be disproportionately involved in the drug trade, or the ways that cuts to social services and government transfer payments left working-class families scrambling. It also discounted another story one could have told about impoverished children in this era: the effects on youth of the steadily expanding workdays that working-class parents had to put in to make ends meet. In its place, the crack baby epidemic offered bad parenting, moral failure, and a criminal recklessness about fetuses.

The other thing the crack baby epidemic did was to produce the contemporary foster care and child welfare system. Between 1985 and 1988, the number of children in out-of-home placement— foster care, psychiatric institutions, and the juvenile justice system— increased by 25 percent. In the five years after that, it reached its 2002 figure: 500,000. At the urging of federal drug czar William Bennett, many hospitals—especially those serving mostly black patients— introduced routine screening for cocaine into delivery rooms, and mothers who tested positive lost their newborns on the spot; some even went to jail, still bleeding from labor. In the post-Reagan social service landscape, these policies initially taxed foster care systems to the breaking point, but crack babies quickly became a rallying point for agencies to lobby for—and get—massive new funding. Congressional reports, hearings, and funding appropriations reflected the new urgency about caring for the 'littlest victims' of crack and built a much larger institutional capacity (at the same time that a massive prison system was also being built, in no small measure for these same children's parents). Foster parents of these so-called crack babies were canonized by the popular press; they were caring for 'babies in pain,' who disrupted families and would never be normal. Although the Supreme Court ultimately found that hospital policies of testing women in labor were unconstitutional—a warrantless search—and, many also argued, racially discriminatory, since very few white women were tested and in some hospitals all black women were, there was also profound popular opposition to 'crack mothers' getting their children back. ...

Once again, we have a redefinition of poverty at a critical policy juncture that rests on an account of children and childhood. ... [T]he narrative of crack babies produced a biologized account of the growing impoverishment of urban communities of color. ...

While fetuses and children are victims in this narrative, and hence innocent, it is an ambivalent kind of innocence. Because they cannot escape the effects of the bad morals and loathsome behavior of their parents, these children grow up to be the terrifying criminals and demonic parents that the discourse holds their parents culpable for being. The possibility is left ever so slightly open that this tedious, rote reproduction of criminality and bad parenting can be interrupted by the extraordinary intervention of heroic (and therefore good and innocent) white and middle-class people.

One should note that there has been a narrowing of the bottleneck into a limited politics of the possible regarding childhood trauma and its emplacement in communities. An 'extract-the-child' solution requires a systematic bypassing of a substantive psychological and sociological literature that locates the traumatized unit at the supraindividual or family level—but attention to the solutions implied by this literature would require the restoration of funds and power to local communities wrested from them in the Reagan and post-Reagan eras. Critical geographers who attend to the cultural construction of social race have also been attending increasingly to trauma; these scholars argue that the behaviors ascribed to crack mothers are best described as adaptive responses to the elimination of safe places in which to live in community, and the intentional disinvestments in areas disproportionately inhabited by racialized minorities, which are allowed to deteriorate into zones of 'urban desertification.'

What is compelling about this scholarship—beyond the fact that it is consistently ignored at the policy level—is that it does take seriously the problems of childhood vulnerability and the psychological sequelae of trauma and explores interventions that break through conventional expectations of efficacy. In noting the absence of community-level solutions that take trauma to birth mothers as seriously as trauma to their children (and the apparently natural and commonsense quality of welfare and adoption reform), we can see the cultural work accomplished by this newly biologized underclass.

References

Chavkin, W. (2001) 'Cocaine and pregnancy—time to look at the evidence', *Journal of the American Medical Association*, vol. 285, no. 12, pp. 1626–27.

Frank, D. A., Augustyn, M., Knight, W. G., Pell, T. and Zuckerman, B. (2001) 'Growth, development, and behavior in early childhood following prenatal cocaine exposure: a systematic review', *Journal of the American Medical Association*, vol. 285, no. 12, pp. 1613–25.

Krauthammer, C. (1989) 'Crack babies forming biological underclass', *St. Louis Post-Dispatch*, 30 July.

Reading C
The cycle of child displacement in the Russian north

Elena Khlinovskaya Rockhill

Source: 'Social orphans and the *neblagopoluchnaia* family: the cycle of child displacement in the Russian north', 2004, *Sibirica,* vol. 4, no. 2, pp. 132–49.

Introduction

Soviet society directly connected childhood with its teleological vision of what a Communist society and the new Soviet man ought to be. This collective vision of the future ended with the collapse of the Soviet Union in 1991. Since then, public discourse has shifted from representing childhood as 'our only privileged class' and 'our future' to the emergence of numerous groups of 'children at risk' growing up in conditions of severe deprivation.

One such group is 'children without parental care', whose numbers grew steadily throughout the 1990s, reaching some 776,000 in 2003. About one-third of these children[1], or approximately 250,000, have grown up in residential care institutions despite having at least one living family member … They are called social orphans (*sotsial'nye siroty*). The problem of social orphans is tied to the perceived post-socialist crisis in the family with its falling moral standards and is seen as an indicator of the disintegration of the social fabric of society (Rybinskii, 1997, 1998; Rybinskii and Krasnitskaia, 1998). Indeed, social orphans come from families experiencing economic hardships and/or domestic difficulties, and from the *neblagopoluchnye*, or 'problem' families, scornfully viewed by the state agents and many members of society as having reached the point of being unfit to bring up their children. The state often takes drastic actions against these parents: between 1992 and 1998, the number of parents deprived of parental rights increased from 6,700 to 31,790 per year (Karelova, 2000).

Public anxiety encompasses not only concerns for the future of the country in general, but also apprehension about the effect the growing number of homeless, neglected, maltreated children and deviant youth will have on the future of Russian society. Most importantly, there is much concern over what lies ahead for these children who are growing

---

[1] The rest are placed in adoptive and guardian families and thus grow up in a substitute family.

up in 'unfit' families. To ensure a better future for them, the state removes children from such families and places them in institutions. A quick comparison of the conditions within the *neblagopoluchnaia* family, and that of institutional settings in Town-X (my fieldwork site) leaves no doubt, about which conditions provide better care. Often the poor, dirty and small living quarters of unemployed parents are contrasted with the spacious, warm, clean and well-lit residential care institutions.

Opinions regarding social orphans vary. Some voice concern about high rates of unemployment and criminal involvement among care-leavers, their reduced ability to adjust well to the outside society, and personal and developmental problems they experience because of institutional upbringing (Andreeva, 2000; Chepurnykh, 1998; Sadovskii, 1998). Others, such as many state agents and institutional staff, feel that institutional settings are able to provide adequately for all the children's needs and ensure a positive outcome. In other words, a well-adjusted individual who can be 'a useful citizen and repay the state for what the state has given you' (in the words of a 22-year-old former resident). This view is held not only by a number of state agents, but also by some of my informants, former residents. Hence, the authorities are often genuinely surprised as to why these children, to whom the state 'had given everything', often do not correspond to the state agents' imagined outcome. ...

The reluctant northerner

Town-X is a regional and administrative centre in northeast Siberia, with a predominantly non-native population. Many people came to this town to work between the 1960s and 1990s and left their extended families behind in the western part of the Soviet Union, called the *materik* ('the mainland'). Attracted by high wages, sizeable northern benefits and the prospect of retiring early with savings to afford a comfortable life back on the *materik*, they viewed their move to this area as temporary. By the 1980s, Town-X had well-developed educational, medical and social welfare infrastructures. The climate in the area is severe: long cold dark winter months give way to cool short summers. For their well-being, newcomers in Soviet times often travelled for holidays to places with a more temperate climate. In those days, air transportation was still affordable, allowing regular vacations and visits to the extended family.

The post-Soviet period introduced dramatic changes to all aspects of life in northern communities. State trade gave way to private enterprise resulting in very high food prices in such a remote area. State employment was reduced; private jobs offered higher wages but no social benefits such as maternity or sick leave. This area has one of the highest rates of unemployment and alcoholism in the Russian Federation, a high percentage of people living in communal flats and houses without 'conveniences', and considerable gaps in the area of child welfare. The number of day-care centres (kindergartens) was cut in half while the remaining ones became expensive (even with a 50 per cent discount many poor or unemployed could not afford them). For many, the combined effects of economic hardship, isolation, and severe climate outweighed the benefits of living in this region.

These changes brought on a wave of out-migration from the Far North. Many well-off residents and young and mobile specialists left for the *materik*, resulting in the loss of a well-trained workforce. Some wanted to remain in northern towns (Thompson, 2003), whereas a considerable segment of the population had nowhere to go and no means to do so even if they wanted to. During a casual conversation, some of my former colleagues who still live in Town-X, explained how they felt abandoned and depressed: 'We don't live', they say, 'but only survive; we are prisoners of the North'. ...

The child welfare network

... A number of administrative agencies deal with child welfare. The Guardianship Department (GD) of the city administration is the main decision-making agency. It comprises four employees, all women. The Centre for Temporary Isolation of Juvenile Delinquents and the Committee for Juveniles focus on delinquent/vagrant children and youth. Since the mid-1990s, the Temporary Children's Shelter has provided residence and schooling for children aged three to sixteen years for up to six months. Local financial constraints have prevented the setting up of a post-institution adaptation centre.

There were also remarkably few state-funded support services for families. The city administration has limited subsidised housing, most of which consists of rooms in dormitories. The Centre for Assistance to Low-Income Families provides some benefits such as reduced transportation fares, kindergarten fees, and school lunches. Two Family Assistance Centres and the Temporary Children's Shelter provide a valuable alternative to the state institutions by working with the 'unfit' families but they were only able to serve a very small portion of the population. Significantly absent were citywide social services providing ongoing emotional, psychological and daily support for families in need.

Indeed, many of my informants felt completely alone. Thus, even though the infrastructure for child welfare was well established and still operated relatively successfully, a system of family welfare was largely absent.

Focus on the family: the struggle of the *neblagopoluchnaia* family with the state

… I found Marina, a small, thin 26-year old woman, through the file on her two-year-old son, Vitia, who had been growing up in the baby home since birth. We were sitting in her poorly furnished, unkempt one-room flat talking about her own childhood spent in various residential care institutions, her relationships with her mother, and the loss of her son. At the time of Vitia's birth, she was single and unemployed:

> At first, they [the Guardianship Department] tried to talk me into having an abortion but it was too late. When Vitia was born, the doctors in the Maternity Home asked me if I had food and clothes for the baby and what my living conditions were. They told me, 'Why don't you leave your baby in the Baby Home for a while so you can find a job and buy everything necessary for the baby and in a few months you can take him home? Meanwhile,' they said, 'your son will gain some weight, get stronger and healthier.'
> This is what I did. I visited him in the Baby Home but then the Guardianship Department came to my flat and they said that my living conditions were not acceptable, and that the baby would get sick here, and that they would not allow me to take Vitia, and that I might as well forget about him.

… The moment when Marina agreed to leave her child in the baby home on the seemingly caring and understanding advice from the doctors is of crucial importance and is fraught with ambiguity. The authorities conceptualise this kind of child placement as a form of *assistance* and *support* to a woman. If a mother refuses such assistance, she may be considered a bad mother because she is subjecting her child to possible deprivation. At the same time, the acceptance of an institutional placement may indicate to the state agents a possible ambivalence in the mother's relationship to her child. This is because good mothering is based on two assumptions. First, a good mother should not be willing to separate herself from her child and she is expected to *overcome* successfully her existing *difficulties*. The focus on the ability to achieve one's goals despite overwhelming difficulties is assigned significant cultural value, and it places the responsibility for failure on the person, not the environment. This maternal devotion constitutes the essence of the prevailing Russian discourse on 'maternal instinct'. Second, if a woman has not lost her 'maternal instinct' then even after her child is placed in an institution, she must be able to quickly overcome any difficulties, both her own and those created by the state's requirements. Thus, even after the placement there is still a chance to prove one a good mother by meeting the state agents' two sets of requirements.

The importance of home 'conditions'

Many women do not know that these requirements constitute a 'trap' that many unsuspecting families fall into, given that initially only the state agents know the rules of the game. At the beginning of the placement, the institutional authorities tell a mother that she is expected to come and visit her child, bring gifts, and take him/her for walks. To the state agents, adherence to this first set of requirements indicates a mother's devotion to the child. It is only *after* the placement that the mothers become aware of another set. At this time, women realise that the conditions upon which their children will be returned to them are much more difficult to meet. This is because they are required to provide acceptable family living 'conditions' based on culturally assumed value judgements of their lifestyle.

These adequate 'conditions' include a well-furnished, warm and well-lit, clean and orderly flat or a room. There must be a separate room or a room corner prepared specifically for the baby and enough baby clothes and food. In addition, parents should hold permanent employment, preferably in the state sector, not be too young, and have some post-secondary education. Evidence of the mother's determination and desire to raise her child must be demonstrated through what I call the 'performance' of love during her visits to the baby home, together with the display of acceptable living 'conditions'. Having a permanent state job, living in a registered marriage rather than in a common-law marriage, possessing material wealth, and being a well-educated, hard-working, self-reliant, conscientious and purposeful individual, are still considered the desired 'norm'. Taken together these still reflect bourgeois Soviet values (*cf.* Dunham, 1976; Fitzpatrick, 2000). Hence, *moral qualities* are revealed through the *outward form of material sufficiency*, which is assumed to ensure the psychological and emotional wellbeing of a child.

Considering the current severe economic and social problems, many families are currently experiencing, more and more families fail to correspond to these requirements. However, the state agents conceptualise the inability of mothers to overcome problems such as unemployment and poor living 'conditions' as the loss of 'maternal instinct' and lack of desire to raise their children. Implicitly, being young, inexperienced, single, and poorly educated contributes to state agents' conviction that a mother lacks vital resources to ensure the wellbeing of her child. These parents will be judged as unsuitable and categorised as *neblagopoluchnye*, an umbrella term for a range of family situations where numerous risk factors are believed to harm a child. Inherited from Soviet times, this term readily evokes the image of a low-income family, poor and dirty dwellings, poor hygiene, diet and health, unkempt personal appearance, alcoholism, and a lack of material goods and status. This image is so powerful that it has become a label with a social role attached to it. Yet as one judge said, 'Nobody is trying to understand what is happening in the family and why'.

The authorities' view of child development therefore has a conspicuously 'environmental' character. Individuals are considered products of their social environment. This philosophy is the basis for removing children in order to eliminate the undesirable influence of such a family. In prioritising a child's placement, the state agents recognise the importance first of a 'good' family, followed by institutions, and only then of the 'unfit' family the child was born into, because, as one GD employee said, '*Such* a mother cannot give a child anything'.

References

Andreeva, N. (ed) (2000) *Psikholog v Uchrezhdenii Sirotskogo Tipia: Opyt Practicheskoi Raboty* [A psychologist in an orphanage: experiences based on practical work], Moskva, Eslan.

Chepurnykh, E. (1998) 'Puti resheniia problem sotsial'nogo sirotstva v Rossiiskoi Federatsii' [Ways of solving the problem of social orphanhood in the Russian Federation], in Rybinskii, E. and Krasnitskaia, G. (eds) *Vse Deti – Nashi (Sbornik Materialov II Vserossiiskikh Pedagogicheskikh Katolikovskikh Chtenii, 12–17 Oktiabria 1998g.)*, Moskva, Presidentskaia programma 'Deti Rossii'.

Dunham, V. (1976) *In Stalin's Time: Middleclass Values in Soviet Fiction*, Cambridge, Cambridge University Press.

Fitzpatrick, S. (ed) (2000) *Stalinism: New Directions*, London, Routledge.

Karelova, G. (2000) *Gosudarstvennyi Doklad 'O Polozhenii Detei v Rossiiskoi Federatsii' 1998* [State report 'On the state of childhood in the Russian Federation' 1998], Moskva, Sinergiia.

Rybinskii, E. (1997) *Sirotlivoe Detstvo Rossii: Chto Delat'?* [Orphaned childhood of Russia: what to do?], Moskva, AO Russkii Mir; KB Prem'er.

Rybinskii, E. (1998) *Detstvo kak Sotsial'nyi Fenomen* [Childhood as social phenomenon], Moskva, Nauchno-issledovatel'skii institute detstva RDF.

Rybinskii, E. and Krasnitskaia, G. (1998) *Vse Deti – Nashi (Sbornik Materialov II Vserossiiskikh Pedagogicheskikh Katolikovskikh Chtenii, 12–17 Oktiabria 1998 g.)* [All children are ours (collection of papers from the Second All-Russian Katolikov Readings, 12–17 October 1998)], Moskva, Presidentskaia programma 'Deti Rossii'.

Sadovskii, N. (1998) *'O rabote ministerstva obrazovaniia i vysshei shkoly po sozdaniiu sotsial'no-pedagogicheskikh uslovii podderzhki detei v respublike Komi'* [On the work of the Ministry of Education and Higher Education for the creation of the social and pedagogical conditions of support for children in the Komi Republic], in Rybinskii, E. and Krasnitskaia, G. (eds) *Vse Deti – Nashi (Sbornik Materialov II Vserossiiskikh Pedagogicheskikh Katolikovskikh Chtenii, 12–17 Oktiabria 1998g.)*, Moskva, Presidentskaia programma 'Deti Rossii'.

Thompson, N. (2003) 'The native settler: contesting identities on Russia's resource frontier', *Polar Geography*, vol. 27, pp. 136–58.

Chapter 2

Children, poverty and social inequality

Heather Montgomery

Contents

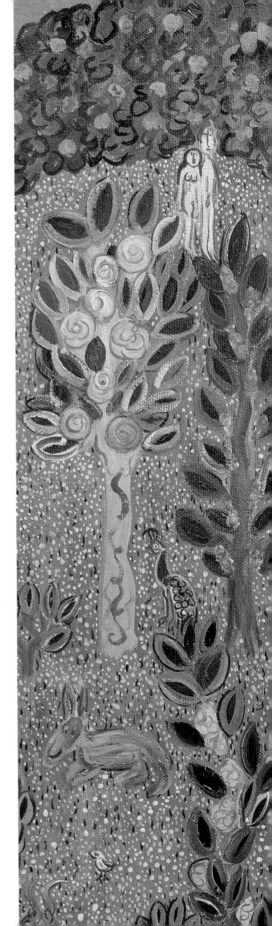

In this chapter, you will:

- explore the concepts of relative and absolute poverty and relate these to children's experiences
- examine the differing effects of poverty on children
- analyse some of the causes of child poverty and their relation to inequitable economic and social relations, within and between states
- consider the inequalities within families that contribute to children's different experiences of poverty, related to age and gender.

1   Introduction

Throughout the world, millions of children live in poverty. In both the minority and majority worlds there are children who go without adequate food or health care because they and their families are poor. This chapter will examine why this is so and will look at children's experiences of poverty. It will start by looking at how poverty is defined, focusing in particular on the differences between absolute and relative definitions of poverty. It then looks at the causes and impacts of poverty in countries throughout the minority and majority worlds, drawing on children's own experiences and understandings. Interwoven with this discussion is an analysis of various forms of social inequality and the impact these have on children's physical and emotional well-being.

2   Definitions of poverty

This chapter is concerned with the different ways in which poverty affects the lives of children throughout the world. Yet deciding which children are poor is not straightforward and one of the first issues encountered when examining this is how to define poverty.

Activity 1   Definitions of poverty

Allow about 30 minutes

Read through the two descriptions below of children's experiences of living in poverty, the first of Linda, a 14-year-old Angolan girl, and the second of Kim, an 11-year-old girl living in the UK. Then answer the following questions:

- Do you think that both Kim and Linda are living in poverty?
- How do you define this poverty?
- What are the impacts of living in poverty in each case?

Linda

Linda is 14 years old and a refugee from Angola. She has fled from fighting in her home town between the government and the UNITA rebels. When interviewed by the BBC she was living in a shack in the port city of Libito.

> [Linda lives] in miserable poverty where clean water is rare, [she] makes do with 'filthy rags' for clothes.
>
> She describes an existence of appalling suffering: 'We're all dirty. If you can find water it's never clean, and I don't sleep well here.
>
> 'We have to lay out pieces of paper on the ground and lie on them.
>
> 'Sometimes we don't even have paper because rain comes in through our roof and everything gets soaked.'
>
> Linda's poverty has taken its toll on her education.
>
> She used to study before she was driven from her home, but now most of her time is taken up preparing food, keeping the shelter clean and caring for her six brothers and sisters.
>
> Other opportunities for self-improvement are few. Linda explains: 'If you can find work, they hardly pay you anything.
>
> 'You can't afford clothes or shoes because they cost too much.'
>
> *(BBC News Online, 2001)*

Kim ← case study

Kim is 11 years old; she lives with her mother and two brothers on a council estate in a small rural town. Kim was unhappy and isolated in her neighbourhood and she felt that people on her estate did not like her or her family. She wanted to move to another area, nearer her school, where she could see her friends after school. She rarely played outside. 'We sometimes play at the park but without the other kids'.

Sustaining friendships out of school hours was problematic for her as she was isolated in a small village, poorly served by public transport. Her only opportunity for meeting with friends was by attending Guides, the sole organised activity available for children in her village. Initially she had problems buying the guide uniform because it was too expensive, but eventually she managed to buy a cheaper second-hand one. However, although she regularly attended Guides, she was unable to join in with the summer Guide Camp because her mother could not afford the costs. Missing out on Guide camp compounded Kim's feelings of difference and because she rarely got the chance to go away on holiday with her family, she felt the lack of opportunity keenly.

'If you have money you can go on loads of holidays and that, when if you've got less money you've kind of got to stay in all the time and limit how much you spend an' that.'

Kim's concerns about not having enough money and fitting in and joining in with friends affect her overall sense of wellbeing and security and this is reflected in her anxiety about the future.

'I worry about what life will be like when I'm older…because I'm kind of scared of growing older, but if you know what is in front of you then it's a bit better, but I don't know.'

(Ridge, 2009, p. 27)

Comment

Both Linda and Kim are poor but their poverty takes different forms. Linda has no access to clean drinking water and there is no money to spare. Her poverty manifests itself in food insecurity and lack of adequate shelter, housing and drinking water. However, the family's poverty also has less obvious effects. Linda has to take on a great deal of responsibility for her family, which means she cannot work to earn money. She cannot sleep properly and is constantly worried about the future. Drinking dirty water is dangerous and it is only a matter of time before it makes her or her siblings ill. It is also highly probable that this will affect her future health and have long-term consequences. Linda does not go to school. She cannot therefore gain any qualifications which might improve her chances of getting a better job and increasing her longer-term prospects. Her siblings, in their turn, will have to work from an early age and forego school. The effects of poverty, therefore, are manifold and encompass both the short and the long term. They are also likely to be passed on through the generations as it is hard to break out of the cycle of deprivation.

Kim is also poor but in contrast to Linda has a home and access to free medical care and education. However, compared to her peers she lacks the things that are important to her, which means she feels different, unwelcome and deprived of the things that other children take for granted. Her experience of poverty, therefore, is a comparative one in that she is poor in relation to other people. She feels different from others and humiliated by her poverty, which threatens her well-being and psychological health.

2.1 Absolute poverty

The two stories in the activity above underline a very important distinction that exists when defining poverty – that of absolute and relative poverty. Linda lives in absolute poverty, a situation defined by the Copenhagen World Summit on Social Development in 1995 as: 'a condition characterised by severe deprivation of basic human needs, including food, safe drinking water, sanitation facilities, health, shelter, education and information' (quoted in Gordon et al., 2003, p. 5). The World Bank's definition of absolute poverty is based on an 'international poverty line' of between $1 and $2 per day per person, which is deemed to be the minimum amount that purchases the goods and services necessary for basic survival. Using this definition, it has been calculated that 'Over a third of all children in developing countries (37 per cent or 674 million) are living in absolute poverty' (Gordon et al., 2003, p. 10).

This measure of absolute poverty is usually used when discussing majority-world countries. The USA, however, also uses an absolute

Figure 1   Site of a former shanty town and market in Liberia which was cleared in 2010, making almost 1 million people homeless

standard when assessing child poverty. It defines its child poverty threshold by identifying the cost of a food basket and estimating from that how much income is necessary for members of a family to survive. In 2008, 15.45 million children, or 20.7 per cent of all children, lived in families with incomes below the federal poverty level – $22,050 a year for a family of four (National Poverty Center, University of Michigan, 2011). Despite the USA being one of the world's richest countries, nearly one in seven children there experience hunger or inadequate shelter.

2.2   Relative poverty

Relative poverty is defined as follows:

> Individuals, families and groups in the population can be said to be in poverty when they lack the resources to obtain the types of diet, participate in the activities and have the living conditions and

amenities which are customary, or are at least widely encouraged or approved, in the societies to which they belong.

(Townsend, 1979, p. 31)

In contrast to the USA, most other minority-world countries define poverty in relative rather than absolute terms. Most governments set the poverty level as a percentage of the average income rather than a set figure. In the UK, different measures of relative poverty are used but the most common one defines a family as living in poverty if their household income is below 60 per cent of the national average. Using these figures, in 2009, 13.4 million people in the UK (22 per cent) were income poor and 4 million children lived in families experiencing poverty (Save the Children, 2010). In terms of the UK nations, 32 per cent of children lived in poverty in England, compared to 30 per cent in Scotland, 27 per cent in Wales and 27 per cent in Northern Ireland (Bradshaw and Mayhew, 2005).

Analysing poverty relatively not only allows for measurement of an individual or household's lack of material resources, but also aids analysis of wider issues of social inequality. Furthermore, it enables the depth and degrees of poverty to be measured. In contrast, measures of absolute poverty simply set a cut-off point and anyone living below that point is seen as poor regardless of the severity of their poverty. Within the UK, many children live in families that have an income of significantly less than 60 per cent of the national average and one in six children live in a household which has an income less than 50 per cent of the national average, placing them in deeper and often more persistent poverty. In this category of deep poverty children from certain groups are over-represented and these children face some of the most acute risks. In 2006, over 100,000 children were living in temporary accommodation as a result of being classed as homeless and around half a million lived in homes unfit for human habitation (Hirsch, 2006, p. 18). The children of asylum seekers are likely to live in some of the very poorest households, where parents cannot work while their claims are being processed and they are excluded from several of the anti-poverty measures available to other children in the UK. Traveller children face particular risks of poverty, deprivation and discrimination, and have some of the lowest educational and health outcomes of any children in the UK. Children of disabled parents are also vulnerable to persistent poverty. Their parents are more likely to be unemployed and even when they do work, they face discrimination and barriers to progress (Hirsch, 2006). All these figures indicate how certain groups experience particular forms of poverty and social exclusion. These differences are not simply concerned with material wealth but are based on patterns of social inequalities and the differences between groups. Measuring relative poverty is therefore always a comparative exercise, looking at children in relation to other children (and adults), and looking at quality of life as well as income.

Figure 2   Youngsters play football up against a boarded-up pub in the Gorton area of Manchester

In 2010, the Child Poverty Action Group (CPAG) compared the ability of the poorest and richest fifth to participate in community activities.

Parents wanted but could not afford ...	Poorest fifth	Richest fifth
a hobby or leisure activity for their children	14%	1%
to have friends round for tea or a snack once a fortnight	15%	0%
to send their children on a school trip at least once a term	14%	0%
to have a one-week holiday away from home with family	55%	4%

(Source: CPAG, 2008, p. 10)

Such activities add to a person's quality of life. They are not concerned with survival but with a person's well-being and hopes for the future. Having a holiday once a year, going out to eat, to a show or the cinema occasionally, or having friends round to eat, are markers of a person's ability to participate in activities that are taken for granted by others in the community. Not being able to afford them is a mark of poverty. Yet these figures also need some careful interpretation and may reflect parental choices as much as lack of income. For example, many of these families in the top fifth may be prioritising independent school fees or mortgage payments on larger houses which means that they cannot afford holidays. For many in the bottom fifth, it may be that they cannot afford a holiday without compromising on the basic necessities for living.

Activity 2   Reading A

Allow about 30 minutes

Turn to Reading A, 'A child's eye view of poverty' by L. Sutton, and, after reading the extract, answer these two questions:

- How do the children themselves define poverty?
- Why do you think some children reject the label 'poor'?

Comment

Perhaps the most surprising aspect about the study was that none of the children regarded themselves as either rich or poor. Instead, all of them identified themselves as average and used the terminology of poverty or wealth to differentiate themselves from disliked 'others'. Poverty was identified only in the case of homeless tramps or starving people in Africa. In their own lives children were determined to be seen as average. In the case of the estate children this sometimes meant 'talking up' what they had while the privately educated children were more likely to 'talk down' their background or their parents' wealth.

This reading also suggests some of the problems of researching child poverty and looking at its impacts on children. Although designed to highlight the problems children face, such studies can reinforce negative views of poor children. With every correlation drawn between poverty and low educational achievement, criminality or social exclusion, the more likely it becomes that the problem is seen as being with the child and not with their circumstances. As Ridge (2002, p. 144) has argued, 'the labels that society attach to poor children will have a profound impact on how children see themselves and on how other children see them'. It is hardly surprising, therefore, that few children wish to identify themselves as poor or claim membership of such a highly stigmatised group, and strive instead to portray themselves as normal. Indeed, the worst fear that the children seem to express in this study is not that they should be poor but that they should be different.

This is not to claim that children in this study are unaware of, or do not care about, social difference and social inequality. Instead, they re-label it and differentiate between people in particular ways, notably by categorising other children as 'chavs' or 'posh' and identifying themselves in opposition to these labels.

Figure 3   In 2012 the Child Poverty Action Group claimed that children and young people in Britain have higher rates of poverty than children and young people in most other European countries (Nastic, 2012)

While relative definitions of poverty are popular in social policy discourse, it is worth noting that they can be contentious. Some commentators have vociferously opposed the concept of relative poverty, arguing that the idea is fundamentally flawed and confuses poverty (income inadequacy) with inequality (income distribution). Peter Saunders argues that:

relative poverty has nothing to do with hunger, homelessness, illiteracy, sickness or dirty drinking water. Nor does it reduce as the economy grows and people get better off. Indeed, in a market economy, relative poverty is unlikely ever to disappear, no matter how rich the country becomes, for if food, housing, healthcare and schooling become universally available, the definition of being poor simply shifts to other things.

This is an infinitely elastic understanding of poverty which is immune to disconfirmation, for as people become more affluent, the poverty line gets raised to compensate. Yet despite this obvious flaw, the idea that poverty is about having less than other people has moved into the mainstream of political thinking in the last 40 years. ...

The problem at the core of the idea of relative poverty is that, for as long as incomes and assets are unequally distributed, there will *always* be people who have less. Defined in relative terms, the poor will always be with us, no matter how much overall living standards improve.

(Saunders, 2009, p. 6)

In other words, relative poverty has no cut-off point. It would be possible to live in a community of billionaires and be defined as poor if you were only a millionaire. Saunders argues therefore that poverty and social inequality are different concepts and must be treated differently. He argues that absolute standards of poverty are the best way to measure how many people are 'truly' poor and that these standards are how the majority of people in the UK understand poverty. Such a view stands in contrast to several of the surveys mentioned above in which people clearly did think of themselves and others as poor if their quality of life was impaired, and they felt deprived if they could not afford things that others took for granted. It is clearly difficult to separate poverty and social inequality conceptually despite Saunders's attempts. These links will be further discussed in Section 3.

Summary of Section 2

Poverty can be understood and measured in two ways: absolute and relative.

Absolute poverty is defined as the inability to purchase or consume a fixed minimum of goods and services.

Relative poverty is when people lack the resources to obtain the types of diet, participate in the activities, and have the living conditions and amenities which are customary in the society to which they belong.

Perceptions of poverty held by children are often unrelated to the kinds of data gathered by researchers.

Children negotiate experiences of poverty on a daily basis but strive to see themselves as normal rather than poor in order to avoid stigmatisation.

Relative poverty is a contentious definition of poverty which has been rejected by some academics.

3 Impacts of child poverty

Although definitions and measures of poverty differ, it is clear that poverty has significant impacts on children's lives, in all parts of the world. In both rich and poor countries, children who live in poverty generally have worse health, worse educational opportunities and worse access to services than wealthier children. In the majority world in the early years of the twenty-first century, around 7 million children under the age of five died every year, 600,000 million lived in poverty, 129 million were underweight, 121 million were not in school, 376 million used unsafe water sources, and around 265 million children were not immunised against any diseases or had suffered a recent illness for which they did not receive any medical advice or treatment (UNICEF, 2009). Although there has been some improvement in these figures since, more than 1 billion children are severely deprived of at least one of the essential goods and services they require to survive, grow and develop (UNICEF, 2009). Such children are also likely to live in families where any unexpected or unplanned situation can prove disastrous. A child becoming sick and needing medical care may mean

that other children in the family cannot eat, or that siblings have to drop out of school to run the household or take on more paid labour. It may also mean that parents have to decide to devote time and resources to a sick or disabled child, at the expense of other children.

Figure 4 A child in Guiyu, Guangdong province, China, pumps water that has been polluted by all the surrounding electronic waste scrapyards

In the UK large-scale and longitudinal studies have shown correlations between living in poverty, ill-health, lower educational attainment and poorer access to medical care. This has impacts in terms of both current and future well-being. Research by the Child Poverty Action Group (CPAG) found that:

> 18% of children [in the UK] (around 2.4 million) suffer from multiple deprivation, even after the sacrifices made by their parents. These children go without two or more necessities such as 'a warm waterproof coat' or a 'properly fitting pair of shoes'.
>
> 1 in 6 families fall into poverty as the result of the birth of a child.
>
> Babies born to poorer families are more likely to be born prematurely and to be of low birth weight. The implications include a greater likelihood of impaired development and of certain chronic diseases later in life. ...

Poverty
Affect
in UK.

Children whose parents do unskilled work are five times more likely to die from accidents than children whose parents have professional occupations.

Children living in temporary accommodation or poor quality social housing are at greater risk of fire. ...

Poverty in childhood can leave a long-term legacy. Children raised in poverty are, as adults, more likely to be unemployed, in low paid employment, are more likely to live in social housing, get in trouble with the police and are at greater risk of alcohol and drug abuse.

(CPAG, 2001, p. 1)

Both in the UK and internationally, longitudinal evidence suggests that poor children suffer disproportionately from ill-health, accidents, racism, violent neighbourhoods, environmental pollution or nuclear testing, and institutional or communal violence (Montgomery, 2008). They go to worse schools, attain lower educational qualifications than their better-off peers and are less likely to go to university (Machin and McNally, 2006). Even before birth they are disadvantaged and as one report concludes:

Poverty in and soon after childbirth is associated with a much higher risk of a low birth-weight birth, maternal depression in infancy and lower chances that the mother will try breastfeeding. All these are known to be associated with poor outcomes in the rest of childhood and in adulthood.

(Mayhew and Bradshaw, 2005, p. 16)

As well as these problems, there is increasing evidence to suggest that poverty has devastating impacts on a psychological level and studies have shown that difficult early life experiences, social marginalisation, feeling undervalued, and being seen as socially inferior inflict long-term psychological damage, which is reflected in children's performance at school, the level of violence they suffer in their daily lives and the quality of their home and community life (Wilkinson and Pickett, 2010).

Young Lives is an international study of childhood poverty, partially funded by DFID (the UK Department for International Development),

Figure 5 Young Lives examines the long-term effects of child poverty, including the impacts of children's work on their well-being

following 12,000 children in Ethiopia, India, Peru and Vietnam over 15 years between 2002 and 2017. It researches different aspects of children's lives and uses this research to improve policies and programmes for children. One of the children it has followed is six-year-old Deepak who lives in India, for whom poverty has many overlapping and devastating impacts:

Deepak's father has had three wives but they all died, two in childbirth. He works as a casual farm labourer, leaving the house at 6am, and does not come back until 8pm, by which time all the children are in bed so they see little of him.

Deepak helps to look after the younger children and can often be seen carrying his younger sister, who is 18 months old, on his back, even in school. He says he likes her better than his brother and that he takes good care of her. He helps to fetch water from the bore well with a small plastic pot in the morning and in the evening. He and his siblings and friends wash themselves in a nearby stream.

His elder stepbrother, aged 12, does most of the household work including cleaning, washing and cooking. His grandmother, who lives just a few houses away, also helps when she can. Deepak's father says his wife died 18 months ago giving birth to Deepak's little sister 'during the mango season', while Deepak says it was 'when he was small'. Deepak's father's second wife also died in childbirth. …

Deepak is a bright child but his family is very poor. He says that the family had to sell their tape recorder and he is sad about this as he liked to listen to songs while working.

Deepak's father is employed under the Government's National Rural Employment Guarantee Scheme, which provides 100 days' employment a year on demand, as a right, for poor rural households whose adult members volunteer to do unskilled manual work. He receives 80 rupees a day (about US$1.55) for this work, which leaves him little money to provide for the children. He also receives oil and lentils as part of a Government Public Distribution System (PDS) and says that it is thanks to this scheme that he can feed his children.

His father says that Deepak often has a fever: 'I don't know why – maybe due to mosquitoes or due to food. We don't know what the problem is.' …

Deepak's grandmother thinks he is less healthy than other children and Deepak says he is bullied at school because he is so thin. His grandmother says this is because they don't have a mother to look after them and there is only so much she can do to help. 'They have no mother and so no proper care. I am old. I cannot take care of small children at my age. He is not what he should be at his age. But what can I do?' She says that the children have to bath themselves and wash their own clothes and hair and that they are too young to do this for themselves. 'All this would be done by their mother if she was alive. I think that compared to other children they are not clean, there is no one to comb their hair, they are shabby. I try and do it for all of them but it is too much for me.'

(Young Lives, 2009, pp. 1–2)

Reading through the case studies of children given so far in this chapter – Kim, Linda and Deepak – it is evident that their poverty has multiple impacts and multiple causes. Deepak's poverty, for instance, is caused not only by his father's low wages, but by other factors such as his caste, his mother's death, his family size and ill-health. All of these are closely related to each other and interact with and exacerbate child poverty. It is rarely easy to point to any one specific cause of child poverty without resorting to simplistic generalisations or judgements. Usually there is a complex series of reasons and circumstances that keep children in poverty.

Activity 3 Lek

Allow about 15 minutes

The following passage is a case study taken down by the author of this chapter during anthropological fieldwork in Thailand in the mid-1990s (for full details see Montgomery, 2001). Read the story of 13-year-old Lek and, as you do, note down all the factors that caused, or exacerbated, her and her family's poverty.

Lek is a 13-year-old girl who lives with her family in a makeshift slum house a few miles outside a major tourist resort in Thailand. She is one of 13 children born to her mother, Saew, although only four of these children are still alive and only seven survived infancy. Her mother married very young, at around the age of 12, and while her family were rice farmers in the poorer north-eastern part of the country, Saew and her husband found that they could not grow enough rice on their small, over-cultivated plot to make a living through farming.

Saew and her husband decided to migrate to a tourist resort in the south of the country and planned to sell food and sweets on the streets to tourists. When they arrived in this resort the children did indeed manage to find this sort of work while Saew took a job as a rubbish collector, going round the streets and picking up waste to sort out for re-sale. For a while they survived and built themselves a breeze-block house with a tin roof on a piece of land near a supermarket. They did not own the land, however, and had no permission to build there, so security was always tenuous.

After several years of doing this work, Saew was hit by a car while collecting rubbish and never fully recovered. She could not walk properly or push her cart, and so she gave up this work. Lek and her other children tried to continue selling sweets and chewing gum but this did not bring in enough money to cover Saew's medical bills or make up for her lost revenue. They started instead to scavenge for scrap metal on a local rubbish tip but quickly began to hate this work and were frightened by the risks they took. They were regularly bitten by rats, picked up infections and the smell was insufferable. Lek is often ill which means that she cannot always work. The family survives because when the children are not working on the rubbish heap they beg from tourists; although this means running the risk of being arrested, or being fined, by the police.

Comment

Clearly Lek and her family are living in poverty but it is extremely hard to point to only one identifiable cause. Instead, it is necessary to look at the impact of multiple causes of poverty and how they amplify and reinforce the family's poverty. It is also important to note how tightly bound up children are in their parents' circumstances. Lek would not be poor if her parents were not. Therefore child poverty is very dependent on adult poverty, and indeed many poor adults may have been poor children.

The downward spiral began when Lek's mother could no longer grow sufficient rice on her family's land and had to move away. This too had social origins rather than being a 'natural' cause of poverty. The silting up of rivers due to modern agricultural practices, deforestation, land enclosures and global warming all contribute to flooding or to drought, while population pressure, over-farming and diversion of land to modern agribusiness make crop failure more likely.

Ill-health also contributes to the family's poverty. Saew's accident increased her family's poverty, both through limiting her earning capacities and through diverting scarce resources to pay for medical care.

There are also other social causes of Lek's poverty. Neither she nor her family have much education, or access to school, which would improve their ability to earn. There is also a lack of legal and adequately paid earning opportunities, forcing the children into illegal or dangerous employment which is much more insecure than legal work. The lack of state-funded social security payments, or free hospital treatment, also plays a part in keeping Lek's family poor.

Finally, we might note the global distribution of wealth: children in certain parts of the world never have to do the badly paid, dangerous and illegal jobs that Lek and her siblings have to take on in order to survive.

Just as poverty has numerous impacts on children, so it also has numerous causes. The small vignette above suggests the complex mesh of individual, local and global factors that cause children to be, and stay, poor.

Figure 6   The slum village in Thailand where Lek's family lives

Summary of Section 3

Poverty has an impact on a child's health and well-being.

There are multiple factors that contribute to, and exacerbate, children's poverty.

Poverty has multiple, cumulative and long-lasting effects on children, including on their health as adults, their educational achievement, and their current and future mental health.

> Poor children suffer disproportionately from ill-health, accidents, racism, violent neighbourhoods, environmental pollution or nuclear testing, and institutional or communal violence.

4 Social inequality

One idea that came up in the previous section was that poverty cannot be understood simply in absolute terms and that the most useful explanations as to what causes child poverty are to be found by examining patterns of inequality; between countries and communities and within individual families.

4.1   Social inequality within countries: 'The Spirit Level'

← research study

In their influential book, *The Spirit Level* (2010), Richard Wilkinson and Kate Pickett argue that poverty cannot be understood simply in terms of the personal circumstances of individual people and that instead it is necessary to look at the gap between rich and poor in any society. Taking the size of the gap between the richest and poorest 20 per cent of the population as an indicator of inequality, they found that people who live in countries with high levels of income inequalities do worse than those where there is a more equal distribution of income. This, they argue, holds true for all aspects of life and they go on to show the differences between highly unequal and more equal countries in terms of child well-being, infant mortality, literacy, obesity and school achievement.

The UK is one of the richest countries in the world and yet it has wide disparities of income between rich and poor, and one of the highest percentages of children who live in relative poverty in the industrialised world. One 2010 study found that the top 10 per cent of households had wealth above £853,000, while the bottom tenth had less than £8,800, and the disparities between rich and poor have been getting worse (Hills et al., 2010). By the late 1990s relative poverty was twice the level of the 1960s and three times the level of the late 1970s. In 1979 the richest tenth of the population received 21 per cent of total disposable income. By 2003 this figure had risen to 29 per cent (Giddens and Diamond, 2005, p. 102). The UK also has one of the worst incidences of child poverty, child obesity, child unhappiness and ill-health of all the rich nations. In contrast, countries in the European Union with the smallest gap between richest and poorest, such as the

Scandinavian countries, are also those with the lowest levels of child poverty. In Sweden the child poverty rate is around 5 per cent and its infant mortality rates are among the lowest in the world (lower even than among the better off in the UK). Swedish people are six times less likely to be obese or end up in prison than in less equal countries.

Another major difference between groups within countries is based on ethnicity, and for many children, poverty and ethnicity are closely linked. In the UK and the USA, ethnic minority children are more likely to live in poverty than their white counterparts. In the USA, 16 per cent of white children are officially poor, while for Hispanic and African American children, the figure is 40 per cent. In the UK 20 per cent of white people are poor compared with 60 per cent of Pakistanis and 70 per cent of Bangladeshis (The Poverty Site, 2011). In other countries this pattern in repeated. In Brazil, and throughout South America, children of African heritage tend to be poorer and live in worse conditions than white children; they have worse schooling, access to health care and to state benefits. If they do not speak the majority language they may not be able to access welfare services, even if these do exist.

Figure 7 The UK has some of the highest childcare costs in the world, as well as some of the worst child poverty and child well-being indicators

The Spirit Level concludes that both rich and poor benefit from a more equal society and from wealth redistribution. Perhaps not surprisingly, this has generated much debate and controversy. Sociologist Peter Saunders, who was quoted earlier objecting to the concept of relative poverty, has claimed that the statistical analysis on which the data is based is flawed and that cultural and historical factors, as much as economic ones, have an impact on children's educational achievements, the status of women or the overall well-being of a society. He concludes that:

> Wilkinson and Pickett think that America or Britain could be made to look just like Sweden, if only the income distribution were changed. ... But Sweden and Japan have the income distributions they have because of the kinds of societies they are. They are not cohesive societies because their incomes are equally distributed; their incomes are equally distributed because they are cohesive societies.

(Saunders, 2010, p. 121)

Activity 4   Reading B   ← *Good case study.*

Allow about 30 minutes

Turn to Reading B, 'Nothing bad intended' by Donna M. Goldstein, and read the extract about poor and rich children in Brazil. Then answer the following question:

*   What differences do you note between the childhoods of the urban middle classes and those of children of the favela (slum)?

Comment

Brazil is a society of extremes with a highly unequal distribution of wealth. Pockets of absolute poverty exist alongside a wealthy middle class. In this extract, Goldstein makes the point that poverty and social inequality change the very nature of poor children's childhoods. Because of their poverty, slum children are conceptualised differently from rich children; they are treated differently, even by their own families, and are valued significantly less.

Figure 9 Ahead of the G8 summit, an estimated 225,000 campaigners joined the Make Poverty History march in Edinburgh on 2 July 2005

Activity 5   Reading C

Allow about 30 minutes

Turn to Reading C, 'Suffering child: an embodiment of war and its aftermath in post-Sandinista Nicaragua' by James Quesada, at the end of the chapter. This reading describes the causes and effects of poverty on Daniel, a young boy growing up in Nicaragua in the 1990s in the aftermath of civil war and revolution. The majority of the reading focuses on the impact of war and violence on Daniel's physical and mental health, but it is clear that these cannot be separated from Daniel's experiences of poverty. This extract concentrates on the political causes of Daniel's poverty and how economic policies imposed on poorer countries by richer ones (through organisations such as the International Monetary Fund), as well as the choices that particular governments make about where to spend money, have an impact on individuals.

Read through this extract and comment on:

- the impact of the war and revolution on Daniel, and his mother's experience of poverty
- the impacts on Daniel and his family of political and policy decisions taken at an international level.

Comment

This reading uses the experiences of one boy to stand for the experiences of many in Nicaragua. The author draws direct parallels between Daniel's suffering, and the events and decisions that take place on a global and international level – about which he can know nothing and cannot control.

The family's poverty is closely tied to the political situation in Nicaragua. Having fought to depose the US-backed dictator, Somoza, Maria did well under the subsequent Sandinista government, receiving a home, training, education and some help with childcare. After the government fell, however, Maria and her family found themselves on the losing side. Their house was publicly and humiliatingly taken away, and Maria could not get work. The new pro-US government instituted a series of financial reforms which severely curtailed social welfare payments, leaving Daniel and Maria almost destitute.

Even in this brief extract, it is possible to see the impact of international policy on an individual child. It is not enough to say that Daniel is poor because of the individual choices that his parents made. He is poor as a direct consequence of policies and decisions made thousands of miles away, which have an enormous impact on him. Large-scale financial restructuring programmes, as required by international organisations, and supported by the USA and other countries, mean that the safety net of a welfare system has been withdrawn from him and that his life has become unbearable. These reforms also mean the end of the wealth redistribution programmes, which, in attempting to reduce social and economic inequalities, had produced great benefits for Daniel's family.

It may, of course, be possible to point to other Nicaraguan children who had very different experiences or who did much better after the Sandinista government fell. However, this reading illustrates the linkages between international political and economic policies, and an individual child's experiences of poverty.

4.3   Social inequality within families

Another area to examine is that of inequality within families. Poverty levels are traditionally measured in terms of income per household, and child poverty levels are extrapolated from that. However, this says little about the distribution of wealth among individual household members. It is possible that while households may be poor, parents may sacrifice things for themselves to protect their children from poverty; while in other instances, children might be materially rich but emotionally have less to do at home and it is more profitable for them to work and send money home to their families.

Other cases also show the differential experiences of poverty, depending on age, within a family. Due to international pressure, countries such as Pakistan and Bangladesh have forbidden children under the age of 14 to work in clothes factories. However, poor families cannot afford to support non-productive children and therefore children are placed into sweatshops and carpet weaving factories by illegal arrangements. The conditions in these places are often worse than in the legal sector and as a result younger children are more vulnerable to abuse and exploitation than their older siblings who are able to work legally. Similar effects can be seen by looking at the impact of the 1992 Harkin Bill, which proposed a ban on the import to the USA of all Bangladeshi products, especially clothes, made with child labour. Although well meaning, it had disastrous consequences for children in Bangladesh. 50,000 children were immediately fired from factories but without education or skills, they did not return home or to school. While older children continued to work legally in the garment factories, and were afforded some legal protection in these jobs, their younger siblings were forced to find new sources of income. The majority ended up working as stone-crushers, street hustlers and prostitutes, doing work that was infinitely more exploitative, hazardous and difficult than garment production (Rahman et al., 1999).

Summary of Section 4

Poverty occurs as a result of political decisions made at international and national levels, and can have devastating consequences on individual children.

There are also important historical and structural factors which need to be taken into consideration.

Social inequalities can be found between nations, within nations and within families.

Within families, girls and boys often have different experiences of poverty, as do younger and older children.

5 Conclusion

The relationship between children and poverty is complex and, as this chapter shows, it cannot be understood in isolation from social inequalities, as well as from international policy and global economic forces. The numbers of children living in poverty worldwide are extremely high and while the bulk of these children live in the majority world, there are also pockets of deprivation in the wealthy countries of the minority world. Although there are differences in the types of poverty these children experience, the distinction between relative and absolute poverty is helpful in understanding the experience of both. By understanding poverty in relative terms, it is also possible to see that at the heart of discussions about poverty lie issues of social justice, and that it is difficult to analyse issues of poverty critically without acknowledging economic and social disparities.

References

BBC News Online (2001) *A Sheet of Paper for a Bed* [online], http://news.bbc.co.uk/1/hi/world/africa/1186527.stm (Accessed 6 April 2011).

Bradshaw, J. and Mayhew, E. (eds) (2005) *The Well-Being of Children in the UK*, 2nd edn, London, Save the Children.

Burdon, T. (2000) 'A clear case of relief,' *CRIN (Children's Rights Information Network) Newsletter*, no. 13, pp. 28–9.

Child Poverty Action Group (CPAG) (2001) *An End in Sight? Tackling Child Poverty in the UK. Background Briefing and Summary*, London, CPAG.

Child Poverty Action Group (CPAG) (2008) *Child Poverty: The Stats. Analysis of the Latest Poverty Statistics*, London, CPAG.

Giddens, A. and Diamond, P. (eds) (2005) *The New Egalitarianism*, Cambridge, Polity Press.

Gordon, D., Nandy, S., Pantazis, C., Pemberton, S. and Townsend, P. (2003) *Child Poverty in the Developing World*, Bristol, Policy Press.

Hills, J., Brewer, M., Jenkins, S., Lister, R., Lupton, R., Machin, S., Mills, C., Modood, T., Rees, T. and Riddell, S. (2010) *An Anatomy of Economic Inequality in the UK*, London, HMSO.

Hirsch, D. (2006) *What Will It Take to End Child Poverty?*, York, Joseph Rowntree Foundation.

Machin, S. and McNally, S. (2006) *Education and Child Poverty: A Literature Review*, York, Joseph Rowntree Foundation.

Mayhew, E. and Bradshaw, J. (2005) 'Mothers, babies and the risks of poverty', *Poverty*, vol. 121, pp. 13–6.

Montgomery, H. (2001) *Modern Babylon? Prostituting Children in Thailand*, Oxford, Berghahn.

Montgomery, H. (2008) *An Introduction to Childhood: Anthropological Perspectives on Children's Lives*, Oxford, Wiley-Blackwell.

National Poverty Center, University of Michigan (2011) *How Many Children Live in Poverty?* [online], http://www.npc.umich.edu/poverty/#5 (Accessed 21 July 2011).

Nastic, D. (2012) 'Why we need a relative income poverty measure', *Poverty*, vol. 143, pp. 13–7.

Rahman, M. M., Khanam, R. and Absar, N. U. (1999) 'Child labor in Bangladesh: a critical appraisal of Harkin's Bill and the MOU-type schooling program', *Journal of Economic Issues*, vol. 33, no. 4, pp. 985–1003.

Rende Taylor, L. (2005) 'Dangerous trade-offs: the behavioral ecology of child labor and prostitution in rural Northern Thailand, *Current Anthropology*, vol. 46, no. 3, pp. 411–31.

Ridge, T. (2002) *Childhood Poverty and Social Exclusion*, Bristol, Policy Press.

Ridge, T. (2009) *Living with Poverty. A Review of the Literature on Children's and Families' Experiences of Poverty*, London, HMSO.

Saunders, P. (2009) *Poverty of Ambition: Why We Need a New Approach to Tackling Child Poverty*, London, Policy Exchange.

Saunders, P. (2010) *Beware False Prophets: Equality, the Good Society and The Spirit Level*, London, Policy Exchange.

Save the Children (1995) *Towards a Children's Agenda*, London, Save the Children.

Save the Children (2010) *Poverty Kills Childhood: Save the Children's UK Programme Annual Report 2009*, London, Save the Children.

The Poverty Site (2011) *UK: Low Income and Ethnicity* [online], http://www.poverty.org.uk/06/index.shtml (Accessed 21 April 2011).

Townsend, P. (1979) *Poverty in the United Kingdom: A Survey of Household Resources and Standards of Living*, London, Allen Lane.

UNICEF (2000) *State of the World's Children*, New York, UNICEF.

UNICEF (2009) *State of the World's Children*, New York, UNICEF.

Wilkinson, R. and Pickett, K. (2010) *The Spirit Level: Why Equality Is Better for Everyone*, London, Penguin.

Young Lives (2009) *Deepak's Story: A Profile from Young Lives in Andhra Pradesh* [online], http://www.younglives.org.uk/files/others/childrens-voices-pdfs/india/deepak (Accessed 6 April 2011).

Reading A
A child's eye view of poverty

L. Sutton

Source: 'A child's eye view', 2007, *Poverty*, vol. 126, pp. 8–11.

Introduction

Research previously undertaken with children who experience poverty has predominantly drawn them from a pre-existing sample of families living on a low income (Ridge, 2002; Roker, 1998), or through charitable organisations (Daly and Leonard, 2002), and has focused directly on asking children – in one-to-one interviews – about life on a low income. This research project was different in that it focused directly on what children from contrasting backgrounds felt to be most important to them *per se*, how they identified themselves, and whether – and how – themes associated with income inequality and social exclusion emerged in their own world views.

The children

Forty-two children, aged 8 to 13 from two contrasting socio-economic backgrounds, took part in a series of group discussions. Nineteen came from a disadvantaged housing association estate and participated in services provided by Save the Children and Groundwork. The children were allocated into four groups on the basis of age and gender with separate groups of older (11–13-year-olds) and younger (8–10-year-olds) boys and girls. Each of these groups participated in five research sessions over a year (2005 to 2006) with each session lasting between two and four hours.

Interviews with parents suggested that most of the children were living in low-income households and had experience of material hardship. Most of the children had lived on, or around, the estate since birth, and many had large, local extended families who, for example, provided childcare and helped their families financially. Most of the children lived in households with more than one sibling and many shared bedrooms. The children attended a range of local primary and secondary state schools. Some children reported that they 'wagged' or played truant from school, and a few of the older boys in particular talked of getting into trouble at school, at home and with their neighbours. Several children had special educational needs and a few had parents with long-term disabilities.

Twenty-three children were recruited to the research from a fee-paying independent school. The school fees ranged from £2,300 to over £5,000 per term. The groups of children were divided in the same way as the estate children, with separate groups of younger (8–10-year-olds) boys and girls and older (11–13-year-olds) boys and girls. Each group was visited four times over the year.

The private school children were a mixture of day students and boarders. Day students mainly lived in the surrounding villages and some had previously attended state schools. Several children's families owned more than one home in the UK. Many had moved house several times during their lives, often having lived in different locations in the UK and abroad. Few of the children saw each other outside school.

Nearly all the children were driven to and collected from school by their parents. They tended to have long school days, staying at school until up to 6.15pm doing 'prep' or homework. They also took part in a wide range of after-school clubs and activities, and a few of the children (mainly girls) kept ponies.

Methodological approach

The research was participatory in approach and design. The aim was to enable children to have input into what issues to research and how best to research them. It therefore focused on exploring the topics that children themselves deemed important from their own perspectives. The children also chose or suggested the methods they wanted to use in follow-up sessions. We began by asking the children what they thought was most important in their lives. Each group of children then constructed a list of their most important things.

All the children (from both backgrounds) identified the same four areas of education, their favourite things, free time, and their family and friends. However, different groups included additional items in their lists. For example, the estate girls identified health and safety as an important issue, and followed this up by designing questions and recording interviews with their peers about health and personal safety. The younger estate boys wanted to explore certain aspects of school life further by conducting role plays about a good and bad day at school. Other groups followed a similar pattern so that we worked through the lists of important issues, exploring topics through using 'draw and write' methods, games, role play, mapping and photography. ...

Similarities between the children

We found some key similarities between the children. For example, although there were differences in the number and size of the material possessions owned by each group, both the estate and private school children owned and valued a similar core of possessions. These included their pets, toys and games. None of the children identified themselves as poor or rich. They considered themselves as 'average' along a continuum of poverty through to affluence.

The children's desire to avoid differentiating themselves from others was reflected in how they presented their circumstances. The estate children tended to 'talk up' what they owned; as one estate boy said, 'I've got all the stuff I want'. The private school children sometimes 'talked down' their material possessions and, particularly, played down their relative economic status.

> 'We live in a nice big house with a drive, but I wouldn't say I was more highly put than anybody else really. We are moving in to a big house with a drive, but I wouldn't really be like that to anybody else. There are some children who get, like, absolutely everything they ask for, but like I don't get everything I ask for...'
>
> (Older private school girl)

Having too much or too little, therefore, was viewed by the children in a group setting as something to distance themselves from. Their desire to avoid standing out as being different highlights how important it is to children to fit in with their own peer group.

The 'otherness' of poverty and affluence

Terms such as 'poor' and 'rich' were rather alien to the children and applied to 'others', particularly those who lived in extreme and absolute circumstances. Poverty was viewed by both groups of children, for example, as either belonging to those in the Third World or, in the UK, to homeless beggars referring to people who were homeless and hungry. During role play sessions with the estate children, poor people were always represented as beggars living on the streets and desperate for food and money. Being rich was associated with having larger material possessions, and more of them, by both groups of children. For example, the rich were perceived to own very large houses and lots of cars. Their houses would have numerous bathrooms, 'golden baths' and spacious rooms. They would have an enormous garden, usually complemented with a swimming pool, a conservatory and invariably a huge trampoline.

The children presented a richer and more in-depth discussion about social difference through their references to 'chavs' and 'posh people'. These terms were associated with lower and higher socio-economic circumstances respectively. The children's perceptions of both these groups were often antagonistic. For example, the estate children perceived being rich to equate with 'poshness'. Being rich and posh meant having few friends, being 'snobby', spoilt, mean and greedy. Estate children also believed that 'posh' children would have little fun in their lives, whilst they were able to have lots. This was primarily because the estate children perceived richer children to be required to work hard. They were also perceived as having few friends mainly because they would 'show off' with their money and have to stay in and do their homework.

By contrast, private school children often perceived children who lived in council estates to be 'chavs', who they considered to be badly behaved and had parents that did not care about them.

'Their parents would be a bad example, they would smoke in front of them and they would swear and drink, you know.'

'The parents wouldn't care about them, would they? They wouldn't care what they do and just let them go off.'

(Older private school boys)

The private school children also perceived poorer children to attend what they considered to be 'rougher' schools.

There were some stark contrasts in the lived experiences between the private school and estate children. For the purposes of this article, we have chosen to focus on their play or free-time activities.

Play and free time

The estate children's free time was dominated by street play and socialising with friends unsupervised in open public spaces within their estate. They enjoyed and valued street play tremendously. Their games were played communally, were physical, and were predominantly based around hiding and chasing.

> 'With Kickstone, someone is at a lamppost and you have all got to hide and you have to count to 30 and you go and look for them and they kick them if they are caught. Manhunt is where there are two teams and you have to catch each other and then when they have caught all of them they have to catch the other team.'

(Older estate girl)

The younger estate boys also enjoyed building 'dens'. Although unsupervised, the estate children's street play was governed by rules set down by their parents. Parents warned their children about which areas in the estate to avoid and set times for their return. This allowed the children the responsibility to make decisions for themselves, and enabled them to be 'street-wise'. The estate children also talked about the range of parental sanctions they received if they got into trouble in the wider community. These generally involved being sent to bed early or being 'grounded'.

Open space was vitally important to the estate children and they expressed real sense of anger at the loss of some of their land to local developers. The loss of this land made it harder for them to congregate and play with their friends in the relative safety of being near home and off roads. The children's frustration was evident on our 'walkabouts' in the estate with the older boys who heckled and abused the builders on site and placed obstacles in the paths of construction machinery. The loss of their land highlights the tension between developing on and maintaining public space, with direct consequences for how children live their lives.

Street play was all the more important to the estate children owing to a lack of space and resources within the home, and limited opportunities to access more organised activities, which were perceived to be too costly to parents. Street play made the children visible and liable to be perceived as trouble within their estate.

> 'There's only one park and no one goes on anything because the 18-year-olds go on and vandalise everything. There's a playground

near the shops and if the police catch you they take you back to your house. You're not allowed to go in.'

(Younger estate girl)

The private school children, on the other hand, led more 'chaperoned' lives than the estate children. They spent more of their free time indoors at home, or involved in organised activities which were accompanied by adults. They were often driven to and from friends' houses, clubs and activities.

'I do quite a lot of riding lessons, I have tennis lessons, I have gymnastics lessons.'

(Older private school girl)

'Well, I have riding lessons and I sometimes have fishing lessons, I go with my dad on fishing lessons… and I go for shooting lessons.

(Older private school girl)

They also emphasised the importance of their own personal space within their homes and tended to play with their friends more at home than the estate children did. They took part in a wide variety of organised activities which frequently emphasised learning. These included: riding, shooting, fishing, tennis and gymnastic lessons.

The private school children's parenting styles differed from the estate children's in that they were based on perceptions of latent risks to their children's safety. The private school children explained that their parents worried about them getting attacked or 'mugged' when out and about. Their perceptions appeared to be heightened by incidents in the media of anti-social behaviour, gun crime and 'rough' hooded youths picking on other children to 'mug' them for their mobile phones. This fear for their safety was transmitted to the children, making them wary of other children when out and about.

Subsequently private school children perceived their parents to 'baby' them, allowing them less freedom to go out unaccompanied than they sometimes would have liked.

> 'I am allowed down to the post box at the bottom of our close but I am not allowed past there and I am set times so like if you are not back within ten minutes they'll call the police.'
>
> ['How does this make you feel?']
>
> 'Strange, my friend, who lives in the village next to the graveyard she has been able to walk the dog as far as she wants since she was 5 or 10 and I am not allowed to go further than the post box.'

(Older private school girl)

Conclusion

One overarching finding from this research was the extent to which both groups of children prioritised issues of importance to them. For example, both the estate and private school children identified relationships and activities as more important to them than their material circumstances. Both, despite their different backgrounds, also emphasised the importance of education, free time, favourite things, and friends and family in their lives. The similarities between children from different socio-economic backgrounds serve as a reminder of the everyday experience of being a child. This is especially important when children from low-income households are often regarded as problematic and different. They are first and foremost children.

A unique strength of this project is the participation of children from contrasting backgrounds and the research clearly identifies the dimensions of social difference from the perspective of children themselves. It therefore helps us to develop a child-centred view of the themes and issues which are associated with, and result from, social disparity and relative disadvantage in childhood.

References

Daly, M. and Leonard, M. (2002) *Against all Odds: Family Life on a Low Income in Ireland*, Combat Poverty Agency.

Ridge, T. (2002) *Childhood Poverty and Social Exclusion*, The Policy Press.

Roker, D. (1998) *Worth More Than This: Young People Growing Up in Family Poverty*, The Children's Society.

Reading B
Nothing bad intended

Donna M. Goldstein

Source: 'Nothing bad intended: child discipline, punishment, and survival in a shantytown in Rio de Janeiro, Brazil', 1995, in Scheper-Hughes, N. and Sargent, C. (eds) *Small Wars: The Cultural Politics of Childhood*, Berkeley, CA, University of California Press, pp. 389–95.

Childhood is a privilege of the rich

In the early evening, along the beachfront in a city in Northeast Brazil, people are out strolling. A well-dressed white man of the upper class and his son, probably about the age of seven or eight, decide to stop and have their shoes shined by a dark-skinned boy, shoeless and not more than seven or eight years old himself. I was close enough to hear the father instructing his son how to speak to the other boy, how to demand a certain polish to be done in a certain way at a certain price. The father insisted that the job, both the shine and the orchestration of behavior between his son and the shoe-shine boy, be done to perfection. The shoe-shine boy was keen to show off his dexterity and did not need any instruction about what to do. At the end of the shine, the young son paid the shoe-shine boy with his father's money, and the shoe-shine boy, happy to have earned a few coins, walked off down the beach in search of new customers. The man and his son continued strolling along. (from author's field notes, 1988)

This scene, witnessed during an extended field visit in 1988, captures well the fact that childhood is lived and experienced differently by the disparate classes that characterize Brazilian urban culture. Indeed, in Brazil childhood is a privilege of the rich and practically nonexistent for the poor. ...

In an age in which class analyses are passé, perhaps it is pointless to call attention to the fact that the condition of Brazil's poor children is a direct result of the highly unequal aspects of Brazilian society—aspects that stem from colonialism, slavery, unequal trade relations, and a rigid class and race system[1]. Yet, these legacies have served to create the contemporary masks of domination, and one of the results has been a shortened childhood for much of Brazil's urban poor. ...

Class and the notion of childhood in Brazil

It bears repeating that childhood in Brazil is a privilege of the rich and is practically nonexistent for the poor. This fact is particularly marked in the urban centers, where the middle and upper classes customarily employ domestic help in the form of cooks, nannies, and housecleaners, generally from neighboring favelas or lower-class neighborhoods. The relationship of this domestic help within Brazilian middle- and upper-class households is a key one: their relationship borders, in terms of actual wages, on domestic slavery, but in terms of intimacy and affective nature, it may have the feel of being a quasi-family member. This construction fits easily into what James Scott (1989) has termed the 'euphemization of power relations.' The children of the wealthy learn at an early age how to 'treat' the maid, and this includes ordering her to do various tasks for them. One of the many results of this relationship is that the children of the wealthy are indulged and spoiled, being catered to daily by their parents and the servants in their midst. At the same time, the children of the poor, often accompanying their mothers who are domestic servants in the homes of the rich, are not treated as children in that social milieu. Contardo Calligaris (1991) recounts, for example, how he was always surprised that the domestic worker would serve food to her employers and their children before serving food to her own child, without regard to the age of her child. This etiquette, an obvious leftover of slave relations, is ubiquitous and denies poor children the privileges that they might otherwise receive merely for being children. In this example, poor children learn early on that their needs are secondary to those of the rich. In contrast, the children of the upper classes are superprivileged: they are welcomed at social functions and generously accepted and appreciated in the public sphere, such as at restaurants and shops, certainly more than their counterparts are in comparative settings in western Europe and the United States.

In the favela, children are expected to be productive and to begin working at a very young age. By the age of five or six, children are participating in various chores, such as cleaning, washing clothes and

---

[1] The World Bank recently reported that Brazil has the most disproportionate income distribution of any major nation in the world, with the top 20 percent of Brazil's population earning twenty-six times what the bottom 20 percent earn (see article by James Brooke, 'Inflation Saps Brazilians' Faith in Democracy,' *New York Times*, 25 July 1993).

dishes, sweeping, and taking care of younger siblings. By the age of nine or ten, young girls are often taking primary care of their baby siblings. Girls, especially, are frequently sent out as domestic workers or as wageless helpers. Favela children may accompany their parent to the home of a rich person, where they will aid in all of the tasks their parent is involved in. In contrast, the children of the rich are usually prohibited from entering the kitchen. There is absolutely no encouragement or value placed on learning to clean or cook since these are tasks carried out by the domestic help. Because these tasks are taken care of by the domestic help, it is a class marker to be inept at these tasks. Moreover, there is a disturbing discourse, sometimes heard among domestic workers in the favela, which at times speaks more lovingly of the children of their *patroa* (employer) than about their own children. The existence of this discourse is perhaps explicable in terms of Albert Memmi's analysis (1965) of the colonized mind: he describes the psychological process of the damage that is done to those who are colonized and that is embedded in their desire sometimes to emulate the colonizer (or dominant class), to prefer their company, and to find them more beautiful, and their habits more respectable than people of their own family or class. Indeed, the favelados prefer, to some extent, the way of being of the children of their employers to that of their own children. Additionally, it seems that the love of the domestic worker for the employer's children has something to do with the differing standards of behavior for middle- and upper-class children and lower-class children. Middle- and upper-class children can be loved and adored as children, while lower-class children are hastened into becoming adults in order to survive.

Children learn the manners of their parents. Middle- and upper-class children never need to learn any kitchen skills, for example, but they must learn how to eat using a knife and fork correctly and how to behave at the table. As Norbert Elias (1978) points out in his analysis of the history of manners, class differences become marked by such habits as table manners. The favela child may never learn to eat with a knife and fork, since a spoon is more commonly used for eating beans and rice, the daily fare of the poor. More importantly, children of both classes are taught by adults of their class the survival skills that their backgrounds require—child discipline and punishment included. Just as knowing the appropriate table manners is part of a small tradition passed on from adult to child, the favela mother knows intuitively that in order for her own children to survive, toughness, obedience, subservience, and street smarts are necessary; otherwise, the child can end up dead. It is important to learn these survival strategies at an early age—by five or six years old. But from the perspective of the domestic worker, the children of the employer do not need to learn the same skills that her children do. They can be pampered, spoiled, and infantilized, and such treatment would not harm or alter their survival capabilities.

Rich children must adhere to the habits and regulations of their class or be 'excluded from the life of that class.'[2] They can be more childlike and be so for longer periods of time, since it is part of their class training to be spoiled and even helpless. In contrast, the younger children in a typical favela household are often parented by their older siblings, since their parents are out working so much of the time. They cannot afford to be childlike, spoiled, or helpless. There is thus collusion at the societal, household, and individual levels in creating these two distinct forms of childhood.

References

Calligaris, C. (1991) *Hello Brasil! Notas de um psicanalista europeu viajando ao Brasil*, Sao Paulo, Escuta.

Elias, N. (1978) *The History of Manners: The Civilizing Process*, vol. 1, New York, Pantheon.

Memmi, A. (1965) *The Colonizer and the Colonized*, Boston, MA, Beacon Press.

Scott, J. (1989) 'Prestige as the public discourse of domination', *Cultural Critique,* no. 12 (Spring), pp. 146–66.

---

[2] Elias (1978, p. 141) points out that '[a] child that does not attain the level of control of emotions demanded by society is regarded in varying gradations as "ill," "abnormal," "criminal," or just "impossible" from the point of view of a particular caste or class, and is accordingly excluded from the life of that class.'

Reading C
Suffering child: an embodiment of war and its aftermath in post-Sandinista Nicaragua

James Quesada

Source: 'Suffering child: an embodiment of war and its aftermath in post-Sandinista Nicaragua', 1998, *Medical Anthropology Quarterly*, vol. 12, no. 1, pp. 51–73.

What follows is a story of a ten-year-old boy, Daniel, and his 33-year-old mother, Maria del Carmen, who live in a squatter settlement perched above the city of Matagalpa, Nicaragua. Together they embody the contemporary history of Nicaragua over the last 25 years: the Sandinista insurrection and revolution, the contra war, and the postrevolutionary neoliberal reform era of today. The department of Matagalpa is located in the northern central highlands of Nicaragua and is the primary coffee-growing region of the country. It was also one of the principal war zones during the U.S.-supported 'Contra war' (1981–90). The socioeconomic status of this particular family is the direct outcome of the rapid social and structural changes they have endured over an extended period of time. …

When I met Maria del Carmen, she was living with her two sons on top of a hill in a dilapidated wooden, cardboard, plastic, and zinc two-room dwelling. She had been a strong, resourceful woman and mother during the Sandinista revolution; since the 1990 Nicaraguan presidential elections, however, she had suffered an abrupt reversal of fortunes. Now unemployed, at times physically ailing and living in near total destitution, she was willing to share the poignancy of her current situation with me. …

Maria del Carmen had participated in the war of insurrection that led to the defeat of the Dictator Somoza in 1979. Beginning in 1976, she became a FSLN (Sandinista National Liberation Front) collaborator and combatant. Her participation in the revolution ultimately alienated her from her more conservative parents and siblings. After the Sandinistas took control in July 1979, Maria del Carmen learned agronomy and beekeeping, and was trained as an elementary school teacher. Her parents left Nicaragua for Mexico in the mid-1980s and her siblings scattered throughout Nicaragua, and Maria became the only member of her natal family to remain in Matagalpa. In the late 1980s she married Pablo, an active-duty Sandinista military officer. She continued to work.

According to Maria, they lived comfortably in the house of a *confiscado* (a property owner whose home or land was confiscated during the revolution). Yet she was often forced to leave her sons, Daniel and Omar, with her mother-in-law, friends, or in local child care centers, Centros de Desarollo Infantil (CDIs), in order to work for extended periods of time in the countryside. By her own account, they lived well in spite of the war, the separations, and economic difficulties. But their world began to fall apart around the time of the 1990 Nicaraguan Presidential elections.

After the 1990 election of UNO (National Opposition Union) and Dona Violeta Chamorro, Maria was laid off as a result of a national neoliberal structural adjustment program that the Chamorro administration devised in conjunction with the IMF and the U.S. Agency for International Development. Two months later, her husband Pablo was discharged from the army as part of the internationally brokered mandatory military reduction plan. Principal among the numerous measures to which the state had agreed was a massive reduction in the public sector labor force (IHCA ENVIO 1992:16–22). Maria's last position had been as an elementary school teacher in an Association of Agricultural Workers (ATC) agricultural cooperative located in the municipio of San Ramon, southeast of the city of Matagalpa.

The transition that followed the defeat of the Sandinistas in the 1990 Presidential elections resulted in changes in property rights (Jonakin 1997:100–101). The former property owner of Maria's house was able to successfully evict her family from their home following his victory in the first national court rulings that allowed former property owners to reclaim their original property. This was particularly traumatizing because their eviction was one of the first forced evictions by authorities to follow the Sandinista electoral defeat. The police actually physically forced them out of their home and threw out all of their personal and household belongings. Now jobless, homeless, and openly humiliated, Maria del Carmen and her family first lived with different friends before having to squat on the large hill northeast of the house where my family and I lived.

Pablo began to drink steadily and their relationship became increasingly estranged. He stayed with his mother who lived nearby and only occasionally gave his wife money, food, or help around the house. Maria was engaged in a daily, sometimes desperate, search for work. At her request, I often gave her aspirin and Tylenol when she came by; she coveted this pharmaceutical to ease her chronic headaches. …

I witnessed the considerable love between Maria and her boys. In spite of poor housing, lack of amenities, and low income, there was a palpable sense of 'pulling together.' Daniel and Omar would dig a ditch around their house to prevent flooding and transforming the dirt-packed floor to mud. They collected firewood and hauled precious water from a communal spigot a half mile from their home. The boys carried their clothes to a nearby stream where Maria would hand wash them. They showed incredible initiative in scavenging for anything that could be put to use. ...

The 1980s saw the rise and fall of the Sandinista revolution. This was due in large part to the U.S government, which sought all along to inflict a total war at the grassroots level (Kornbluh 1988). U.S. policies encouraged disaffected Nicaraguans to organize politically and militarily and to destabilize the Sandinistas, if not to topple them outright (Kornbluh and Bryne 1993). The reverberations of the contra war were felt throughout society and exacted a mixed effect that had real lived consequences for practically all Nicaraguans. ... For Maria del Carmen's family, the war resulted in repeated separations between parents and children, continuous shortages of food and goods, rampant inflation, faltering infrastructures, limited life options, and a state of chronic uncertainty. ...

Often the boys came to visit me on their way home from school in the early afternoon. They usually arrived shortly after siesta with the excuse of asking for glasses of water. They often left my house with gifts of food, pencils, or other things for which I suspected they had really come. ...

One afternoon, Daniel and Omar came to visit after school. As was their habit, they asked for water. I offered them a piece of birthday cake, which they gladly accepted. As Daniel accompanied me to the kitchen to get dishes and forks, he mentioned quite matter of factly that he felt like dying. I stopped immediately and turned to face him. Daniel displayed neither sadness nor alarm. I asked him to repeat what he had said, and he calmly told me that sometimes he felt like dying. I responded that this was a pretty serious sentiment, and I asked him to explain. We were alone in the kitchen, and Daniel quietly, yet flippantly, told me that everyone would be better off with him dead:

> look at me, I'm all bones anyway, I'm already dying. I'm too small and I've stopped growing and I am another mouth to feed. My

mother can't keep taking care of my brother and me, and I can't keep taking care of her. I can't do anything. So it would be better if I just died since that would help everyone.

His explanation was stated calmly and very reasonably. His concerns were legitimate, and his thinking was relatively clear. Daniel appeared to have arrived at this conclusion quite logically. I asked him if he had any specific plans to kill himself. He said that he did not, but when the time was right, he would find an appropriate way. I was very distraught yet fought to remain calm. I felt I needed to show some of the same coolness he exhibited but also convey to him that he was a worthy human being who deserved to live and had much to live for. This latter point was a particularly difficult proposition; talking about hope and the future was difficult when so many Nicaraguans experienced so little of either.

Daniel began to describe how he regularly rationed his meals. His family's daily fare was meager at best. ... He did not remember the last time he had eaten beef or chicken although he ate eggs approximately once a week. Daniel explained that he routinely served himself small portions while generously serving his mother and brother, assuring them that he had served them all equal portions. He explained that sometimes he hid his food, and when his mother was bedridden, he took his food to her. Daniel gave his brother a tortilla a day because Daniel thought his younger brother was the stronger of the two of them, and he wanted to make sure his brother got enough food. In fact, Omar did appear more robust than his older brother.

Daniel said that he was physically exhausted from not sleeping well. He lay awake trying to think of ways to make money such as shoe shining or selling newspapers. He protected his brother from the leaking roof by moving him or holding up a flap of plastic from the wall whenever it rained. Sometimes he stoically allowed himself to get wet, because he did not want to worry his mother or make her get up and go outside to fix the roof. He engaged in daily improvised rituals of sacrifices to contribute in whatever way he could to keep his family from falling apart. Daniel mentioned that he had thought of running away, but to him that would be too cowardly and a betrayal of his mother and brother. So in the end, he thought it would be best to die. He looked at me squarely and said, raising his arm and pinching the skin of his forearm, 'besides, I'm already withering away.' ...

Daniel's desire to die could be viewed as his last act of selflessness, aid, and protection for his family. Objectively, Daniel is imperiled simply by living under conditions of scarcity that are particularly difficult for older children (McDonald et al. 1994). These conditions of scarcity were socially produced and were not merely the product of a dysfunctional family or maternal neglect. In a society where over 50 percent of the population are unemployed, and the state has withdrawn from a commitment to social welfare (FIDEG 1992; Walker 1997), the negative consequences of these circumstances have immediate and direct effects on people. Daniel was very conscious of his predicament, of his 'skin and bones.' Yet, although he spoke about his body, his concern was for his family.

He was primarily concerned about his body's relation to his family. His was another mouth to feed in the face of chronic scarcity.

References

Fideg (Fundacion Internacional Para El Desafio Economico Global) (1992) *El Impacto Diferenciado de Genero de las Politicas de Ajuste Sobre Las Condiciones de Vida en el Area Rural y Concentraciones Urbanas Intermedias*, February 1992, Managua, Nicaragua, Norad.

IHCA ENVIO (1992) 'Se trato el despegue economico', *Instituto Historico Centro-Americano Envio*, vol. 11, no. 129–30, pp. 16–22.

Jonakin, J. (1997) 'Agrarian policy', in Walker, T. (ed) *Nicaragua Without Illusions*, Wilmington, DE, Scholarly Resources Books.

Kornbluh, P. (1988) 'Nicaragua: U.S. proinsurgency warfare against the Sandinistas', in Klare, M. and Kornbluh, P. (eds) *Low Intensity Warfare*, New York, Pantheon Books.

Kornbluh, P. and Bryne, M. (eds) (1993) *The Iran-Contra Scandal: The Declassified History*, New York, The New Press.

McDonald, M., Sigman, M., Espinosa, M. and Neumann, C. (1994) 'Impact for a temporary food shortage on children and their mothers', *Child Development*, vol. 65, no. 2, pp. 404–15.

Walker, T. (ed) (1997) *Nicaragua Without Illusions: Regime Transition and Structural Adjustment in the 1990s*, Wilmington, DE, Scholarly Resources Books.

Chapter 3

Achieving health for children

Catherine Panter-Brick

Contents

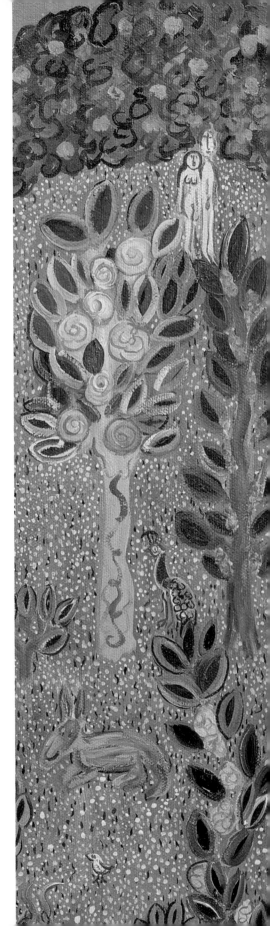

In this chapter, you will:

- recognise why children's health matters globally and identify the important goals set for improving children's health
- evaluate definitions of health and critically appraise the economic, social, cultural and political contexts affecting the treatment of ill-health
- recognise why children suffer from preventable and curable conditions
- examine how inequality affects children's health
- discuss what makes interventions in children's health successful.

1 Introduction

This chapter will discuss some of the major health issues for children and, most importantly, the policies developed to try to improve their health. Issues regarding the health of young children, especially those aged under five, have long been the focus of international efforts, as it is widely acknowledged that they are particularly vulnerable, dying unnecessarily of largely preventable malnutrition and curable infectious diseases. The health of adolescents is also receiving increasing attention, in the 'age of opportunity' for health-related investments (UNICEF, 2011a; Sawyer et al., 2012). The present-day agenda is thus to consolidate the historic gains achieved for children under five and to expand investments in adolescents, in order to strategically step up investments in health and development for all children. This chapter will review some of the goals and the challenges in achieving good health for children, in light of the inequalities that still remain. It also examines why world views about the causes and treatment of illnesses matter in shaping access to health care, and why the international agenda has focused attention on tackling the wider socio-political causes of health inequalities.

2 Child health matters

Child health has long been a matter of international concern and intervention. The 1924 Geneva Declaration of the Rights of the Child stated that: 'The child that is hungry must be fed; the child that is sick must be nursed' (Article 2, League of Nations, 1924). The United Nations Convention on the Rights of the Child (UNCRC) declared that States Parties 'shall ensure to the maximum extent possible the survival and development of the child' (Article 6, United Nations, 1989) and 'recognize the right of the child to the enjoyment of the highest attainable standard of health and to facilities for the treatment of illness and rehabilitation of health. States Parties shall strive to ensure that no child is deprived of his or her right of access to such health care services' (Article 24, United Nations, 1989).

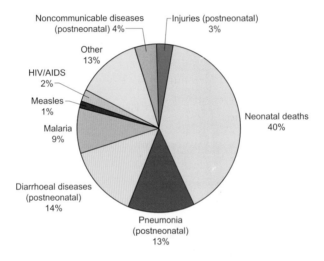

Figure 1 Major causes of death in neonates and children under five globally, 2008 (data from the WHO)

Children's health is the focus of major international institutions such as the World Health Organization (WHO) and UNICEF, which monitor and promote health issues on a global scale. These organisations collect systematic information about health and health inequalities – the relative chance to live, die and fall sick, across geographical areas and socio-economic groups. They also design and promote large-scale health interventions (the eradication of smallpox in 1980 is the best example of a successful worldwide campaign). Both produce annual reports, with the WHO focusing on selected health problems and UNICEF producing *The State of the World's Children* annually, which gives an up-to-date review of health statistics, identifies key aspects of children's lives or issues for special consideration, and reports on the progress of specific health interventions.

Children's health matters for many reasons. At the most extreme end, ill-health leads to death for many millions of children, who are most at risk in their earliest years. Several of the diseases to which children are most prone – respiratory infections, diarrhoeal diseases and measles – could be readily prevented or treated. The loss of such high numbers of young children, from largely preventable causes, is not just a tragedy for their families, but is also significant in socio-economic and demographic terms, as the loss of the future workforce and the 'human capital' necessary for social development.

Many young children have reduced resistance to infections as a result of mild but chronic malnutrition. Among the various possible forms of malnutrition, chronic mild-to-moderate under-nutrition is a largely 'silent and invisible emergency, exacting a terrible toll on children and their families' (Bellamy, 1998, p. 1). It is silent and invisible because it commands less attention than severe under-nutrition in famine situations, yet it is a real emergency, because it is implicated in more than half of all child deaths worldwide.

Figure 2   Child survival: the annual number of global deaths in children under five dropped from 12.5 million in 1990 to less than 9 million in 2008

Even if children survive their early years, there is plenty of evidence that episodes of ill-health and malnutrition affect future development. For example, a malnourished infant can be listless and have slow social and cognitive development, which affects school performance and opportunities for education. Such a child will be less able to resist infections, and will show retarded growth, which can affect work performance and future income. These effects can also damage the next generation. When a malnourished girl becomes an adult, she will be more likely to have low birth-weight babies and, given her short stature and small hips, suffer complications from childbirth.

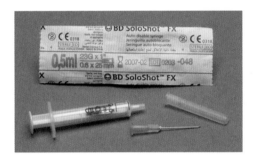

Figure 3 Vaccines: these save millions of lives and have helped reduce global measles deaths by 74 per cent since 2000

Since the 1990s there have been marked advances in child survival and social development. UNICEF has pointed out that since 1990 there has been a '33 per cent reduction in the global under-five mortality rate, the near elimination of gender gaps in primary school enrolment in several regions and considerable improvements in access to primary schooling, safe water, routine immunizations and critical medicines such as antiretroviral drugs' (UNICEF, 2011a, p. 1). However, although these improvements are significant, there is still a long way to go and while improving children's health has a global mandate, the implementation of health programmes at regional, national and local levels has proved challenging. Furthermore, some groups remain overlooked. A great deal of money and attention has been paid to infant and child mortality but adolescents' health has not always been seen as so important. It was only in 2011 that UNICEF devoted its *State of the World's Children* report to older children, calling it *Adolescence: An Age of Opportunity* and arguing that 'investing in adolescents provides our best hope of breaking the intergenerational cycle of poverty and inequity that weakens communities and countries and imperils the development and rights of countless children' (UNICEF, 2011a, p. 2). In 2006, over a third (2.2

Why? not seen as innocent. Not part of romanticism??

billion) of humanity was under the age of 18, and just under half was under 25, meaning that the demographics of youth are currently driving outstanding changes in education, the economy and social transformations across the globe. Yet despite their social and demographic importance, adolescents are still rarely given great attention in health matters, especially in the fields of reproductive, sexual and mental health, which remain overlooked and underfunded (McManus and Fox, 2007).

Figure 4   Improved drinking water: more than 1.6 billion people gained access to improved drinking-water sources between 1990 and 2006

Summary of Section 2

Children have rights to health and to access health care, but fulfilling these rights is challenging.

Children are particularly vulnerable in the first five years of life when they die from preventable and curable conditions such as respiratory infections, diarrhoea and malnutrition.

Adolescents' health has also been the focus of concern but it remains underfunded, and issues such as mental or sexual health have not always been given a high priority.

Figure 5 Primary school enrolment: the number of children out of school declined from 115 million in 2002 to 101 million in 2007

3 What is good health?

We can see in the bald statistics on infant and child mortality the extreme effects of ill-health on children. But not all child ill-health leads to death and there are certain forms of ill-health that are harder to identify. The same is true when looking at good health which the World Health Organization has defined as 'a state of complete physical, mental and social well-being and not merely the absence of disease or infirmity' (WHO, 2006 [1946]).

Activity 1   Concepts of good health
Allow about 10 minutes

Answer the following questions:

*   What do *you* think constitutes good health in children?

- What advantages and what problems can you see with the WHO definition?

Comment

When describing good health in children, you might have thought of the obvious and clinically measurable physical signs of child health, such as a lack of disease, as well as a steady pattern of physical growth and development. You might also have thought of less tangible qualities – children's emotional health – their happiness or the quality of their home life, how far they feel secure and raised with love. These are all important issues and of course contribute to children's overall health and development, but they are harder to appraise.

The WHO definition captures the idea that health is a holistic concept encompassing mental, physical and social dimensions. This definition has been significant in broadening a vision of health beyond the idea of mere physical survival and promoting a positive concept of health.

However, there have been criticisms of this definition for being an idealistic and unrealistic one that 'puts health beyond everyone's reach' (Lewis, 2001, p. 59). It would be difficult for anyone to be truly healthy by this definition and extremely hard work to stay that way. The WHO definition, with its emphasis on complete physical, mental and social well-being, seems to correspond more closely to 'happiness' than to 'health'. However, the distinction between these two concepts is crucial: only health is a universal human right, happiness is not (Panter-Brick and Fuentes, 2010).

The definition is also difficult to put into practice. For instance, how does one evaluate the 'social' dimension of health? If social well-being means social adjustment and 'fitting in' socially, then it would strongly depend upon the values promoted by a particular culture or by particular groups within that culture. Ideas about social well-being tend to be controlled by dominant groups in society, who uphold a particular norm of social adjustment. A good example here relates to diagnoses of child hyperactivity: whether a lively child's behaviour is seen as normal, boisterous or pathological depends in part on what is expected or indeed found disruptive at home, at school or in the wider society.

Despite these complexities, it is worth noting that a holistic definition resonates with understandings about health in many cultures. For example, the Huli, who live in Papua New Guinea, have no single word for 'health', but characterise health as the absence of disease, resilience (to illness) and social effectiveness (the ability to become wealthy and influential). The Huli perceive efforts to promote a good physique as entwined with efforts to attract wealth and social distinction. The converse of a person with 'good skin' is said to be *ibatari*: 'a shabby, sickly, impoverished recluse' (Frankel, 1986, p. 58). For the Huli, 'health is as much a social as a physical state' (Frankel, 1986, p. 55). This brings Huli notions close to the WHO definition of health.

Figure 6 A Huli boy from Tari Valley, Papua New Guinea

While the WHO has promoted a broad definition of health, child health statistics collected by state and international organisations have tended to focus on a narrow range of indicators: disease, malnutrition and mortality amongst children under five. In practice, promoting health has often been equated with ensuring physical health and survival. For some, this emphasis was justified, given the high child mortality statistics across the globe. Others have argued that priorities in terms of physical survival should be considerably shifted to broader issues about child development and quality of life. Epilepsy, for example, appeared to be a relatively unimportant priority for children's health when diseases were ranked according to their impact on child mortality, because it rarely killed. Yet when the World Bank introduced a new ranking system for diseases (the Disability-Adjusted Life Year, or DALY), which measured the disabling potential of diseases, epilepsy was recognised as one of the ten most important diseases among 5–14 year olds in poorer countries – leading to school withdrawal, social isolation, and inability to find work. Although happiness or well-being are not human rights, there is an increasing recognition that children's rights to health care must take into account social requirements such as education or social inclusion.

3.1   Culture, medicine and health

It is often argued that the Western biomedical model prevalent in minority-world countries sees a healthy body as functioning like a machine, with all the constituent parts in good working order. Conversely, many non-Western medical systems in the majority world focus on the personal, spiritual or social experiences of illness rather than the 'faulty' part of the machine. Furthermore, where Western biomedicine tends to demarcate between the physical and mental causes of ill-health, other explanatory systems may not. It follows that views about ill-health and appropriate treatment can be very different across cultures.

With respect to the physical dimensions of well-being, society plays an important role in defining what is 'healthy' and 'not healthy' in light of ideas of what is 'normal' in society. A dramatic example of a cultural redefinition of normality is the belief that red urine is a sign of sexual maturity in adolescent boys – the equivalent of menstruation in girls – among the Bozo in Mali. Red urine is caused by a parasitic infection (schistosomiasis) that begins in childhood and becomes progressively heavier, causing internal bleeding around the time of adolescence. Because this affects the whole community, it is perceived by the Bozo as normal – so much so that it is celebrated as a rite of passage (Dettwyler, 1998). Another example of local definitions of normality is 'teething diarrhoea.' In a study of market women in Nigeria, 71 per cent of mothers perceived that diarrhoea was caused by teething – a normal sign of growth and development accompanying the milestone of tooth eruption (Ene-Obong et al., 2000). In both instances, what would be defined in Western biomedicine as a symptom of disease and ill-health, is reclassified as a normal part of healthy child development. Such beliefs have major implications for the management of disease: in

Nigeria, mothers did not share the biomedical explanations of diarrhoea causation, such as poor personal and environmental hygiene practices, or seek prevention or treatment, as they believed there was nothing anybody could do about it. Achieving good health for these children, therefore, entails understanding local definitions about health and ill-health and reconciling disparities of world views.

Figure 7 Mother with a one-year-old child in Nigeria. Many people think the diarrhoea their children suffer from is a consequence of teething

There are also significant cross-cultural differences in the way individual parents understand the significance of a child's ill-health – differences related to ideas about children and their roles in society. In some societies, a focus on child survival, growth and nutrition is seen as self-evident and sufficient in itself: in the face of poverty, disease or malnutrition, the cultural imperative is to save children's lives. By contrast, many other societies find such emphasis on child survival, without alleviating poverty and improving quality of life, misplaced. In a famine situation, such as that found in the Sahel region of Africa, the tension between 'saving lives' and 'saving livelihoods' was acute (Hampshire et al., 2009). In a situation of food shortage, the dilemma here for a family was whether it was more important to feed the adult breadwinners so they could work their lands and ensure the long-term survival of the family – even if this meant children went without – or whether to feed their children, who were more vulnerable and less able to survive without adult help, but who could not ensure the longer-term survival of the family or the community. When it comes to feeding young children, this contrast of world views has been expressed as the 'needs versus contribution' approach. While some people feed children according to their biological *needs* for growth and physical development, others allocate food according to their real or perceived, actual or future, *contributions* to society (Engle and Nieves, 1993).

Other aspects of child health are viewed very differently cross-culturally. When it comes to the 'mental' dimension of ill-health, the distinction between being mentally well and mentally ill is far from clear-cut, and therefore a matter of interpretation in both medical and social terms. The difficult cultural demarcation between healthy and disturbed behaviour in lively, active children has already been mentioned. Another example would relate to children reported to be 'hearing voices'. This is a characteristic symptom of schizophrenia in European or North American diagnoses, yet hearing voices is normal for shamans (spiritual healers) when they enter a trance during rituals. In Inuit and Amazonian societies, or indeed any society with a belief in the spirit world, a child hearing voices may well be trained as a shaman and invested with a large amount of ritual authority, rather than treated as ill.

Activity 2   Reading A

Allow about 30 minutes

Turn to Reading A, 'The spirit catches you and you fall down', at the end of the chapter. In this reading Anne Fadiman describes the experiences of Lia Lee, a Hmong girl, and her parents Foua and Nao Kao, who had settled in Merced County, California, after a year in refugee camps in Thailand.

Lia and her family were originally from Laos in South East Asia. The period described in Fadiman's book is the early 1980s, when almost all Hmong living in America had, like Lia's parents, recently arrived as refugees. The spiritual beliefs Fadiman writes about, including views on the causes of epilepsy, were prevalent among the Hmong at that time but have adapted to a certain extent as the Hmong have assimilated into American society. Today, younger Hmong (especially Christian converts) are more likely to subscribe to biomedical based beliefs or to a combination of the two. However, the Hmong beliefs about epilepsy at this time provide a useful example of the different ways in which particular forms of ill-health are understood and the implications this has for treatment.

As you read the extract, make notes on the traditional Hmong views of illness and compare them with the ones held by the American doctors. What do you think might be the implications of these beliefs for treating Lia's condition?

Figure 8 Hmong girls in Xieng Khang province, Laos. Many Hmong became refugees during the Vietnam War (1965–75) and emigrated to the USA

Comment

Ideas about illness are intricately bound up in cultural beliefs, so that different people have profoundly different explanations of the causes and effects of illness. Both Lia's parents and her doctors noted the same symptoms, but ascribed them to very different causes: the doctors to an electro-chemical storm inside Lia's head and her parents to soul loss. The Hmong, in this extract, emphasised epilepsy's spiritual origins in contrast to the American doctors who looked to its physical causes.

Lia's parents did not reject medical intervention entirely and recognised that it had saved their children's lives in the refugee camp. However, while they recognised that American medicine could treat the symptoms of their daughter's illness, they did not think it could do anything about its cause. Fundamentally, they had very different ideas about the nature of illness and did not share the biomedical model that sees epilepsy in terms of brain dysfunction and neurological disorder. Indeed, they did not necessarily share the idea that epilepsy was a problem or a disorder, and saw it as a potential entrée into the vocation of shamanism, although they still worried about its impact on their daughter and wanted to find a cure. The doctors they consulted perceived epilepsy very differently, focusing entirely on its debilitating physical aspects. Such differences in world views matter when it comes to treating children's ill-health. If the physical, mental and social significance of these different world views are not reconciled, diagnoses may be contested, treatment may be interrupted and distrust or tension may arise between doctors, parents and children.

3.2   Malnutrition and obesity

Another example of the different ways in which health issues can be understood, including the links between medical and social understandings of health, can be seen in discussions of malnutrition. Malnutrition has many meanings, covering aspects of inadequate health from starvation to poor diet more generally, and does not always mean not having enough food – it can also mean having the wrong sort of food. In the richer countries of the world, such as the USA and the UK, obesity rates are rising among children, linked to low levels of physical activity and a diet of high-fat, cheap, 'fast' foods. In the UK, in 2011, one in ten children aged 2–10 were classified as obese (Department of Health, 2011).

China is also currently facing increasing numbers of children who are obese. In urban centres like Beijing, where couples are forbidden to have more than one child and where four grandparents might have only one grandchild, the health consequences of over-indulging children – known as 'little emperors' – are striking. There are plentiful treats in the form of minority-world 'junk food' and sugar drinks and children are living increasingly sedentary lives associated with home video games and transport by motor car. Child malnutrition in China, far from being a consequence of parental powerlessness to secure good resources, arises out of parental indulgence of children at a time of a strictly enforced policy for population control.

Figure 9   Obesity is a growing problem for children

Perhaps counter-intuitively, however, obesity mostly affects the poor who live in the richest countries, as well as people experiencing a nutritional 'transition' in rapidly modernising countries such as Brazil and South Africa, partly because they are less able to afford a varied, nutritious diet and come to rely on cheap and readily available 'fast foods'. There is also increased evidence of a particular genetic susceptibility for obesity – making the bodies of some children and adults particularly efficient at depositing fat. Children raised in very poor conditions who have this genetic make-up – advantageous under conditions of adversity – become caught in a 'fat trap' when fat-laden foods become plentiful and physical activity for subsistence is reduced in conditions of rapid socio-economic development. Thus, rather surprising associations have been found between nutritional deprivation in early life (even foetal life) and obesity in later life. For instance, studies of the Dutch famine of 1944–45 (due to an embargo by the Nazi occupiers) have noted a high prevalence of obesity in adult men who had been exposed to under-nutrition during the first half of their mothers' pregnancy (suggesting a developmental response that prioritised the deposition of fat, leading to a tendency to obesity when food sources became plentiful). The risk of obesity was less for those exposed to under-nutrition in the last trimester of pregnancy and the first few months of life (a period of development for laying down fat cells). The association between under-nutrition at critical periods of

Figure 10   Five generations of the Yang family in China. Many grandparents have only one grandchild. These children are indulged as 'little emperors'

development and later obesity is a particular concern in lower-income countries, where maternal and early child malnutrition exists along with rapid changes in socio-economic conditions (Martorell et al., 2000). Indeed, stunted growth in childhood has been associated with being overweight in four countries, specifically in Russia, Brazil, South Africa and China (Popkin et al., 1996).

Activity 3   Reading B

Allow about 30 minutes

Obesity among children has been identified as a pressing medical problem. Studies have drawn attention to the links between obesity and behavioural factors such as watching television, not exercising, or eating poor-quality foods. In Reading B, 'The obesity epidemic: medical and ethical considerations', Jantina de Vries examines how obesity is constructed as a children's health issue and what this tells us about political and social relationships within society.

Read through the extract and comment on:

- how de Vries understands contemporary concerns over obesity
- how health interventions into obesity entail a form of social control or lead to stigmatisation of the socially marginalised.

Comment

de Vries is less concerned with the issue of obesity as a medical problem and concentrates instead on how the issue came to prominence in the early twenty-first century. She relates modern concerns about obesity to wider issues about how ideas of beauty and physical attractiveness are constructed in contemporary societies. She claims that there has been a shift in what is considered beautiful, from the plump or cuddly to the very thin. Even though being underweight also has serious health implications, being overweight is considered the more urgent problem. But, she argues, this may well have less to do with medical risk and more with stigmatising the socially undesirable who are labelled as gluttonous, lazy and feckless.

Weight issues are a way of defining and reinforcing social divisions. Although the effects of the 'wrong' food choices are presented in terms of health or ill-health, moral connotations serve to stigmatise the poor. de Vries is concerned with the use of obesity as a form of social control and how it is used as a way of marking out children (and their parents) who do not conform to white, middle-class values and to the 'proper' body shape, and do not make the 'right' choices. In this line of argument obesity is not a problem because it makes children ill, it is a problem because it marks out certain children, usually poor ones, as different. This speaks to a fundamental challenge in public health: successful interventions must be socially embedded and also address the harmful unintended consequences of social action, such as stigmatising obese children, blaming poor families and inadvertently widening social inequalities.

Summary of Section 3

The World Health Organization promotes a holistic view of health that covers physical, mental and social dimensions.

Notions of health and ill-health are culturally interpreted. World views about ill-health matter, because they shape people's views about the appropriateness of different kinds of treatment.

Medical systems that focus on the biological causation of disease and biomedical treatment often clash with approaches which take a more holistic view.

Medical and humanitarian interventions often place the emphasis on saving lives, while local communities may put their priority on sustainable lives or quality of life.

Notions of health and disease are not fixed entities and alter as viewpoints in both medicine and culture change. They are affected by global changes in social, economic, political and media-driven contexts.

4 The social determinants of health: the role of social inequality

High levels of child ill-health are not found throughout the world but are concentrated in particular, poorer parts of the world, especially in sub-Saharan Africa. There are also great regional variations in children's chances of surviving until the age of five and growing up healthy after that. In almost all aspects of health care, poor children do worse than richer ones and, as suggested in Section 1, many forms of ill-health from which children suffer could be prevented if resources were available. Understanding ill-health therefore means analysing these patterns of social inequality and the impacts that these have on groups of children.

4.1   Global inequalities

There is now substantial evidence that social inequalities go hand in hand with variations in ill-health and access to health care within and across nations (Wilkinson and Pickett, 2010). One of the clearest ways to illustrate this is by looking at data on infant and child mortality. The number of deaths for the age group 0–5 years of age (per thousand live births) is known as the under-five or child mortality rate (U5MR), while deaths for the 0–1 year olds are called infant mortality rates (IMR). Such mortality rates are considered very sensitive indicators of social development, including the adequacy of public health services, and are also used as a yardstick for measuring poverty. These figures illustrate the unequal chances of survival for children depending on where they live. Sub-Saharan Africa has the highest rates of child mortality and one in eight children born in that region dies before the age of five, more than double the rates in Southern Asia (where 1 in 15 children die before their fifth birthdays). However, about half of under-five deaths occur in only five countries: India, Nigeria, Democratic Republic of Congo, Pakistan and China. India (22 per cent) and Nigeria (11 per cent) together account for a third of all under-five deaths. Sub-Saharan Africa has made progress in reducing U5MR but changes in its rates have been slower than elsewhere and in some aspects of child health, these statistics have got worse. The proportion of deaths that occur within the first month of life (the neonatal period) has increased by about ten per cent since 1990 to more than 40 per cent (UNICEF, 2011b).

Figure 11 Providing children with a meal each day is a high priority for this early childhood centre in rural India

In contrast, some countries have managed a substantial reduction in child mortality. Bangladesh is one of the poorest countries in the world but, unlike countries within sub-Saharan Africa, it has achieved a striking decrease in child mortality. The under-five mortality rate declined from 143 per thousand live births in 1990 to 48 per thousand in 2010 (UNICEF, 2012). The reason for this is simple: there was a national commitment to invest in basic social services that would directly benefit mothers and children. Thus, in 1999, 25.7 per cent of the national budget was spent on social services, boosting adult literacy and primary school enrolment (UNICEF, 2001, p. 5). This is compared to the 12 to 14 per cent of national budgets usually allocated to basic social services by countries outside Europe, North America and Australasia (UNICEF, 2001, p. 22).

Activity 4   Reading C

Allow about 30 minutes

Although infant and child mortality might appear as straightforward indicators of ill-health on a national level, looking behind the figures reveals the need for more complex understandings and the necessity of taking into account patterns of social inequality, as well as examining the impact of children's deaths on their families.

Turn to Reading C, 'Death without weeping: the violence of everyday life in Brazil', at the end of the chapter. Anthropologist Nancy Scheper-Hughes spent many years working in a district called Bom Jesus in the slums of Brazil – in a community she calls Alto – with poor women and children. Infant mortality rates are high in this community and this reading looks at how they are explained and understood.

Read through this extract and answer the following questions:

* Why do so many children die in the slums?
* How do mothers explain these deaths?
* Why do mothers not do more to save their children?

Comment

Children die in the slums through lack of food, from diarrhoea, respiratory infections and other infections. Mothers are well aware of this and attribute their babies' deaths to these causes. However, they are also aware that children do not 'just' die and that their deaths would be preventable if they had greater resources. Women in Alto are well aware that poverty forces them into making fated choices, such as going to work and leaving children behind without proper food or supervision, or being unable to afford nutritious food. Their children do not die simply because they are ill, therefore, but because of the lack of support given by government or health authorities and the lack of provision of clean water and waste disposal.

In this situation mothers feel powerless to save their children and Scheper-Hughes describes, with much sympathy, the underinvestment in the very young. Poor mothers are ambivalent about very young children whom they do not 'trust' to survive, and therefore they invest little emotional energy in them. Mothers feel that some children do not want to live and cannot be kept alive, and that there is nothing they can do for them. This is not callousness or helpless passivity, rather a way of dealing with high levels of infant mortality, which occur against a backdrop of social inequality and poverty.

4.2   Differences within nations

The modern world is characterised by significant disparities both across nations and across groups within nations. Health differentials are significant both in developing countries such as Brazil – one of the economic success stories of Latin America – and in countries like the United States, where child health varies significantly by ethnic group and relative wealth or deprivation. Over three-quarters of children with HIV/AIDS in the USA are from ethnic minorities. These children may also be disadvantaged by factors such as poverty, inadequate housing, lack of access to basic welfare services and a struggle with the dominant language. The UK also sees great disparities in health between different groups so that, for example, in parts of Glasgow life expectancy for men is only 67.7 years compared with 78.3 years in East Dunbartonshire (BBC News, 2010a); while in Wales, men born in deprived areas such as Blaenau Gwent can expect to live until 73.8 – five years less than in parts of Monmouthshire, where life expectancy is 78 years (Welsh Centre for Health, 2006, p. 5).

These examples emphasise once again the point that health has political and economic dimensions. Countries where the income differentials between rich and poor are large tend to have worse health among the overall population than countries in which such differences are small. Inequality is 'bad' for national health, because social and material inequalities generally go hand-in-hand with poor investment in human resources, including education and health services. According to Wilkinson:

> Countries in which the income differences between rich and poor are larger (meaning more or deeper relative poverty) tend to have worse health than countries in which the differences are smaller. It

The idea that all people are equal and need equal rights and opportunities

is ... the most egalitarian rather than the richest developed countries which have the best health.

(Wilkinson, 1996, p. 75)

The effects of social inequality on child health in the UK can be demonstrated by comparing statistics about children's health and accidents across the social classes. Throughout childhood, deaths from accidents, respiratory disease and, to a lesser extent, infectious diseases, show steep class gradients: for example, in 2000, a child in the lowest social class was twice as likely to die before the age of 15 as a child in the highest social class (Roberts, 2000).

4.3   Health inequalities within families

Another aspect of the complex relationship between ill-health and poverty is enacted within families at the household level; this too has dramatic consequences for children. People who live in poverty have to allocate scarce resources and may find themselves obliged to establish priorities in terms of access to health care or access to nutritious food. Research has shown that discrimination against children within a household occurs between siblings of a different age, gender, birth order or perceived health/disability (Panter-Brick, 1998). Gender inequalities are amongst the most striking.

In many parts of the world, but particularly in South Asia, girls have significantly higher rates of malnutrition, reduced access to health care services and greater rates of mortality. In India and China, they are at risk of being aborted before birth on the grounds of their gender. The increased availability of prenatal screening has meant that parents can now know the sex of their child long before it is born. In India, where there is a strong preference for boys, as well as concern over dowries that must accompany a daughter's marriage, the results of these tests have been dramatic:

In one of the first hospitals to offer low-cost tests, a study by a Bombay women's organisation between 1979 and 1982 found that of 8,000 women who came from all over India, 7,999 wanted an abortion if the test revealed a female child. Many advertisements set the costs of the sex tests and abortions against the future costs

Figure 12 Photo of three children of the same age in rural Nepal. The one to the left has severe protein-energy malnutrition largely due to maternal neglect (he is the last-born son in a household of six children). The girl in the middle is an only child whose mother cannot have any more children. The one to the right is a boy whose father has a steady income

of a daughter, including that of her dowry, with slogans such as 'better 500 rupees now than 50,000 rupees later on'.

(Croll, 2000, p. 95)

Summary of Section 4

There is a socio-political dimension to children's health and the subject cannot be discussed without reference to social inequality.

Between and within nations, there are significant differences in child health as poverty structures exposure to risks and access to health care.

Within families, there exists further discrimination against children – well documented in the case of gender – which affect their health.

5 Achieving health in practice

Understanding the importance of social inequalities for children's health has led to calls for a change in world view, and a shift in emphasis to take into account the socio-economic and political factors which exacerbate health problems for children. This shift can be seen in the WHO's report called *Closing the Gap in a Generation*, which argued powerfully that a push for greater social equality and social justice would be the best way forward for reducing widespread ill-health among children in the poorer countries of the world (CSDH, 2008). This report calls on countries to close the health gap between the richest and poorest children in a generation. It demands concerted action to reduce the differences in life expectancy between richer and poorer countries (and regions within countries) through improving daily living conditions (the report argues that healthy places make for healthy people), tackling the worldwide inequalities in power, money and resources, putting claims of social justice at the heart of all policies, and through understanding the evidence and evaluating action with a stronger focus on the social determinants of health.

5.1   Tackling social inequality

In response to such calls, there has been an international push towards 'closing the gap'. Governments throughout the world have pledged to achieve specific goals concerning children's health and to reduce the inequalities between different regions of the world. Backed up by the idea that children have a right to health, the UN Millennium Summit of 2000 set out eight Millennium Development Goals (MDG), which countries pledged to fulfil by the year 2015. These goals were to be achieved through partnership with the richest states (including the UK) making a commitment to donate 0.7 per cent of their gross national income to development aid. Although there were criticisms that these goals were too ambitious and that governments in fact only paid lip service to them, it was still a considerable achievement for the United Nations to secure international consensus on specific deliverables, and to insist on a review of each nation's achievement of these goals. Eight goals were agreed and within each of these, particular indicators were set to measure and monitor how far the stated goal had been reached. The goals were:

Goal 1:   Eradicate extreme poverty and hunger

Goal 2: Achieve universal primary education

Goal 3: Promote gender equality and empower women

Goal 4: Reduce child mortality

Goal 5: Improve maternal health

Goal 6: Combat HIV/AIDS, malaria and other diseases

Goal 7: Ensure environmental sustainability

Goal 8: Develop a global partnership for development

(United Nations, 2012)

Since these were agreed, there have been some notable successes: most notably that fewer children are dying. Annual global deaths of children under five years of age fell to 8.1 million in 2009 from 12.4 million in 1990. Also, fewer children are underweight. The percentage of underweight children under five years old is estimated to have dropped from 25 per cent in 1990 to 16 per cent in 2010. Fewer people are contracting HIV and treatment for this, and for other diseases such as tuberculosis, is now more successful. Almost all countries of the world are on track to achieve the MDG target on access to safe drinking water. By 2012, however, there were still some areas which needed improvement. While access to drinking water had improved, the sanitation target had not been met and there were still not enough toilets. As diarrhoeal diseases remain one of the main killers for children under five, this is clearly a crucial area for improvement. There have been tangible successes, therefore, but also disappointments. Olivier De Schutter, the UN's Special Rapporteur on the right to food, has argued:

> The MDGs have been useful in mobilising money and energy ... [b]ut they attack the symptoms of poverty - underweight children, maternal mortality, HIV prevalence - while remaining silent on the deeper causes of underdevelopment and hunger.

(BBC News, 2010b)

Millions of children still go hungry, maternal death rates have not fallen as hoped and the richest states have failed to meet their commitment to give 0.7 per cent of their gross national income to development aid. The UK gives 0.51 per cent of its national income in aid. Italy gives just 0.15 per cent. The USA gives only 0.20 per cent but because of the size of its economy, it gives more aid than any other country (BBC News, 2010b). There is still reluctance by the richer countries in the world to redistribute wealth more fairly and, as a consequence, chronic poverty combined with economic, social and health inequalities remain obstacles to fulfilling an international mandate to give first call to the interests and rights of children.

5.2   'Magic bullets'

Some interventions in children's health care – vaccinations, adequate food or life-saving operations – might appear to be 'magic bullets' which can bring about all sorts of cures and improve children's health demonstrably. They might be seen as an unquestioned and unquestionable 'good thing'. However, while a medical technological breakthrough might lay the ground for a 'magic bullet' intervention, this alone does not address other important causes of child ill-health or respond to community concerns that may undermine the success of an intervention. Availability of medical treatment cannot in itself guarantee that children will sidestep preventable and curable diseases or malnutrition. This is well illustrated by debates surrounding vaccination of young children in the UK.

Activity 5   MMR vaccination in the UK
Allow about 10 minutes

Measles is a disease that can have devastating consequences on children, causing blindness, mental health problems and death. There is a highly effective vaccine against it – conferring life-long immunity – currently taken as part of a triple vaccination against measles, mumps and rubella (the MMR vaccine). Yet there has been some resistance to vaccinating children in the UK after an article in the medical journal, *The Lancet*, claimed that the MMR vaccination was linked to bowel problems, infections and to the onset of autism in otherwise healthy children. Many parents were reluctant to have their children vaccinated with MMR despite vigorous reassurance by the National Health Service about the safety and importance of this triple vaccine.

- Why do you think that some people hesitated or refused to have their children vaccinated?

- How might the government or health services have better promoted vaccinations?

Comment

Childhood infectious diseases in the UK have been largely conquered. Few individuals die of measles, smallpox, diphtheria or any other disease that would have been fatal even 50 years ago. At the same time, childhood autism is on the rise, for reasons still needing explanation. Thus, many UK parents did not appreciate the devastating consequences of children contracting measles, giving greater weight to the possible (but unproven) risk of childhood autism. Because parents did not perceive the gravity of the risk of measles, they were reluctant to expose their children to the well-publicised but unconfirmed risk of autism. Parents were told by the medical establishment that the claimed links between MMR and autism were without foundation, but were suspicious of this information; they looked to other (non-medical) sources of information, trusting their own judgement rather than the 'official' information presented to them.

'Non-compliance' posed a great dilemma for the government and health services in the UK. Because the measles virus is so infectious, 90 per cent of all children must be vaccinated in order to avoid a measles epidemic; this target was not reached in many areas. The Department of Health needed to persuade parents that its advice was unbiased and that it was concerned about the well-being of all children without sacrificing the good health of a few, but at times appeared as if its main objective was preserving public confidence rather than investigating suspected adverse consequences. Trust was a key issue that the government could have tried to address better in order to promote vaccines more successfully.

'Magic bullets' can be highly effective technological interventions, but making them available within health services cannot constitute the be-all-and-end-all of an intervention. Technological breakthroughs, or education of the lay public, are necessary but not sufficient to achieve good health. The eradication of childhood infectious diseases also requires full community endorsement. This necessitates trustworthy information and sensitive communication on the part of the officials in charge, in addition to the provision of health infrastructure and social development. MMR serves as a reminder that even well-informed parents may reject a procedure which is a highly effective way of preventing a killer disease. Non-compliance with a 'magic bullet' treatment can follow from a lack of trust in information presented to

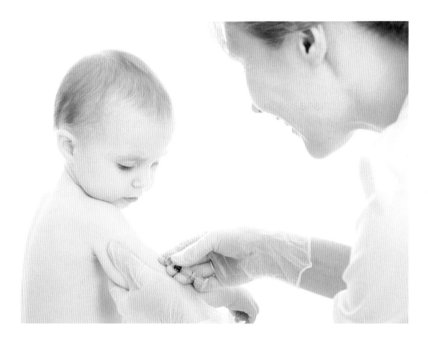

Figure 13 Vaccinations have been seen as a 'magic bullet' approach, but technological or medical interventions are not always enough and community endorsement and acceptance are also central

parents as well as being a symptom of a risk-averse society where, no matter how small the perceived risk, many people are simply not prepared to take it.

In a different context, the case of diarrhoea well illustrates some of the complexities of health care intervention. Diarrhoea is a major killer of children throughout the world, and parents (as shown in Reading C) recognise its devastating impact on children. Diarrhoea kills by dehydration when the body cannot keep enough fluids in it and so the child dies. The symptoms can be treated with an extremely low-cost intervention. Oral rehydration salts (ORS), which are a solution of salt and sugar, provide essential water and electrolytes for the body to combat dehydration. ORS restore the necessary salts to the cells of the body, which enables the cells to retain water and the child to stay hydrated. ORS are very cheap (less than five pence a dose) and have been promoted worldwide in a campaign to reduce deaths from dehydration. ORS might therefore be seen as a prime example of a 'magic bullet' cure which can have an enormous impact on children's lives.

However, the effectiveness of rehydration salts depends to a very large extent on parents' willingness to administer them as part of rehydration

Figure 14 A mother in Conarky, Guinea brings her child to a health centre which promotes the use of oral rehydration salts for young children with diarrhoeal disease

therapy. This point was well argued in a study monitoring the success of an ORS treatment programme among the Huli of highland Papua New Guinea (Frankel and Lehman, 1984). Huli mothers initially complied very well with this programme, and diarrhoea-specific mortality fell significantly. However, mothers began showing less compliance. To understand why, the authors undertook a careful evaluation of the Huli's beliefs and practices regarding diarrhoeal disease.

The Huli understood an illness episode at different levels. First, they sought a pragmatic explanation in terms of immediate causes, to address the question 'How did this illness occur?' Second, they asked the critical question 'Why me?' – or 'Why did this particular child become ill at this time?' – seeking more complex explanations which draw on wider social and religious understandings. What is significant is that the type of explanation influenced their choice of treatment (foods given or withdrawn, the use of spells, prayer readings and other healing ceremonies). When their child became ill, mothers tried minority-world medicine alongside other traditional treatments. But they expressed increasing dissatisfaction with ORS, eventually coming to health posts only if children with diarrhoea also had other symptoms such as fever, for which minority-world treatment was perceived as very effective.

Dissatisfaction occurred because minority-world biomedical explanations and courses of treatment seemed irrelevant in the case of diarrhoea, when mothers did not share the biomedical explanatory model. They had real difficulty getting sick children to drink an adequate quantity of ORS, or even plain water. Mothers said that their children refused to drink the solution, finding its taste unpleasant, or that the fluid made the diarrhoea worse over the next few days. In fact, a mother's first requirement for diarrhoea treatment was the control of its symptoms. She would attempt to dry the child's stool – by withholding fluids and by offering dry, firm, solid foods such as taro or plantain scorched in fire. By contrast, the ORS provided did not block the flow of diarrhoea: it prevented dehydration. The Huli initially tried ORS, given the proven efficacy of other health post treatments. But since they did not embrace the concept of rehydration in their own world views for diarrhoea treatment, it is not surprising to find that people were becoming sceptical of ORS efficacy. When a child had a very runny stool, Huli mothers were reluctant to follow the advice 'give it lots of water'.

Furthermore, such interventions did not address the causes of diarrhoea. If children 'saved' from diarrhoea died a few weeks or months later from malnutrition or infection, then had the intervention actually been successful? The case of diarrhoea well illustrates that a single top-down intervention (known as selective, vertical intervention) may well *save* lives (from diarrhoea) but does little to improve the *quality* of lives (in terms of access to water, sanitation, and in terms of reducing mortality and morbidity from other causes). The implementation of low-cost technology might well have seemed an *efficient* campaign in the eyes of officials at the World Health Organization, but it was far from *sufficient* to make a lasting impact on the lives of children at the local level. What would be more effective would have been to provide clean water and proper sewage systems – a package of primary health care also known as comprehensive, horizontal intervention.

In order to achieve a real reduction in child mortality and sustainable improvements in quality of life, attention needed to be focused not just on the availability of ORS to combat diarrhoea, but also on the environmental and social factors that underlie childhood diseases. Thus, with respect to diarrhoea, the most successful child health programmes have used ORS treatment as one strategy among other parallel and complementary interventions. They have tackled the problem of the children's limited access to water and sanitation, and tried to improve children's long-term prospects for good health.

Summary of Section 5

The Millennium Development Goals set out eight pledges to improve human development by 2015.

Progress on redistributing wealth and tackling social inequality has been patchy and there remain vast discrepancies between variations in ill-health throughout the world.

'Magic bullets' will not be accepted by populations unless they trust them and those promoting and administrating them. Top-down interventions are unlikely to be effective if they are insensitive to local priorities in matters of child health.

Effective health care measures need to use 'magic bullets' as part of wider strategies. Causes as well as symptoms of ill-health have to be addressed.

---

6 Conclusion

This chapter has looked at the various reasons why children's health matters and the long-term impacts that ill-health can have on their futures. It has examined in detail some of the different conceptualisations of health and ill-health, and looked at the importance of these in understanding children's health care needs. Specific global campaigns are in place to improve the health of children, meet their needs, realise their rights and guarantee their well-being and opportunities in life. However, poverty and social inequality continue to undermine efforts to improve health for children. Global health interventions currently aim to go beyond promoting the mere survival of children, with a critical commitment to achieve a sustainable quality of life. The lesson of the twenty-first century is clear: achieving health in practice requires taking action on the wider socio-political factors, specifically the social inequalities that create and sustain health inequalities.

References

BBC News (2010a) *Poorest Scots Die 13 Years Early, Report Suggests* [online], http://www.bbc.co.uk/news/uk-scotland-11878212 (Accessed 2 July 2012).

BBC News (2010b) *Uneven Progress of UN Millennium Development Goals* [online], http://www.bbc.co.uk/news/world-11364717 (Accessed 23 March 2012).

Bellamy, C. (1998) *The State of the World's Children 1998* [online], http://www.unicef.org/sowc98/ (Accessed 29 October 2011).

Croll, E. (2000) *Endangered Daughters: Discrimination and Development in Asia*, London, Routledge.

CSDH (2008) *Final Report: Closing the Gap in a Generation: Health Equity Through Action on the Social Determinants of Health*, Geneva, World Health Organization.

Department of Health (2011) *Nutrition* [online], http://www.dh.gov.uk/health/category/policy-areas/public-health/nutrition-nutrition/ (Accessed 2 July 2012).

Dettwyler, K. (1998) 'The biocultural approach in nutritional anthropology: case studies of malnutrition in Mali', in Brown, P. (ed) *Understanding and Applying Medical Anthropology*, Toronto, Mayfield Publishing Company.

Ene-Obong, H., Iroegbu, C. and Uwaegbute, A. (2000) 'Perceived causes and management of diarrhoea in young children by market women in Enugu State, Nigeria', *Journal of Health, Population and Nutrition*, vol. 18, no. 2, pp. 97–102.

Engle, P. and Nieves, I. (1993) 'Intra-household food distribution among Guatemalan families in a supplementary feeding program: behavior patterns', *Social Science & Medicine*, vol. 36, no. 12, pp. 1605–12.

Frankel, S. (1986) *The Huli Response to Illness*, Cambridge, Cambridge University Press.

Frankel, S. and Lehmann, D. (1984) 'Oral rehydration therapy: combining anthropological and epidemiological approaches in the evaluation of a Papua New Guinea programme', *Journal of Tropical Medicine and Hygiene*, vol. 87, no. 3, pp. 137–42.

Hampshire, K., Panter-Brick, C., Kilpatrick, K. and Casiday, R. E. (2009) 'Saving lives, preserving livelihoods: understanding risk, decision-making and child health in a food crisis', *Social Science & Medicine*, vol. 68, no. 4, pp. 758–65.

League of Nations (1924) *Geneva Declaration of the Rights of the Child* [online], http://www.un-documents.net/gdrc1924.htm (Accessed 2 April 2012).

Lewis, G. (2001) 'Health: an elusive concept', in Macbeth, H. and Shetty, P. (eds) *Health and Ethnicity*, London, Taylor and Francis.

Marmot, M., Friel, S., Bell, R., Houweling, T. and Taylor, S. (2008) 'Closing the gap in a generation: health equity through action on the social determinants of health', *The Lancet*, vol. 372, no. 9650, pp. 1661–9.

McManus, M. and Fox, H. (2007) *Making the Case for Addressing Adolescent Health Care*, Washington, Incenter Strategies.

Martorell, R., Kettel Khan, L., Hughes, M. L. and Grummer-Strawn, L. M. (2000) 'Overweight and obesity in preschool children from developing countries', *International Journal of Obesity*, vol. 24, no. 8, pp. 959–67.

Panter-Brick, C. (1998) 'Biological anthropology and child health: context, process and outcome', in Panter-Brick, C. (ed) *Biosocial Perspectives on Children*, Cambridge, Cambridge University Press.

Panter-Brick, C. and Fuentes, A. (2010) 'Health, risk and adversity: a contextual view from anthropology', in Panter-Brick, C. and Fuentes, A. (eds) *Health, Risk, and Adversity*, New York, Berghahn Books.

Popkin, B., Richards, M. and Montiero, C. (1996) 'Stunting is associated with overweight in children of four nations that are undergoing the nutrition transition', *Journal of Nutrition*, vol. 126, no. 12, pp. 3009–16.

Roberts, H. (2000) *What Works in Reducing Inequalities in Child Health? – Summary*, London, Barnardo's.

Sawyer, S., Afifi, R., Bearinger, L., Blakemore, S-J., Dick, B., Ezeh, A. and Patton, G. (2012) 'Adolescence: a foundation for future health', *The Lancet*, vol. 379, no. 9826, pp. 1630–40.

UNICEF (2001) *Poverty and Children: Lessons of the 90s for Least Developed Countries*, New York, UNICEF.

UNICEF (2011a) *Adolescence: An Age of Opportunity. State of the World's Children Report*, New York, UNICEF.

UNICEF (2011b) *Childinfo: Monitoring the Situation of Children and Women* [online], http://www.childinfo.org/mortality.html (Accessed 2 July 2010).

UNICEF (2012) *Bangladesh: Basic Indicators* [online], http://www.unicef.org/infobycountry/bangladesh_bangladesh_statistics.html (Accessed 2 July 2010).

United Nations (1989) *Convention on the Rights of the Child* [online], http://www2.ohchr.org/english/law/crc.htm (Accessed 2 April 2012).

United Nations (2012) *Millenium Development Goals* [online], http://www.un.org/millenniumgoals (Accessed 28 June 2012).

Welsh Centre for Health (2006) *Pictures of Health in Wales: A Technical Supplement* [online], http://www.wales.nhs.uk/sitesplus/documents/888/WCH%20Pictures%20of%20Health%20%28E%29%20LR.pdf (Accessed 2 July 2010).

Wilkinson, R. G. (1996) *Unhealthy Societies: The Afflictions of Inequality*, London, Routledge.

Wilkinson, R. and Pickett, K. (2010) *The Spirit Level. Why Equality is Better for Everyone*, London, Penguin.

World Health Organization (2006 [1946]) *Constitution of the World Health Organization* [online], http://www.who.int/governance/eb/who_constitution_en.pdf (Accessed 25 March 2012).

Reading A
The spirit catches you and you fall down

Anne Fadiman

Source: *The Spirit Catches You and You Fall Down: A Hmong Child, Her American Doctors, and the Collision of Two Cultures*, 1997; reissued with new afterword 2012, New York, Farrar, Straus and Giroux, pp. 10–31.

Although the Hmong believe that illness can be caused by a variety of sources—including eating the wrong food, drinking contaminated water, being affected by a change in the weather, failing to ejaculate completely during sexual intercourse, neglecting to make offerings to one's ancestors, being punished for one's ancestors' transgressions, being cursed, being hit by a whirlwind, having a stone implanted in one's body by an evil spirit master, having one's blood sucked by a *dab* [malevolent spirit], bumping into a *dab* who lives in a tree or a stream, digging a well in a *dab's* living place, catching sight of a dwarf female *dab* who eats earthworms, having a *dab* sit on one's chest while one is sleeping, doing one's laundry in a lake inhabited by a dragon, pointing one's finger at the full moon, touching a newborn mouse, killing a large snake, urinating on a rock that looks like a tiger, urinating on or kicking a benevolent house spirit, or having bird droppings fall on one's head— by far the most common cause of illness is soul loss. Although the Hmong do not agree on just how many souls people have (estimates range from one to thirty-two; the Lees believe there is only one), there is a general consensus that whatever the number, it is the life-soul, whose presence is necessary for health and happiness, that tends to get lost. A life-soul can become separated from its body through anger, grief, fear, curiosity, or wanderlust. The life-souls of newborn babies are especially prone to disappearance, since they are so small, so vulnerable, and so precariously poised between the realm of the unseen, from which they have just traveled, and the realm of the living. Babies' souls may wander away, drawn by bright colors, sweet sounds, or fragrant smells; they may leave if a baby is sad, lonely, or insufficiently loved by its parents; they may be frightened away by a sudden loud noise; or they may be stolen by a *dab*. Some Hmong are careful never to say aloud that a baby is pretty, lest a *dab* be listening. Hmong babies are often dressed in intricately embroidered hats (Foua made several for Lia) which, when seen from a heavenly perspective, might fool a predatory *dab* into thinking the child was a flower. They spend much of their time swaddled against their mothers' backs in cloth carriers called *nyias* (Foua made Lia several of these too) that have been embroidered with soul-retaining motifs, such as the pigpen, which symbolizes enclosure. They may wear silver necklaces fastened with soul-shackling locks. When babies or small children go on an outing, their parents may call loudly to their souls before the family returns home, to make sure that none remain behind. Hmong families in Merced can sometimes be heard doing this when they leave local parks after a picnic. None of these ploys can work, however, unless the soul-calling ritual has already been properly observed. …

… When Lia was about three months old, her older sister Yer slammed the front door of the Lees' apartment. A few moments later, Lia's eyes rolled up, her arms jerked over her head, and she fainted. The Lees had little doubt what had happened. Despite the careful installation of Lia's soul during the *hu plig* [her soul-calling] ceremony, the noise of the door had been so profoundly frightening that her soul had fled her body and become lost. They recognized the resulting symptoms as *qaug dab peg*, which means 'the spirit catches you and you fall down.' …

In Hmong-English dictionaries, *qaug dab peg* is generally translated as epilepsy. It is an illness well known to the Hmong, who regard it with ambivalence. On the one hand, it is acknowledged to be a serious and potentially dangerous condition. …

On the other hand, the Hmong consider *qaug dab peg* to be an illness of some distinction. … Hmong epileptics often become shamans. Their seizures are thought to be evidence that they have the power to perceive things other people cannot see, as well as facilitating their entry into trances, a prerequisite for their journeys into the realm of the unseen. The fact that they have been ill themselves gives them an intuitive sympathy for the suffering of others and lends them emotional credibility as healers. Becoming a *txiv neeb* [healer] is not a choice; it is a vocation. … Although shamanism is an arduous calling that requires years of training with a master in order to learn the ritual techniques and chants, it confers an enormous amount of social status in the community and publicly marks the *txiv neeb* as a person of high moral character, since a healing spirit would never choose a no-account host. Even if an epileptic turns out not to be elected to host a *neeb* [healing spirit], his illness, with its thrilling aura of the supramundane, singles him out as a person of consequence.

In their attitude toward Lia's seizures, the Lees reflected this mixture of concern and pride. …

Foua and Nao Kao had nurtured Lia in typical Hmong fashion ... and they were naturally distressed to think that anything might compromise her health and happiness. They therefore hoped, at least most of the time, that the *qaug dab peg* could be healed. Yet they also considered the illness an honor. ...

During the next few months of her life, Lia had at least twenty more seizures. On two occasions, Foua and Nao Kao were worried enough to carry her in their arms to the emergency room at Merced Community Medical Center, which was three blocks from their apartment. Like most Hmong refugees, they had their doubts about the efficacy of Western medical techniques. However, when they were living in the Mae Jarim refugee camp in Thailand, their only surviving son, Cheng, and three of their six surviving daughters, Ge, May, and True, had been seriously ill. Ge died. They took Cheng, May, and True to the camp hospital; Cheng and May recovered rapidly, and True was sent to another, larger hospital, where she eventually recovered as well. (The Lees also concurrently addressed the possible spiritual origins of their children's illnesses by moving to a new hut. A dead person had been buried beneath their old one, and his soul might have wished to harm the new residents.) This experience did nothing to shake their faith in traditional Hmong beliefs about the causes and cures of illness, but it did convince them that on some occasions Western doctors could be of additional help, and that it would do no harm to hedge their bets. ...

... On March 3, 1983, Foua and Nao Kao carried Lia to the emergency room a third time. On this occasion, three circumstances were different: Lia was still seizing when they arrived, they were accompanied by a cousin who spoke some English, and one of the doctors on duty was a family practice resident named Dan Murphy. ...

Among Dan's notes in Lia's History and Physical Examination record were:

> HISTORY OF PRESENT ILLNESS: The patient is an 8 month, Hmong female, whose family brought her to the emergency room after they had noticed her shaking and not breathing very well for a 20-minute period of time. According to the family the patient has had multiple like episodes in the past, but have never been able to communicate this to emergency room doctors on previous visits secondary to a language barrier. An english speaking relative

available tonight, stated that the patient had had intermittent fever and cough for 2–3 days prior to being admitted.

FAMILY & SOCIAL HISTORY: Unobtainable secondary to language difficulties.

NEUROLOGICAL: The child was unresponsive to pain or sound. The head was held to the left with intermittent tonic-clonic [first rigid, then jerking] movements of the upper extremities. Respirations were suppressed during these periods of clonic movement. Grunting respirations persisted until the patient was given 3 mg. of Valium I.V.

Dan had no way of knowing that Foua and Nao Kao had already diagnosed their daughter's problem as the illness where the spirit catches you and you fall down. Foua and Nao Kao had no way of knowing that Dan had diagnosed it as epilepsy, the most common of all neurological disorders. Each had accurately noted the same symptoms, but Dan would have been surprised to hear that they were caused by soul loss, and Lia's parents would have been surprised to hear that they were caused by an electrochemical storm inside their daughter's head that had been stirred up by the misfiring of aberrant brain cells. …

Lia's seizure was a grand mal episode, and Dan had no desire to do anything but stop it. He admitted her to MCMC as an inpatient. Among the tests she had during the three days she spent there were a spinal tap, a CT scan, an EEG, a chest X ray, and extensive blood work. Foua and Nao Kao signed 'Authorization for and Consent to Surgery or Special Diagnostic or Therapeutic Procedures' forms, each several hundred words long, for the first two of these. It is not known whether anyone attempted to translate them, or, if so, how 'Your physician has requested a brain scan utilizing computerized tomography' was rendered into Hmong. None of the tests revealed any apparent cause for the seizures. The doctors classified Lia's epilepsy as 'idiopathic': cause unknown. …

Lia was discharged on March 11, 1983. Her parents were instructed, via an English-speaking relative, to give her 250 milligrams of ampicillin twice a day, to clear up her aspiration pneumonia, and twenty milligrams of Dilantin elixir, an anticonvulsant, twice a day, to suppress any further grand mal seizures.

Reading B
The obesity epidemic: medical and ethical considerations

Jantina de Vries

Source: 'The obesity epidemic: medical and ethical considerations', 2007, *Science and Engineering Ethics*, vol. 13, no. 3, pp. 55–67.

Introduction

'When a three-year-old girl who weighs 40 kg dies of heart failure brought on by obesity, you know her parents are guilty of gross child abuse', was just one of the comments following the publication of the 2004 UK House of Commons Health Committee report on obesity. In this report that examines the state of obesity in the UK, the committee cited written evidence of a UK-based medical professional who, in her letter to the committee, expressed concern about the number of children in need of medical treatment for obesity. In some ill-chosen words, the doctor detailed to the committee the problems she encountered in her work in an obesity clinic, and also referred to the case of a three-year-old's death 'where obesity was a contributory factor'. As an immediate result, media around the world reported on the excesses of obesity, the lethal consequences associated with childhood obesity, and the relative responsibility of parents and the state to prevent children from growing so big, with one source in particular describing 'this poor little girl' as the *'freakish extreme'* of what is now commonly referred to as 'the obesity epidemic'. ...

Fat is 'freakish'

The question, however, is why contemporary society is so concerned with body weight. How come the slender body has become not only the fashionable, but also the political, scientific and medical ideal, when this body does not rationally represent the 'ideal' body, neither in scientific nor in medical terms?

The most important indication is provided in a quotation earlier ... The deceased three-year-old girl was called the *'freakish* extreme' of a trend of increasing body weight, revealing a glimpse of contemporary social disgust with fat. For one thing, a fat body signals to the observer that its owner is not able to control desire. For centuries, religious protestant teachings have lectured Western societies about the need to be humble and to control desire. Desire, in many ways, was interchanged with sin, and the body itself was conceptualised as a site of temptation. ... Fat and fatness, in other words, signal immorality and are incompatible with a protestant ethic, that continues to inform many of Western societies' norms and values. Over the years, these religious claims have become interlaced with the broader cultural setting, and are now inseparable from it. Values of beauty have thus persisted even in largely secularized societies. Such a disparity with Western religious ethic has given rise to current social stigmatisations of overweight people as lazy, sloppy, dirty and worse.

Related to this, the last century has witnessed increasing incompatibility between fat on the one side, and beauty on the other. Increasingly in the twentieth century, ideals of the body celebrated slenderness as the bodily ideal, and condemned 'fat' as destroying grace and delicacy. This opposed to nineteenth century conceptions of beauty, where slenderness was normally described as 'meagreness', and associated with weakness and ill health. Contrary to trends in the twentieth century, at this time the round body was celebrated as the ideal body shape. ...

Children and aesthetic concerns

Aesthetic concerns are also not irrelevant for children: almost four decades ago, research pointed out that children translate cultural and normative values of beauty into specific body shapes. At that time, researchers found that at the age of six, children started to associate the fat body with a range of negative characteristics, and became concerned about their own body size. More recently, researchers have argued that children develop these concerns at an even younger age ... and readily associate more negative and less positive characteristics with chubby body types. They also indicate that the person they would least like to be is a chubby person. This is consistent with the results of other research projects, and provides an indicator for the age with which social norms about 'normality' and 'deviance' become internalised.

Interesting in this respect are research findings that discuss the ethnic nature of concerns about fat. White and Asian children and adolescents in the US for instance generally appear to be far more concerned with their body weight and shape than black and Hispanic children and adolescents. Such results are repeated for other countries and continents, and are normally explained by making reference to a different cult of beauty where the ideal of thinness is less prominent.

What effect on childhood obesity?

But how does the medical condemnation of fat influence the lives and autonomy of children and parents in deciding what is good for them? The substitution of notions of the healthy but chubby child with unhealthy and unrealistic ideals of thinness and fitness, especially in the light of evidence that holds that being underweight might potentially be more damaging for health than being overweight, can be seen as carrying severe ethical concerns.

First of all, social and normative ideals of body shape and body weight gain hegemony over other, perhaps more sane, relations to the body. In some research, for instance, mothers have indicated to prefer having an underweight child over an overweight or obese child, even when (the image of) the underweight child was given an emaciated appearance. This is not synonymous to saying that offering treatment to obese children is always nonsensical; on the contrary, there are those exceptions of children becoming extraordinarily big, where excess body fat is simply incapacitating the child's activities. However, contrary to what one is made to believe, these children are still the exception to the rule, and represent a small fragment in obesity prevalence data. The majority of children included in such statistics are not exceptionally heavy, and often they are not obese. My concern here is twofold and entails first of all the absence of a good overview of prevalence distribution. Normally, reports about childhood obesity heap together all children that are too heavy without providing the cultural/ historical context of body weight, and without clarifying the percentage of children that actually is obese or morbidly obese. Second, it concerns the notion that the rapid and society-wide spread of an ideology of restriction works as a way of stigmatising all children with excess weight, including all the overweight children, rather than contributing to a solution to the problem. The spread of such an ideology is not without repercussion for the wellbeing of children. As we saw before, knowledge, norms and values about the body and body weight reach and influence children. Children are not immune for such information, and modify behaviour and emotions to fit social expectations. It is naïve to presuppose that a widely diffused logic of restriction does not influence the eating behaviour or well-being of children. With the growing attention for the impact of expanding waistlines on society, we might actually be raising a generation of people with a fear of food and highly disturbed eating patterns, rather than a generation of big people. Reflection about consequences of the diffusion of a logic of anorexia might be warranted, especially since little serious consideration has actually been given to this aspect of the obesity epidemic.

Another area of concern that warrants attention is the apparent association between obesity, social class and ethnicity. Focussing on the composition of prevalence statistics in almost all Western countries, we can observe a strong racial- and class component to weight distribution in modern societies. Namely, prevalence of overweight and obesity is significantly higher in the poorer 'classes' and in the ethnic minorities than in the richer classes and in the native population in almost all Western societies. In the Netherlands, for instance, children from low-educated parents, or from single-parent households, were found to have higher likelihood to be overweight. Also, children from Turkish or Moroccan descent were found to be obese more frequently. In the UK, researchers identified higher prevalence of diabetes and obesity in children of Pakistani and Indian descent, whereas in the United States, children from Hispanic origin are thought to have a significantly higher risk of developing obesity. Various reasons including parental education and behaviour, are normally mentioned to account for such differences but a matter of fact is that the prevalence of obesity appears to follow class structures and segregation in societies that have since long embraced the principle of equality. This fact in itself should trigger profound social reflection not only on the income distribution in society, but also on the moral injustice of an unequal distribution of health and education across society. However, it also carries seeds for contemplation about the close relation between the medicalisation of a condition and drives to eradicate deviance and homogenise society. Previously, I have discussed how the obesity debate could be recast as a debate to convict gluttony and indulgence. Here, I point out the close relation between immoral behaviour and the social and economic outcasts of society; the poor and the immigrants also most readily engage in self-destructive behaviour and are thus in need for regulation that protects them from themselves. In this way, the call to take political action against childhood obesity apparently equals a call for political action against the poor and weak individuals in society. I believe a theoretical reflection on these assertions is necessary.

A third and last remark to be made concerns the best way forward. The frustration of practitioners and family to effectively treat the problem has increased calls for the application of intense intervention measures on obese children and adolescents. Pharmacotherapy and bariatric surgery have come to the focus of the peadiatricians as possible aids in the fight against early onset obesity, although these treatments are not considered for children under the age of ten. Such measures, however, are truly rigorous and cannot be recommended for mildly obese or overweight children. In the light of uncertain scientific knowledge, however, we should question whether any kind of political or medical intervention in children is desirable.

As it is, current political, social and medical attention for excess body weight appears not only to be motivated by real concerns about the negative health effects of excess body fat, but also at least partially by a social condemnation of fat. Indulgence, gluttony and laziness are all characteristics normally ascribed to the obese, and reveal a societal incapability to deal with a variety of body shapes. The medicalisation of the condition confronts the overweight and obese child and his or her parents with a set of fixed expectations, not the least of which is the social expectation of 'getting better'. Failure on the side of the patient, and his or her parents, to reach a healthy, fit and slender body is considered weakness, fat children are considered 'freakish'. Parents failing to make their child lose weight are accused of child abuse, since they are denying treatment (and thus a normal life) to their children.

Reading C
Death without weeping: the violence of everyday life in Brazil

Nancy Scheper-Hughes

Source: *Death Without Weeping*, 1993, Berkeley, CA, University of California Press, pp. 312–6.

Mortal Ills, Fated Deaths

Whereas doctors in the clinics and hospitals of Bom Jesus were unconcerned about properly diagnosing and recording the causes of infant and child deaths for the poor of Bom Jesus, Alto women readily shared with me their notions of the causes of childhood mortality. I posed the question in two ways. I asked a general question: 'Why do so many babies die on the Alto do Cruzeiro?' Then in the course of recording personal reproductive histories, I asked each woman to tell me at length about the circumstances surrounding each child's death, including her perception of the baby's key symptoms, the various steps she took to remedy the illness, and her understanding of the cause of the death. The two questions elicited very different answers.

In response to the general question on the incidence and causes of high child mortality in the community, Alto women were quick to reply with blanket condemnations of the hostile environment in which they and their children were forced to live and die. They responded:

'Our children die because we are poor and hungry.'

'They die because the water we drink is filthy with germs.'

'They die because we cannot afford to keep shoes on their feet.'

'They die because we get worthless medical care.'

'They die of neglect. Often we have to leave them alone in the house when we go to work. So you wash them, feed them, give them a pacifier, close the door, and say a prayer to the Virgin hoping that they will still be alive when you get home. Yes, they die of neglect [*à míngua*] but it's not due to a lack of goodwill toward our children. The problem isn't one of *vontade* [willingness] but one of *poder* [power or ability].'

When asked what it is that infants need most to survive the first and most precarious year of life, Alto women invariably answered that it was *food*, pure and simple. 'Can it be that mothers of ten, twelve, even sixteen children don't know what a child needs to survive? Of course we know! Rich people's children have proper food. Our children are fed catch as catch can. Some days we have one ingredient for the baby's *mingau* [porridge], but we don't have the other. We may have the *farinha* [flour] but not the sugar. Or we have the sugar but not the powdered milk. And so we improvise. What else can we do?'

Another shook her head in perplexity: 'I don't know why so many die. Some babies are born strong and healthy enough. Their stomachs when they are round and full give one such pleasure! But something is wrong with the food we give them. No matter how much we feed them, they lose their fat and turn into toothpicks. It makes one discouraged.'

Still another could identify the exact problem and its remedy: 'They die from the miserable *engano* [ruse] of *papa d'água* [potato water]. Babies need food to live. Most older babies require at least two cans [four hundred grams each] of powdered milk a week. But people here can afford only one can, and so the babies are fed mostly on water. Soon their blood turns to water as well. Money would solve all our problems.'

Many others agreed with her: 'Here on the Alto there are a multitude of children who live in neglect, eating garbage that other people leave behind, sucking on banana skins and on orange peels. It's because their parents don't earn enough to feed them, and the only solution is to set the children out on the streets.'

In short, Alto mothers gave highly politicized answers to the question of child mortality in general, ones that stressed the external constraints on the ability to care for their offspring. But when these same women were asked to explain why any of *their own* children died, their answers were more clinical, and the causes of death were seen as more proximate, sometimes as *internal* to the child. Often the dead infant was judged as lacking a vital life force, his or her own 'will' to live. And not a single Alto mother stated that hunger was the cause of death for any of her own children, although many of the dead babies were described as having 'wasted' or 'withered' away, 'shriveled up,' or 'shrunk to nothing.' In response to what may have caused a particular infant to 'waste away', Alto women often replied that the baby was born with a 'fragile', 'nervous', or 'weak' constitution. Hunger, it seemed, only killed Alto children in the abstract. It may kill *your* children (perhaps) but not any of mine. It may be that Alto mothers had to exercise a certain amount of denial because the alternative—the recognition that one's own child is slowly starving to death—is too painful or, given the role that mothers sometimes play in reducing food and liquid … , too rife with psychological conflict.

Alto women distinguished between child deaths viewed as 'natural' (coming from God or from nature) and those suspected to be caused by sorcery, evil eye, and magical possession. They attributed most of their own children's deaths to natural causes, especially to communicable diseases. But the women also explained child deaths in terms of failures in proper nurturing, including disregard for the normal 'lying-in' precautions for mother and newborn, mortal forms of neglect, and strong and passionate emotions. …

Alto mothers considered simple diarrhea the greatest single killer of their babies, carrying away 71 of the 255 children who died. But more 'complex' and complicated forms of diarrhea were also implicated in the folk category *doença de criança*, 'child sickness,' and in some cases of *dentição* (teething illness), *gasto* (wasting illness), *susto* (fright sickness), and *fraqueza* (general weakness and debility). Were we to include all the folk pediatric diagnoses in which diarrhea was at least a secondary symptom, then as many as 189 of the 255 deaths, 74 percent of all infant and child deaths on the Alto, could be attributed to diarrhea. Mothers distinguished among many different subtypes (*qualidades*) of infant diarrhea (e.g., *intestino*, *quentura*, *barriga desmantelada*), based on color, consistency, smell, and force of the stools. Mothers saved the dirty nappies of their ailing babies to discuss the differential diagnoses with neighbors and elderly healing women of the Alto. In all, mothers recognized the severity of this disease in particular as a primary child-killer on the Alto. Among the other communicable diseases commonly cited by mothers were (in order of importance) measles, pneumonia and other respiratory ailments, infant jaundice, tetanus, fevers, whooping cough, smallpox, and other skin diseases and infections.

Underlying and uniting these diverse etiological notions were the same structural principles that informed Alto people's beliefs about the 'nervous' body. Here, once again, life was conceptualized as a *luta*, a power 'struggle', between large and small, strong and weak. Infants were born both 'weak' and 'hot'; their tiny systems were easily overwhelmed. Poor infants were already compromised in the womb. Born (as the women said) of prematurely aged fathers whose blood was 'sick and wasted' and whose semen was 'tired' and of mothers whose breasts offered blood and infection instead of rich milk, it is little wonder that Alto babies were described as born 'already thirsty and starving in the womb', as 'bruised and discolored,' their 'tongues swollen in their mouths.'

The babies of the rich were described as coming into the world fat and fair and 'greedy' for life. They emerged from the womb with a lusty cry. The babies of the Alto, 'poor things,' came out of the womb 'like wet little birds, barely chirping' and with a 'nausea' for food. 'Our babies,' I was often told, were 'born already *wanting* to die.' Although few Alto mothers could give me the accurate birth weights of their offspring, their descriptions of 'skinny,' 'wasted,' 'pale,' 'quiet' newborns, infants who came into the world with no *gosto* (taste) for life and no will to suckle, seemed very much the descriptions of preterm and low-birth-weight infants, babies all too aptly described by Alto women as born already 'disadvantaged.'

What mothers expectantly looked for in their newborn infants were qualities that showed a readiness for the uphill struggle that was life. And so Alto mothers expressed a preference for those babies who evidenced early on the physical, psychological, and social characteristics of fighters and survivors. Active, quick, responsive, and playful infants were much preferred to quiet, docile, inactive infants, infants described as 'dull,' 'listless,' and spiritless. Although differences in infant temperament were believed to be innate, in a precarious environment such as the Alto parasitic infection, malnutrition, and dehydration reproduced these same traits in a great many infants. A particularly lethal form of negative feedback sometimes resulted when Alto mothers gradually withdrew from listless infants whose 'passivity' was the result of hunger itself.

Conversely, for an Alto mother to say proudly of a child that she or he suffered many 'crises' during the first year of life but 'conquered' or 'endured' the struggle was a mother's fondest testimony to some hidden inner strength or drive within the child. And so fat, resilient babies were described as having *força*, an innate charismatic power and strength. Many frail infants easily succumbed to death from teething because the innate *força* of the teeth straining against the soft gums holding the teeth captive overwhelmed the little body, making the infant vulnerable to any of several lethal and incurable child diseases. Perhaps the ethnopediatric illness *gasto* best captured the image of the beleaguered little body unable to resist powerful forces. In *gasto*, a fatal form of infant gastroenteritis, the infant's body offered no 'resistance' and was quickly reduced to a hollow tube or sieve. Whatever went into the infant's mouth emerged directly in virulent bouts of vomiting and diarrhea. The infant was quickly 'spent,' 'wasted,' used up; her fight and her vital energy were gone.

Chapter 4

Children and violence

Heather Montgomery

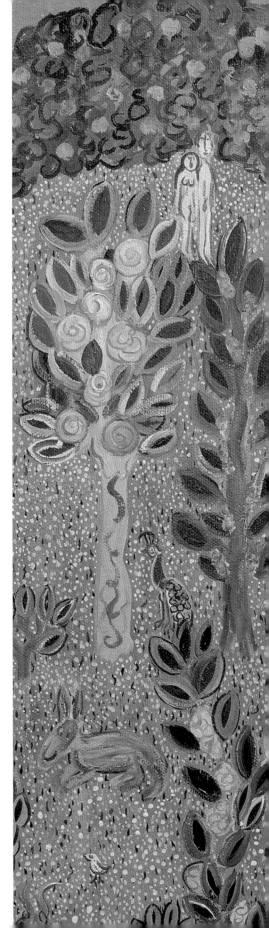

Contents

In this chapter, you will:

- explore the different meanings of the term 'violence' and the various impacts that violence can have on children's lives
- analyse children's relationships to violence in three specific sites – the home, the school and the community
- critically analyse the concept of symbolic violence
- examine the various roles that children play in relation to violence
- discuss children's experiences in war and armed conflict.

1 Introduction

This chapter examines another form of adversity that many children face, that of violence. It starts with an examination of what violence means in children's lives, before focusing on three different sites where children experience violence: home, school and the wider community, especially during times of armed conflict. There is obviously an overlap between these sites and they are not meant to be mutually exclusive. Furthermore, this chapter emphasises that violence against children is not something that occurs only in the majority world. Many children have daily experience of violence whether they live in Europe or in an African war zone.

2 Definitions of violence

Violence at first might seem a simple concept, especially when it refers to children. Anything that damages them, hurts them or upsets them surely constitutes violence. The question of intent is also important, if someone *intentionally* hurts a child, then that constitutes violence, whereas accidentally running into them or unintentionally hitting them does not. The idea of violence is also closely associated with abuse – although abuse is a much wider term, covering neglect and mistreatment. Within these seemingly straightforward definitions, however, there are ambiguities and difficulties. While there is broad agreement that some behaviours are violent – beating a child unconscious or hitting them with an implement – others are highly contentious. For some, smoking cigarettes in front of a child is a form of child abuse, while for others any smacking is a violent abuse of power.

Activity 1   Different forms of violence

Allow about 10 minutes

In 2008 Parentline in Scotland, in conjunction with the Violence Reduction Unit, issued a series of posters suggesting that not only were children victims of violence in the home, but that this violence had long-term effects on children.

Carefully study the two posters in Figures 1 and 2 and comment on:

- how violence is defined in these posters
- whether or not you agree with this definition.

Figure 1   Anti-violence poster from a campaign by Parentline in Scotland from 2008

Comment

These posters are designed to shock and to invoke an emotional response. By transposing such violent language on to the faces of young children, along with their captions, these images suggest that violence is

Figure 2   Poster highlighting the impact of verbal violence on children from Parentline Scotland, 2008

not simply about force and physical hurt but is also concerned with verbal assault. The implication here is that words and threats such as 'I'll skelp you' (I'll hit you), or 'Get out of my sight' constitute a form of violence against children, even if they do not involve physical force. Furthermore, although a phrase such as 'You never get anything right' does not necessarily imply a threat of physical force, it is counted here as a form of violence against children because it humiliates and belittles them, damaging their well-being. Words and actions are seen as equally damaging to children and both are seen as violent.

However, there is no universal agreement on this and some would argue that telling a child they never get anything right is hurtful or upsetting, but that it is not violent. There is a fear that if the word 'violence' is used towards any form of behaviour deemed undesirable then the term loses its meaning and it becomes harder to protect those children who are at risk from the most serious forms of physical violence.

In one sense, therefore, it is impossible to define violence absolutely as definitions depend on personal ideology and social context. Ideas about what constitutes violence change, as ideas about children, families and their relationships to each other, and to the state, change. An example of this can be seen in the issue of corporal punishment. In the 1970s in the UK corporal punishment was widespread in British schools and viewed as an important disciplinary tool for teachers. Now it is banned (in 1987 in state schools and 1999 in private schools) and if it occurred would be classified as assault. However, a poll of 6162 UK teachers carried out by the *Times Educational Supplement* in 2008 found that 22 per cent of secondary teachers would still back caning in extreme cases (Bloom, 2008).

Smacking is even more controversial. Throughout most of the twentieth century (and before) it was generally understood as a positive and necessary way of disciplining children, but is now seen more negatively. Despite attempts to change the legislation by children's rights activists, and criticisms of the UK government for failing to outlaw it in successive reports of the Committee on the Rights of the Child (a body of experts who monitor the implementation of the UNCRC), smacking remains legal. Its legality is based on an 1860 law which allows parents to discipline their children using 'reasonable chastisement'. What is reasonable has never been accurately defined, however, and remains the subject of much debate in national and, more recently, European courts of law. As of 2005, any punishment which causes visible bruising, grazes, scratches, minor swellings or cuts has been outlawed, although smacking, if it does not leave a mark, has not. Some parents in the UK continue to argue that smacking is an acceptable form of discipline and an effective form of training for good behaviour. They do not consider it a form of violence or abuse. Indeed, even some of those parents who do not smack their children argue that it can be a useful tool for other parents and do not want to see it banned completely. The Growing Up in Scotland study (2008) suggested that while only a minority of parents practise smacking (16 per cent of mothers of two year olds), 30 per cent agreed with the statement 'it may not be a good thing to smack, but sometimes it is the only thing that will work' (Centre for Research on Families and Relationships, 2008, p. 2).

There are also other instances where what is considered violent depends on social and cultural norms and beliefs. Often boys are seen as inherently more violent than girls and the norms of acceptable behaviour are different for them as a result. Similar discrepancies are apparent in what is acceptable in younger and older children, and different sections of the community – as well as individuals – will have different standards as to what they consider violent behaviour.

Figure 3   Children on a no-smacking demonstration, England

Furthermore, there are site-specific differences between what are labelled as violent or non-violent behaviours depending on whether they occur in the home, the classroom, the playground or the sports field. A child chasing and deliberately bringing down another child would be unnecessarily violent in the playground but very useful on a rugby pitch.

In the UK, as in other minority-world societies, there is an ambivalent, and much debated, relationship between children and violence. In some instances, children are seen as innocent, in need of protection and the victims of violence rather than its perpetrators. Children in this ideal are naturally good and those who commit violence against them are not only attacking someone more vulnerable, they are also violating cherished notions of innocence and goodness. Children are still thought of (or hoped to be) pure and innocent, and when this vision is violated, either by children themselves or by adult perpetrators of violence or abuse, there is widespread anger and pity.

Running alongside this idealised version of childhood and human nature, however, is another set of imaginings. In this vision, children are not always innocent and have the capacity to act violently, especially towards other children or through cruelty to animals. Children are seen as inherently violent and in need of the control of adults or the state to protect the social order. They are the perpetrators of violence as much as its victims. Books such as William Golding's *Lord of the Flies* (1954), about a group of schoolboys who are stranded on a remote island after a plane crash and gradually descend into savagery, losing all the attributes of civilisation until they run totally wild and commit murder, are often invoked to suggest that children are 'naturally' savage and in need of adult control and civilisation. Golding's vision is one of horror as children degenerate into savagery without adult constraint:

> Ralph moaned faintly. Tired as he was, he could not relax and fall into a well of sleep for fear of the tribe. Might it not be possible to walk boldly into the fort, say – 'I've got pax,' laugh lightly and sleep among the others? Pretend they were still boys, schoolboys who had said 'Sir, yes, Sir' – and worn caps? Daylight might have answered yes, but darkness and the horrors of death said no. Lying there in the darkness, he knew he was an outcast …

> There were sounds coming from behind the Castle Rock. Listening carefully, detaching his mind from the swing of the sea, Ralph could make out a familiar rhythm.

> *'Kill the beast! Cut his throat! Spill his blood!'*

> (Golding, 1954, p. 205)

Figure 4   Scene from 1990 film of *Lord of the Flies*

This might be dismissed as merely fiction were it not for other studies that point out that adults still have very ambivalent feelings towards children and violence.

A survey carried out by Barnardo's in 2008 found that:

- just under half (49 per cent) of people agree that children are increasingly a danger to each other and adults
- 43 per cent agree something has to be done to protect us from children
- more than a third (35 per cent) of people agree that nowadays it feels like the streets are infested with children
- 45 per cent of the public agree that people refer to children as feral because they behave this way.

(Barnardo's, 2008)

Summary of Section 2

Today, violence against children is defined much more broadly than simple physical assault. It also includes emotional violence and humiliation.

Abuse may be a form of violence although it is interpreted more widely to include many forms of mistreatment.

Violence against children is socially constructed. What constitutes violence against children changes over time and place. It also depends on context, and the age and gender of the child. Boys are likely to be seen as more violent than girls, and teenagers more violent than younger children.

Children and violence have an ambivalent relationship to each other in much of the minority world. Children can be perceived as inherently violent and naturally cruel, as well as gentle and lacking in violence.

---

3 Violence in the home

Since Henry Kempe publicised the 'battered baby syndrome' in 1962, the extent and nature of child abuse in the home has become increasingly recognised. Following on from Kempe's claims that some children were routinely beaten and ill-treated within their own families, other issues such as sexual abuse and emotional abuse have also been acknowledged. In 2009, 34,100 children in England were judged to be at risk from their home environment and were the subject of a Child Protection Plan. In Scotland the figure was 2682, in Northern Ireland 2488 and in Wales, 2521 (NSPCC, 2010). In 2008, Ofsted (The UK's Office for Standards in Education, Children's Services and Skills) found that, between May 2007 and August 2008, there were 210 child deaths, or three deaths each week, attributable to violence, abuse or neglect by parents and carers (Gilbert et al., 2008).

Figure 5 Despite fears of 'stranger danger' the majority of abuse occurs within the home

Despite these figures, parental and social fears about violence against children predominantly focus not on members of the family, but on the role of the stranger or the predatory outsider coming into the home to commit violence. The abduction of four-year-old Madeleine McCann in Portugal in 2007 obsessed the media for years, both in the UK and internationally, despite its rarity. The fear of stranger danger remains and, in fact, eclipses many other anxieties. It has been claimed, for example, that parents are more worried about their children being murdered than they are about them getting obese, despite the risk of the latter being very much greater than the former (BBC News, 2010). This unwillingness to recognise the relative risks that children face suggests not just ignorance on the part of society but a deliberate choice to focus on certain issues and to ignore others. Talking of the USA in the 1980s, but still resonant today, Nancy Scheper-Hughes and Howard Stein argued that:

> the 'choice' of child abuse as a master social problem of our times, also includes a strong 'choice' for only certain forms of child abuse – battering and sexual abuse – and a *selective inattention* to other forms – specifically, poverty-related neglect. This selective inattention is a consequence of the need to deny the role of our punitive public policies in contributing to the 'feminization of poverty', and to the problem of childhood mortality in our inner city, minority neighbourhoods.
>
> (Scheper-Hughes and Stein, 1987, p. 353)

Scheper-Hughes and Stein are not arguing that child abuse does not exist or that parents need not worry about child abduction. What they do claim is that certain forms of violence against children are easier to accept and discuss than others and that this is a social choice. Fears are focused on abhorrent individuals, thereby negating the need to look at wider social issues (this point was also forcefully made by Reading B on 'Crack babies' in Chapter 1). It is much easier to blame either poor mothers or outside abusers; much harder to look at the poverty, poor housing and racism which put enormous pressure on vulnerable families, and increase children's vulnerability and risk of witnessing or being a victim of violence.

There remains a reluctance to confront violence against children in the home. Tackling the issue leads to accusations of interference in private family life and the intrusion of the state into the relationships between parents and children. As the previous section suggested, smacking is still seen by some as an acceptable form of discipline, and successive governments have been reluctant to intervene and ban it against the wishes of parents. When it comes to violence against children in the home, there is still a willing blindness on the part of many that it is at home where children are most at risk. As the director of one children's charity, Kidscape, once put it:

> We have found that one of the difficulties about getting across messages about children abused by people they know is that very often it's not a message people want to touch. I think people concentrate far more on the 'stranger danger' aspect of child abuse because […] people are not hideously embarrassed about talking to their children about it; advertisers, people who want to sponsor us, it's a subject they're happy to talk about. People don't want to be associated with child abuse [in the home] as incest […] it's a message we try to get across to the press but they're very wary, […] it's not a fun subject, it's likely to put readers off, may upset readers, and it's easier and safer to concentrate on strangers and bullying.
>
> (Quoted in Kitzinger and Skidmore, 1995, p. 53)

3.1 Self-harm

So far this chapter has looked at overt forms of violence, including emotional violence. It has also noted that violence is a slippery concept and often apparent in the eye of the beholder, so that what is considered violence depends on personal standpoint and social context. This section will now turn to another form of violence – violence manifested in acts of self-harm among children and young people. This might be a controversial categorisation and many might see self-harm as a form of illness rather than an act of violence, but it is included here to give another perspective on children's relationship with violence. It aims to show the complexities of this relationship and to argue that violence is a constant feature of many children's lives, even if it is often overlooked.

Self-harm can be defined as an act with a non-fatal outcome in which a person deliberately:

- Initiated behaviour (for example, self cutting, jumping from a height), which they intended to cause self harm
- Ingested a substance in excess of the prescribed or generally recognised therapeutic dose

- Ingested a recreational or illicit drug that was an act that the person regarded as self harm

- Ingested a non-ingestible substance or object

(Hawton et al., 2002, p. 1208)

Because the problem has only recently been identified and acknowledged as a health issue for children and young people, it is difficult to know whether incidences have actually increased in the last 30 years or whether it is now better recognised and diagnosed. Certainly the secrecy surrounding it and the fact that many young people who self-harm rarely report it to doctors or hospitals makes it very difficult to gain accurate numbers. However, some figures indicate that 250,000 adolescents are treated in hospital each year for self-harm and that many of these young people report previous episodes for which they did not seek treatment (Hawton et al., 2002). There are likely to be even more whose self-harm is never noticed. In 2008, one study suggested that one in three young women in the UK had self-harmed at one point in their lives (Harion, 2008).

The factors that influence self-harm rates are extremely complex but there are some broad generalisations that can be made. Girls are four times more likely to self-harm than boys. Boys and girls worried about their sexual orientation are also more likely to self-harm, as are those who have experienced bullying. It is also strongly associated with physical and sexual abuse, and is more likely to occur after using drink or drugs. Children and young people are also heavily influenced by their peers; if they have a friend or family member who self-harms, they are more likely to do so themselves. Finally, the researchers in one study concluded that: 'Levels of depression, anxiety, impulsivity, and self esteem were all associated with self harm in both sexes' (Hawton et al., 2002, p. 1209).

Although self-harm has sometimes been seen as a minority-world phenomenon, researchers have found incidences elsewhere. One study in Sri Lanka established that there were very high levels of self-poisoning among young people and found similar patterns to the UK, with more young women than men poisoning themselves (60 per cent of those who died having drunk poison were women under 25) and those who knew of someone else who had self-harmed in this way were more likely to self-harm than those who did not (BBC News, 1998).

There is still great debate about whether self-harm indicates suicidal tendencies or is a transient phase of distress. Certainly not all young people who harm themselves go on to commit suicide, but it is an important indicator of extreme distress, however temporary. In terms of understanding children's relationship with violence, however, it needs to be noted that while the home may be idealised as a sanctuary for children, it does not always provide a safe space for them. Indeed, home is the place where children are most likely to experience violence, either that committed by their parents or that which they inflict on themselves.

Summary of Section 3

Children are at most risk of violence in the home, although fears of violence often cluster around the figure of the dangerous outsider.

Home remains idealised as a sanctuary for children; however, it is the place they are most likely to experience violence.

Self-harm affects many children and can be seen as another way they experience violence in the home.

---

4 Violence at school

When confronted with the phrase 'violence at school' the immediate reaction is to think of bullying. Bullying is seen as a serious social problem for children in the UK and one of the major challenges that they face at school. In an interview for the *Observer* newspaper in 2005, the then Children's Commissioner for England, Professor Al Aynsley-Green, said:

> I have no doubt that children are being brought up in a society where violence is the norm in many ways. I include in this the violence on television, in the workplace and in the home.
>
> I have had hundreds of in-depth conversations with children since accepting this post and I can tell you that the one thing every child

I have met has been affected by, with virtually no exceptions, is bullying ...

(Quoted in Hill and Hinsliff, 2005)

Other organisations have concurred with these findings. In 2008, the telephone helpline for children, ChildLine, said that 'Bullying has been the single greatest problem encountered by ChildLine for the past 12 years' (NSPCC, 2008, p. 5) and that around 18 per cent of the calls to the service in 2007/8 (approximately 32,000) were from children worried about bullying (NSPCC, 2008, p. 1). Yet violence at school goes beyond this and before this section looks at the specific issue of bullying at school, it will look at the more general issue of violence in this environment.

Children, Aynsley-Green suggested in the quote above, live in an inherently violent society. They watch violence on the television, they confront bullying in the classroom and they witness it in the home. Others have gone further and suggested that school itself is an intrinsically violent place and that sending children to school is an act of violence which forces children to conform to externally imposed norms and strictures over which they have no control. Mary Jane Kehily has argued that:

> Schools are not egalitarian spaces, despite the discourse of equality to be found in most school based policies, schools are hierarchically structured and struggles for power and privilege are an endemic feature of school life – for teachers and for students. Teacher hierarchies rely upon social position: head, senior staff, classroom teachers, support staff/hard subject teachers v. soft subject teachers; liberals v. authoritarians; career teachers v. committed practitioners. Symbolic hierarchies also exist - where you sit in the staffroom; having the ear of the headteacher; myths, survival stories, tales of resilience form part of teacher culture as well as pupil culture. Student hierarchies exist in various forms: boy/girl; age based hierarchies; popular/unpopular; conformist/ rebel ... Structural inequalities embedded in the school site become interwoven into the feelings and practices of the institution, documented by successive generations of school-based ethnographers. Thirty years ago Paul Willis spoke of the 'caged

resentment' pupils felt as a response to being subject to the authority of teachers.

(Kehily, 2008, p. 1)

This account describes the symbolic violence endemic in schools, in terms of both its structures and the reactions of the children and young people. Schools are sites of violence and resentment experienced by those who feel powerless within the system, and who express this resentment through door slamming, gossiping, insolence, infringing the uniform code and other forms of resistance to the school's regulatory measures. 'Symbolic violence and caged resentment both capture the routine and everyday conflict between teachers and students, the basic injustices that create a "them and us" battleground between teachers and pupils' (Kehily, 2008, p. 2).

Figure 6   Children fighting in a school playground

4.1   Symbolic violence

For Pierre Bourdieu, symbolic violence is closely related to ideas of social capital. Bourdieu used the term 'social capital' to refer to the value created by social relationships and the connections within and between social networks (Bourdieu, 1986). He suggested that not only are some people materially poorer than others, but they also lack

Chapter 4   Children and violence

something less tangible – access to power. They have low social capital and therefore do not have the connections or even the language to secure better resources for themselves or their families. They do not know the 'right' people, speak the same language in the same accent or know how to get things done. Social capital is a source of power, therefore, used to impose the will and beliefs of an elite on to others in order to alter their actions.

Bourdieu used the term 'symbolic violence' to explain how an alien, dominant-class culture was imposed on the working class through the education system. Today, the term is applied more widely to discuss the ways in which all forms of social hierarchy involve symbolic violence through the imposition of categories of thought and perception, and ultimately behaviour, by elites on others. Furthermore, symbolic violence is invoked as a way of explaining how and why the dominated eventually come to see the dominant as 'right' and take on their categories of thought. Symbolic violence can be even more powerful than physical violence because it works in an unconscious way, altering the aspirations of individuals and legitimating a particular social order. Within schools, symbolic violence can occur when teachers privilege the knowledge and attitudes of the middle classes – or of children of one gender or ethnicity – above those of children of a different background, when they consistently ask the same children to speak up in class or ask the type of questions only certain children can answer. As a consequence, social relations are maintained and reinforced by the everyday pedagogic actions of teachers, even if they are inequitable, and even if there are explicit compensatory mechanisms in the curriculum. An example of this in action is given in Reading A.

Activity 2   Reading A
Allow about 30 minutes

The first reading in this chapter, 'Violent youth or violent schools?' by Kathryn Herr and Gary Anderson, examines Bourdieu's theories of symbolic violence in relation to a critical incident observed in a classroom during a year of ethnographic study. It gives a good example of symbolic violence in practice and the difficulties of making this form of violence visible. The incident is drawn from a single-sex classroom of 13–14 year olds (eighth grade in US terms). The school in which they are located draws students primarily from a low-income neighbourhood and the population of the school is made up overwhelmingly of students from ethnic minorities (African American, Latino and Cambodian).

169

As you read through this extract, take notes and then answer the following questions:

- At what points can you see symbolic violence in the exchanges between teacher and pupils?
- Do you agree with Bourdieu's theory of symbolic violence? Can you see any flaws in it?

Comment

The authors of this extract discuss in detail the forms of symbolic violence that they observed in this classroom. They point out that Ms R. is a good, experienced teacher who genuinely wants her pupils to do well and to learn. She teaches on topics such as 'respect' which she hopes will engage the students. Yet Ms R. also makes many assumptions about these boys' learning, their background and their social capital. She assumes that they have limited attention spans and will be disruptive. She attempts to impose her routine on them, which they are not happy about, and makes them copy out pages of a book rather monotonously. She believes that they will amount to nothing, and in her attitude and behaviour she is displaying symbolic violence. This is not simply an individual attitude, however, but a wider social one. The institutionalised practices of the school, the emphasis on copying out, the invitation to the police officers to talk about drugs (in the DARE or *Drug Abuse Resistance Education* programme) are all forms of symbolic violence which position these young people in certain ways and impose the view of the dominant on the dominated.

Young people do not necessarily accept this, however, and often display active resistance. Many do not simply or passively accept the dominant ideology of the school and, even in this short passage, it is possible to identify patterns of resistance. The boys do not do what they are told; they are argumentative and challenging, asking why they should copy out text when they can see no reason for it. They subvert some of the rules, all asking to go to the bathroom until the teacher gets cross and allows no one to go. They pay no attention to her and look out of the windows. All these may be minor infringements but they suggest that these boys do not always play by the rules and show resistance to the dominant ideology.

However, even this is not straightforward and there are, of course, more options than either being passive in relation to symbolic violence or resisting it. The behaviour described here actually reinforces the teacher's idea of the boys so it could be argued that far from resisting control they are in fact contributing to their own subjection. Having been labelled as inattentive, argumentative and challenging young men, they are living up to this label and rather than challenging the ways in which they are constructed by others, they are simply conforming to them.

This extract also raises further questions about the role of the teacher in the classroom and the impact of symbolic violence on her. She could simply be a representative of the elite imposing her own ideology on others, but there are also other interpretations. She too is constrained by imposed social norms and, having limited autonomy to change, is equally a 'victim' of forms of symbolic violence which she has no means of confronting. In trying to keep order she is also encouraging the boys to reject their label as disruptive and argumentative and is therefore challenging the symbolic violence that stigmatises the boys. The multiple meanings and interpretations of what is going on during this 'critical incident' make the notion of symbolic violence, while much used and discussed, problematic.

Activity 3   How useful is the concept of symbolic violence?

Allow about 20 minutes

Having read through this chapter so far, write a brief paragraph or bullet points on why you think symbolic violence is a useful concept. Then write one on why you think it is problematic.

Comment

Useful

- Symbolic violence suggests that violence is an unavoidable part of everyone's life but that children in particular feel its impact through inherently oppressive regimes of schooling and, indeed, socialisation.
- It allows for acts of self-harm, everyday resistance and attempts at control to be analysed as forms of violence.
- It enables the recognition that violence is not always overt or immediate but exists in the symbolic and psychological realm as well as the physical.
- It usefully acknowledges that symbolic violence creates the conditions for other, more explicit forms of physical or economic violence.

Problematic

- Seeing violence everywhere and analysing everything as violent, means that the idea of violence loses its impact. Such an analysis fails to distinguish between the trivial and the profound, equating the slammed door in a classroom with the hitting of a child.

- There could never be a situation in which symbolic violence has not already taken place and affected people's behaviour. It becomes impossible to understand children's resistance as anything other than a reaction to previous 'violence', making it difficult to look at children's agency or own understandings.

- Analysing socialisation, education and adult–child relations as based on symbolic violence implicitly assumes that children are naturally good, and that if they were left to act in an entirely free manner they would not be aggressive towards each other, teachers or other adults.

4.2   Bullying in schools

This chapter has argued so far that violence is an everyday part of children's lives and that school can be an inherently violent place to be. In some parts of the world violence in schools is physical and corporal punishment is still common, despite laws banning it. Corporal punishment is illegal in both Ethiopia and Uganda, for example, yet 98 per cent of children have experienced it in these countries (CRIN, 2005). In other places, violence is symbolic, although this may well create the conditions for more physical and immediate forms of violence. However, once these different forms of violence have been discussed and acknowledged, it becomes easier to understand the prevalence of bullying at school and its importance as an issue for children.

A great deal of research on bullying focuses on the individual child as either victim or perpetrator, looking at the impacts of bullying on the former and focusing on the characteristics of the latter. Dan Olweus defines bullying as 'Negative actions [that] can be carried out by physical contact, by words, or in other ways, such as making faces or mean gestures, and intentional exclusion from a group' (1999, p. 10) and, although there are other definitions of bullying (for a fuller account of these see Oliver and Candappa, 2003), almost all define it in terms of the pathological behaviour of particular children and its impacts on others in their peer group. Other forms of violence are almost never mentioned or labelled as bullying; teachers are rarely accused of bullying children even though many children can feel unfairly picked on and singled out by particular teachers.

Focusing on the characteristics of individual children or on ways of defining bullying by drawing up lists of acceptable or unacceptable behaviours fails to take into account the different roles children play at

Figure 7 Deliberate exclusion is one manifestation of bullying

different times in relation to bullying. Children are rarely only perpetrators or victims but can be both at different times. In some cases bully and victim may be the same person in different contexts, and bullying may be a defensive act prompted by the fear of being bullied. Children may also take on the role of colluders – encouraging the bullying but taking no part in the actual bullying. Other children may be bystanders, knowing what is going on but turning a blind eye, while others can be witnesses – recognising what is happening and informing others. Children can also move between these roles depending on circumstances, and their identities as victim, perpetrator, colluder, etc. are not fixed.

Focusing on the characteristics of individual children also implies that bullying is unrelated to wider social norms of gender and ethnic construction. In his work on masculinities and violence, Martin Mills looks at how boys are socialised into cultures of violence within schools where particular versions of masculinity are modelled and promoted. Boys learn that prowess in sport and powers over women (among other things) are important signifiers of masculinity and represent traits which are valued within the school as well as in the outside world. Based on an ethnographic study of schools in Australia, Mills examines how boys

Figure 8 Although bullying is a problem for many children, it is important to note that children themselves often tackle bullying among their friends

learn to value and deploy violence against others. This is done not necessarily by a show of force or straightforward bullying, but through a culture of denigrating all those who are not white, male, heterosexual and good at sport:

> Dominant images of the 'ideal' man' portray him as competitive, strong, aggressive when crossed and as a good 'mate' (mate here referring to friendships between men as opposed to sexual partner). This image is true of the action hero, the football star, the business magnate and even the popular politician. The physical, sexual and, sometimes, intellectual prowess of these heroic men is beyond the reach of most men.
>
> (Mills, 2001, p. 23)

Not surprisingly, therefore, girls, ethnic minorities, boys who value school work over sport, those who are gay or appear in any way to deviate from this norm, are liable to be bullied. Being a man in this culture means dominating those who do not conform, and being a bully is not about individual traits or characteristics as much as social norms and locally valued ideas of masculinities. This is not to claim that it is only boys who bully, girls too may turn on those who do not conform to particular notions of femininity or who transgress other social norms. They are likely to pick on those who dress in ways they disapprove of or whose sexual behaviour they dislike. Seen in this way, bullying becomes an issue of gender and identity construction rather than individual pathology. It can also be understood as another manifestation of symbolic violence in which the norms and ideology of a dominant group of children and young people are imposed on others through physical and emotional violence.

Summary of Section 4

The notion of symbolic violence can be used to analyse schools as inherently violent institutions.

The concept of symbolic violence can be questioned because it is so all encompassing that almost all actions can be understood in these terms. It is, thus, so broad as to be meaningless.

Symbolic violence can be seen in both children's reactions and resistance to imposed norms.

Bullying in schools is a concern for many children in the UK and elsewhere.

Bullying is not simply an example of individual pathology, it can also be understood in terms of social norms and constructions of social identity.

---

5 Violence in the community

So far this chapter has looked at different forms of violence in two sites – the home and the school. This final section will look at violence in the community and the variety of ways in which children experience violence in this setting, including in armed conflict. However, it is important to emphasise that such violence is not limited to war zones. In some cities in the USA, children are as likely to be affected by violent death from guns as child soldiers. Psychologist James Garbarino refers to these as 'war-zone neighbourhoods' where:

almost every fourteen-year-old has been to the funeral of a playmate who was killed, where two-thirds of the kids have witnessed a shooting, and where young children play a game they call 'funeral' with the toy blocks in their preschool classroom.

(Garbarino, 1999, pp. 17–18)

Nor is this form of violence limited to the inner-cities of the USA. Gang culture and knife crime are prevalent in certain areas of the UK and are a cause of fear for many children and young people. Recent research on young crime and gangs has found that there are over 100 youth gangs, with approximately 2000 gang members aged between 12 and 23, currently active in the Glasgow area. Violence against young men, often by other young men, has been identified as a serious source of health inequality in Scotland, with those of between 10 and 29 years of age seven times more likely to be the victim of homicide than their peers in France, and five times more likely than their counterparts in England and Wales (Scottish Government, 2008):

The analysis of the statistics show the continued disproportionate impact on young men (62% of offenders; 42% of victims), the prevalence of knives (responsible for 3 times as many homicides as any other form of killing), the associated use of alcohol and drugs (47% of perpetrators reported to be on drink or drugs at the time of the offence), and a geographical focus in the West of Scotland (64% in Strathclyde Police force area with the homicide rate in Glasgow twice that of London and more than just about every other European city). The causal and associative factors in relation to violence - alcohol, drugs, deprivation - are all sources of significant health inequality.

(Scottish Government, 2008)

Other parts of the UK show similar problems in terms of young men and their likelihood of being both victims and perpetrators of violence in the community. A recent report on young men's views of safety and violence in Northern Ireland suggested that violence is an ever-present reality for them. While Northern Ireland has specific problems of sectarianism, the young men interviewed did not see this as the main issue they faced, but simply as yet another form of violence in an

Figure 9   Street shrine to young man killed in gang violence in London

already tense situation. The young men told the researchers of their bad relationships with police and with those from different neighbourhoods. Ten per cent of them carried knives for protection, although others claimed that this was an affront to their masculinity and that real men ought to be able to fight without a knife. What is apparent from this report is that concerns about safety constrain these young men's experiences of their own community. There are certain areas they will not go into or will travel to only with a large group of friends. While these young men appear threatening to outsiders and ready to use violence, they are very aware of the threats they face and most take care to avoid areas in which they know they will be unsafe (Centre for Young Men's Studies, 2009). Their relationship to violence in the public space is therefore ambivalent. On the one hand, ideas of masculine status are dependent on perceived ownership and defence of public spaces, and this necessitates occupation of, and public presence in, such spaces. On the other, this is also extremely restrictive – while young men may claim ownership of 'their' territory, they are unable to travel freely into others and there is no neutral space for them.

from ideological motivation or political involvement. Yet this ideal does not always match the reality and there may be circumstances in which children can fight for a cause in which they believe. It is also possible that some children have no choice but to fight. If children are in peril, then they have a right to self-defence and to protect their families. To keep them out of the army may compromise other rights, such as the right to have an opinion, to bodily integrity, or to protection of life and property. This is a problematic position, however. Allowing children the possibility of fighting infringes other rights and is a violation of international law. It is also highly debatable if any meaningful distinction can be drawn between forced and voluntary recruitment in many situations for either adults or children, and there is often little difference between recruitment and coercion.

5.2 Children's engagement with violence

The question of children's innocence in war is a problematic one. Children may well need protection in times of war as the innocent victims of adults who manipulate them for their own ends. They may also take a more active role. How far children and young people are able to act as political agents or are simply the unwitting perpetrators of adult-led violence remains a complex and controversial issue. Many armed conflicts today do not involve wars between states but between militant groups, rebels or diverse internal forces. In these circumstances, both children and adults need the protection of one faction or the other if they are to survive. In many cases the military, or some sort of extra-governmental militia, may well be the safest place for children to be. David Rosen argues:

> In some circumstances, becoming a soldier may be a necessary and positive choice for children. Indeed, where there is a total breakdown of society, armed groups may provide the only source of refuge and safety for children. This was certainly the case for Jewish children during the Holocaust, in which partisan units in countries like Poland, Belarus, and the Ukraine incorporated into their ranks many Jewish children who were fleeing for their lives from German execution squads.

> (Rosen, 2007, p. 298)

In other cases children and young people become involved in armed conflict when they are targeted by their enemies. For example, children took an active part in the struggle against the apartheid regime in South Africa. They were often specifically targeted by the police and subject to arbitrary whippings, detentions, tear-gassing or shootings. Between 1984 and 1986, 300 children were killed by the police, 1000 wounded, 11,000 detained without trial, 18,000 arrested on charges related to protesting and 173,000 held in police cells (Simpson, 1993, cited in Cairns, 1996, p. 113). Given these statistics, it can be argued that South African children had no choice but to fight back.

After the end of apartheid, the Truth and Reconciliation Commission was set up in South Africa to examine the injustices of the previous era. While it documented the ways in which children had been actively engaged in the struggle, and the extent to which they were the targets of state suppression and brutality, it has been heavily criticised by some who feel that rather than celebrating children's resistance and important role in the struggle, it reduced many to the role of victim, looking at crimes against them but not always recognising their organisation, their political commitment or their bravery (Reynolds, 2008).

Activity 5   Children's induction into violence

Allow about 20 minutes

Read through the extract below and make notes on the following issues:

- Do you see throwing stones at soldiers, as described in the extract, as 'childish' behaviour or is it an example of political violence among children?

- Do you think these Palestinian children are victims or perpetrators of violence, or are they both?

- Should this affect the ways in which they are treated by the Israelis?

> In Palestine rioting and stone throwing brought the local children to the attention of the world's media. However, far from being a childish behaviour ... stone throwing amongst children in Palestine has been elevated to a military art with specific roles assigned to children of different ages. Those aged 7–10 years are given the job of rolling tyres into the middle of the road. These tyres are then set alight in order to disrupt traffic and attract Israeli soldiers. The next youngest age group (11–14 years) use slingshots to attack passing cars. These two groups are used to prepare the ground for ... the

Figure 10 Drawing by a six-year-old Palestinian child depicting Israeli tanks and soldiers

'veteran stone throwers'. These young people use large rocks and inflict the worst damage on passing traffic and hence 'they are the most sought after by the Israelis'. This command structure is coordinated by older youths who from the vantage points they occupy determine which cars to attack for example, or when to retreat when the soldiers advance.

(Cairns, 1996, pp. 112–13)

Comment

These children have been raised in an atmosphere of violence and, to them, the Israelis are the enemy. They have suffered both direct violence in the form of family members killed or arrested, and indirect violence in the form of prolonged curfews and ongoing tension. Given this, it seems naive to dismiss their stone throwing as a childish game. Many soldiers, and the states they protect, have rejected this idea and arrested or even shot at such children, seeing them as legitimate targets – often causing outrage in the outside world.

It is hard to know how politically aware and astute these children are – and therefore how knowingly violent – or whether they have been persuaded to take part by peer pressure or the chance to join a group activity. For them it may be a game or it may be a form of violent political protest. Reacting to such actions depends not on what the children do, but on the perceptions of these children and their behaviour. If they are seen as innocent of bad intent and of ideological motivation, then stone throwing is simply game playing. If, however, they are politically motivated and committed to a cause, then throwing stones is an act of political violence, which might invite retaliation.

Yet this need not be an either/or question. The answers to all three questions depend largely on context. It is possible to see children both as political agents and as people who have been inducted into a culture of violence and know of no alternative. Furthermore, taking part in political violence should not necessarily mean that shooting or imprisonment is a justifiable response.

In all forms of armed conflict, therefore, children have an ambivalent relationship to violence. As Rosen and others have pointed out, a child soldier is not necessarily only a victim and may have made an active choice to join a militia. In other instances children may be coerced, or feel they have no choice, or lie somewhere else on the continuum. What is clear, however, is that the image of the child engaging in war, political struggle or simply doing what they need to in order to survive, challenges notions of children's innocence and of childhood being a safe space which protects them from violence.

5.3   Child soldiers in Sierra Leone

In 1991 civil war broke out in Sierra Leone when the Revolutionary United Front (RUF) attempted to overthrow the military rule of the All People's Congress. Around 10,000 children fought on both sides in the conflict; some were kidnapped from their villages, having been brutalised by seeing family members killed. Both boys and girls were abducted and while boys were used on the front line, girls were made to become 'wives' and sexual partners to the commanders. Other children had a more decisive relationship to the conflict and to the side they fought on, joining through political conviction, and finding in these armies a sense of purpose and comradeship, learning skills of loyalty,

Figure 11 A child soldier in the Sierra Leone civil war (1991–2002)

teamwork and independence. For others, one side or the other was a much needed source of protection, food or shelter. These multiple and complex reasons for why so many children fought in this conflict are distilled in the account of one young man discussed below.

Activity 6 Reading C
Allow about 30 minutes

Reading C, 'A long way gone', is an extract from a book written by a former child soldier from Sierra Leone, Ishmael Beah, who describes how, aged 13, he became involved in the civil war in his country in the 1990s. He writes this account as a 25 year old, who escaped from Sierra Leone and made his way to the USA. The book recounts how he was separated from his family and escaped with friends into the countryside, where he tried to avoid the rebel soldiers who were fighting a war against the government. Eventually he was found by soldiers from the government and joined their army.

Read through the passage, in which he describes being recruited, and then answer the following questions:

- To what extent are Ishmael and his friends perpetrators or victims?
- What options did they have in this situation?

Comment

Ishmael is only 13, and he and his friends have sought refuge in this village. They believe that the soldiers will protect them and recognise that they are only children. However, they are also very aware of the violence going on around them; they have seen death and destruction and become aware that they will have to fight. It is left very ambiguous in this passage as to whether or not they choose to fight. Appeals to avenge their parents' deaths obviously have great resonance with the boys. They are also easily caught up in the rhetoric of the lieutenant who paints a clearly delineated picture of the world where the rebels are evil and must be destroyed by the government army. It is clear, however, that the government soldiers are equally capable of carrying out atrocities, and it seems as if they might have shot the child and old man themselves as a warning to other villagers who might refuse to join them. Even so, it is still a shock at the end when Ishmael says that two of the children called up to fight are only seven and 11 years old.

These young boys, like the rest of the group, and indeed the adults in the village, are aware they do not have any options. They have to stay in the village because they will be killed if they do not. Even if they do escape, without food or shelter they will quickly die. The army therefore offers them the only possibility of safety – although the death rate among both soldiers and civilians is clearly high.

This brief extract suggests the complexities of the issues and the difficulties of talking about children choosing to fight or being nothing but victims. These children have been brutalised and the rest of the book details the killings that they carry out. They may have had no choice but to fight, but they go on to do so and, in some cases, appear to enjoy it. At the end of the war, they are treated with fear and repugnance by the communities they have fought in and against. It is equally clear, however, that given other options they would not have fought – none of these children made an active choice to do so but found themselves in a situation where bearing arms was a necessity.

Whatever their reasons for fighting, child soldiers provoked particular fear in this conflict and came to be regarded as exceptionally brutal and lacking pity or mercy. Reintegrating them into the communities after the war has proved difficult and they have been seen by many as the perpetrators of appalling violence for which they must be called to account. Describing such young people as 'child soldiers' draws on minority-world notions of political and moral ignorance in children, but may well obscure a more complicated reality. David Rosen goes on to argue that:

the 'child soldier' is conceived of as a deviant product of adult abuse; such a conception presupposes that children are dependent, exploited, and powerless. However, taking this position also means that children cannot be held responsible for the war crimes they commit, because they are considered to have no legally relevant agency. This view often contradicts the real-world experience of the victims of crimes committed by child soldiers and also may violate local understandings of blameworthiness and justice.

(Rosen, 2007, p. 297)

Bearing this in mind, in the closing stages of the war in Sierra Leone, Kofi Annan, the then Secretary-General of the United Nations, asked the United Nations Security Council to approve the prosecution of those child soldiers in Sierra Leone over the age of 15 who were involved in murder, mutilation and rape. This compromise was bitterly contested by those who believed that children were protected under the UNCRC – whatever they had done – and must be thought of as children, and those who argued that justice for victims was equally important and that Sierra Leonean society could never recover unless those who were responsible for atrocities – whatever their age – were held to account (Ramgoolie, 2001).

Summary of Section 5

Violence in the community affects children and young people both within and outside the context of armed conflict.

Although childhood is perceived in minority-world thought as a time of innocence, children who fight complicate this ideal and raise awkward questions about how far children can choose to be violent.

Children can be both victims and perpetrators of violence in wartime and other armed conflict.

6 Conclusion

This chapter has concentrated on three main sites of violence: the home, the school and the community. It has looked at both individual and social experiences of violence, and focused on the concept of symbolic violence to help understand the background of violence in children's lives. In doing so, it has suggested that children suffer from both physical and symbolic forms of violence, and that while certain forms – such as child abuse by strangers or bullying in schools – are widely acknowledged, other forms are hidden, with both adults and children remaining silent about them. What is obvious from this examination is that children at both a local and a global level experience multiple and complex forms of violence, which shape their experiences of childhood and which constitute, for many, a daily form of adversity.

References

Barnardo's (2008) *The Shame of Britain's Intolerance of Children* [online], http://www.barnardos.org.uk/news_and_events/media_centre/press_releases.htm?ref=42088 (Accessed 27 November 2010).

BBC News (1998) *Third World Faces Self-harm Epidemic* [online], http://news.bbc.co.uk/1/hi/health/129684.stm (Accessed 23 March 2011).

BBC News (2010) *Parents 'More Worried About Murder Than Obesity' Threat* [online], http://www.bbc.co.uk/news/10120160 (Accessed 23 March 2011).

Bloom, A. (2008) 'Survey whips up debate on caning', *Times Educational Supplement*, 10 October.

Bourdieu, P. (1986) 'The forms of capital', in Richardson, J. (ed) *Handbook of Theory and Research for the Sociology of Education*, New York, Greenwood.

Cairns, E. (1996) *Children and Political Violence*, Oxford, Blackwell.

Centre for Research on Families and Relationships (2008) *Parenting Practices and Support in Scotland*, Edinburgh, University of Edinburgh.

Centre for Young Men's Studies (2009) *Stuck in the Middle (Some Young Men's Attitudes and Experience of Violence, Conflict and Safety)*, Coleraine, University of Ulster.

Child Rights International Network (CRIN) (2005) *Ethiopia: Physical and Psychological Punishment Does Not Teach Children To Be Good Citizens* [online], http://www.crin.org/resources/infodetail.asp?ID=5300 (Accessed 23 March 2011).

Garbarino, J. (1999) *Lost Boys*, New York, The Free Press.

Gilbert, C., Hart, M., Howlison, V. and Rosen, M. (2008) *Uncorrected Transcript of Oral Evidence – Taken Before the Children, Schools and Families Committee: The Work of Ofsted, 10 Dec 2008* [online], http://www.publications.parliament.uk/pa/cm200809/cmselect/cmchilsch/uc70-i/uc07002.htm (Accessed 2 July 2012).

Golding, W. (1954) *Lord of the Flies*, London, Faber and Faber.

Harion, N. (2008) 'Survey finds worrying number of young people self harm', *Nursing Times*, 6 May, pp. 23–4.

Hawton, K., Rodham, K., Evans, E. and Weatherall, R. (2002) 'Deliberate self harm in adolescents: self report survey in schools in England', *British Medical Journal*, vol. 325, no. 7374, pp. 1207–11.

Hill, A. and Hinsliff, G. (2005) 'Children's czar warns of huge leap in bullying', *The Observer*, 13 November [online], http://www.guardian.co.uk/society/2005/nov/13/childrensservices.pupilbehaviour1 (Accessed 2 July 2012).

Kehily, M. J. (2008) 'Patterns of violence and caring across three social sites: young people in the school, the community and the nation state', paper given at *From Violence to Caring Conference*, University of Oulu, Finland, 4–5 December 2008.

Kitzinger, J. and Skidmore, P. (1995) 'Playing safe: media coverage of child sexual abuse prevention strategies', *Child Abuse Review*, vol. 4, no. 1, pp. 47–56.

Mills, M. (2001) *Challenging Violence in Schools: An Issue of Masculinities*, Buckingham, Open University Press.

NSPCC (2008) *Children Talking to ChildLine about Bullying*, London, NSPCC.

NSPCC (2010) *ChildLine Casenotes: Child Protection Register Statistics* [online], http://www.nspcc.org.uk/Inform/research/statistics/child_protection_register_statistics_wda48723.html (Accessed 27 November 2010).

Oliver, C. and Candappa, M. (2003) *Tackling Bullying: Listening to the Views of Children and Young People*, Nottingham, DfES Publications.

Olweus, D. (1999) 'Sweden', in Smith, P. K., Morita, Y., Junger-Tas, J., Olweus, D., Catalano, R. and Slee, P. (eds) *The Nature of School Bullying: A Cross-National Perspective*, London, Routledge.

Ramgoolie, M. (2001) 'Prosecution of Sierra Leone's child soldiers: what message is the UN trying to send?', *Journal of Public and International Affairs*, vol. 12, Spring, pp. 145–62.

Reynolds, P. (2008) 'On leaving the young out of history', *The Journal of the History of Childhood and Youth*, vol. 1, no. 1, pp. 150–6.

Rosen, D. (2007) 'Child soldiers, international humanitarian law, and the globalization of childhood', *American Anthropologist*, vol. 109, no. 2, pp. 296–306.

Scheper-Hughes, N. and Stein, H. (1987) 'Child abuse and the unconscious in American popular culture', in Scheper-Hughes, N. (ed) *Child Survival: Anthropological Perspectives on the Treatment and Maltreatment of Children*, Dordrecht, D. Reidel.

Scottish Government (2008) *Equally Well: Report of the Ministerial Task Force on Health Inequalities – Volume 2* [online], http://www.scotland.gov.uk/Publications/2008/06/09160103/8 (Accessed 23 March 2011).

Simpson, M. A. (1993) 'Bitter waters: effects on children of the stresses of unrest and oppression', in Wilson, J. P. and Raphael, B. (eds) *International Handbook of Traumatic Stress Syndromes*, New York, Plenum.

UNICEF (2007) *The Paris Principles: Principles and Guidelines on Children Associated with Armed Forces or Armed Groups*, New York, UNICEF.

WarChild (2011) *Key Facts and Statistics About Child Soldiers* [online], http://www.warchild.org.uk/issues/child-soldiers (Accessed 23 July 2011).

Reading A
Violent youth or violent schools?

Kathryn Herr and Gary Anderson

Source: 'Violent youth or violent schools? A critical incident analysis of symbolic violence', 2003, *International Journal of Leadership in Education*, vol. 6, no. 4, pp. 415–33.

Critical incident 1: 'They've been terrible'

Many teachers in the school struggled with their all-male classes and Ms R. was no exception. The classes throughout the school are large, with 35 students jammed into classrooms intended for smaller numbers. Ms R. was initially squeamish about giving permission for observations in the boys' class, explaining 'they've been terrible'. Nonetheless, she did grant permission and as our relationship developed, she often asked for feedback or suggestions. Although departments had instructional coaches who were to be resources for the teachers, they also evaluated the teachers, something both coaches and teachers saw as being at cross purposes. As one coach put it, when he came into the classrooms he felt as welcome as Typhoid Mary.

Ms R. was an experienced teacher, but at the elementary, rather than middle school level; in the suburbs, rather than in an urban setting. A white woman, Ms R. had little experience with students of colour and confessed to being a bit intimidated by the boys in her class, many of whom were larger than her. In fact, there had been a fight in her girls' class the week before and Ms R had cried; one of the girls told her that it was 'almost worth the fight for them to see how much she cares about them'. Ms R. said she 'really, really wants her students to learn' but she has been struggling to create a learning environment in her classroom; it has, in fact, been near pandemonium. Ms P., an African American educational assistant, has been assigned to the room to help out.

The following incident is drawn from field notes of Ms R's class, a 2½-hour math/science block. It is mid-November of the school year. The first 15 minutes are homeroom time and, on this day, all the homerooms are to discuss the school's 'word of the week': respect. Teachers have a lot of latitude regarding how they conduct the homeroom time.

Description of critical incident 1

Boys come spilling into the room, some leaping over desks on their way in. Ms R. insists they go back out and enter the room all over again. Once they are in the room she tells them that today there will be no warnings, that the first infraction will earn them a call home. She switches on the overhead where the word respect is written; the rest of the page is covered up. 'Respect', she announces, 'copy this definition in your notebooks'. She uncovers the rest of the overhead and reads aloud, 'Respect is doing what the person in charge of you tells you to do'. Boys are opening notebooks and looking for writing utensils. Ms R. continues, 'The first thing you've got to learn here is to respect the teaching going on and the learning of fellow students'. She tells them they are not to question assignments and suggests that outside of class they confront those who are 'pulling the class down – talk to them outside of class, tell them what they're doing'. The room is now somewhat quiet and the boys are writing.

Ms R. has written their assignment on the board – to copy pages of the science text into their notebooks. 'The first thing I've asked you to do is a no brainer. Hopefully something will stick in your head'. Ms R. went on to say that the second assignment will be a 'bit more'; it involves looking up a word. Boys are grumbling and one asks Ms P. why they need to copy pages from the book. 'Cause these are her instructions and you can't question what she tells you'. Marvin, one of the students, replies, 'I'm not doing this; it's too much'. Ms P. tells him 'You've got to face reality; you come to school to work. We're not going to discuss this; you're too argumentative'.

The room is quiet. Some boys are not writing at all; they have their heads down on their desks, eyes closed. There's an occasional noise in the classroom but overall it is 'peaceful'. The boy beside me has been diligently copying pages of the science book; he looks to see how much more there is, sighs, puts down his pencil for a little while and stretches his hand. Fifty minutes pass and the boys are writing or dozing. Some are being pulled out of class by Ms R., for some infraction I deduce, since phone calls are being placed to these boys' homes. The phone is near the classroom door and the cord stretches to the outside; the calls home can be overheard in a sort of stage whisper and are a backdrop to the continued copying of the science book.

I notice that a group of boys in the back of the room are stretching to see something outside the window; the window looks out over an entrance to the school and the school's parking lot. I must have looked curious because one of them mouths to me, 'There's cops out there'. The room starts to stir as boys notice the scene outside the window. Finally, Ms P. says 'it's probably the DARE officers; the sixth and seventh graders have DARE [*Drug Abuse Resistance Education*]'.

Soft murmuring begins in the room; Ms R. reminds them she'll call home. The boys are getting their names on a list on the board to go to the bathroom. It seems like most of the boys want to go to the bathroom and the list grows. More boys stop writing and talk to those around them. Ms R. says, 'Okay, no bathroom!' The boys groan.

There's excitement in the back of the room as the boys watch the unfolding scene outside the window. Sergio, a fellow 8th grader at the school, is being led away by two policemen. The whole room is trying to see what's happening. Sergio gets in the police car and it pulls away. Ms R. calls the room to order, 'Sit up straight! Feet on the floor! Let me see everyone's feet flat on the floor. Everyone put your pencil in the tray ...'

She begins a math lesson, passing out a math work sheet, but the boys are not paying attention. Ms R. tells the boys 'I can't go any lower in math; make an honest effort to solve them'. But by now the boys are talking among themselves, speculating on why Sergio has been taken away by the police and no one appears to be paying attention to Ms R. who is trying to get them to work on the math work sheets. A boy calls out, 'Hey quiet! Administrators are here!' An assistant principal pops her head in the door; the room is quiet and she moves on.

Epilogue to critical incident 1

Ms R. never returned after the school's winter break in December. An African-American male teacher was hired to take her place; he had previously worked at the youth detention centre and it was commonly thought that he was brought in to restore some order to the classroom. After a few weeks he was fired because he threw one of the boys up against a wall and had his hands around the boy's neck. A third teacher was hired, a young African-American male teacher, who remained with the class for the rest of the school year. Two of the boys transferred out of this class and moved into Mr Y's classroom ... ; in looking back at their classroom experience these boys observed: 'They had three different teachers already because the way the students act ... they just act up how-they-want-to-act-wise. It's like they don't have no self-esteem for themselves ... The teachers, they didn't really care. They the one that was getting paid. It wasn't their education that was lost'.

Discussion of critical incident 1

This classroom will sound familiar to those who have spent time in low-income schools. Of all the classrooms observed in this school, this one was only slightly worse than many. Symbolic violence is perhaps exacerbated in this case by differences of race, class, and gender. A white, female, middle-class teacher attempts to teach a group of low-income, male students of colour. However, while these differences undoubtedly contribute to the incomprehension between teacher and students, symbolic violence is embedded in the 'explicit pedagogy' of the educational system. In this sense, teachers are largely interchangeable. According to Bourdieu, an 'implicit pedagogy' consists of those practices that teachers have acquired informally as well as the particular habitus they, largely unconsciously, model for students. In this latter sense, race, class and gender are implicated, but as we saw above, two middle class, African-American men followed the same explicit pedagogy (Character Counts: 'respect', etc.) and one appeared to have the same general view of the students that the white, female teacher had.

Here the symbolic violence is seen in the failure on the part of the teacher to recognize the students' abilities. Through her behaviours and statements, she makes it clear that she does not believe that these students have a primary habitus that provides them with the tools to be high-achieving students. Images are of students with heads on their desks, getting their names on the board for bathroom breaks – anything to get out of the classroom – taking themselves out, in effect; and why not, since the day-to-day dynamic is one that violences and denigrates their sense of selves?

As Ferguson (2001) points out, Bourdieu's concept of symbolic violence

> is particularly useful for an examination of punishment practices as symbolic enforcers of a cultural hegemony in the hidden curriculum. He directs our attention to the manner in which this type of violence operates through taken-for-granted notions of the form and content of 'proper' behaviour overlooked by liberal notions of schooling. For example, 'politeness', in his view, 'contains a politics, a practical immediate recognition of social classifications and of hierarchies between the sexes, the generations, the classes, etc'. (p. 51)

The very means by which the boys take themselves out of the violence – heads down, long lists to get out of the room by going to the bathroom – become incorporated into the punishments of the classroom: 'Heads up! Feet on the floor!' No bathroom privileges. Definitions of respect reinforce dominant rules and privileges without being open for questioning or alternative constructions. All of these are instruments of symbolic violence in this particular class, while serving as a means to create a 'respectful' classroom environment. The police car pulling up outside the classroom window seems an all-too-ready metaphor for the end results of this kind of education; as pointed out at the beginning of this [reading], all violence is ultimately paid for, 'matched sooner or later in the form of ... a whole host of minor and major everyday acts of violence' (Bourdieu, 1998: 40).

References

Bourdieu, P. (1998) *Acts of Resistance: Against the Tyranny of the Market*, New York, The New Press.

Ferguson, A. A. (2001) *Bad Boys: Public Schools in the Making of Black Masculinity*, Ann Arbor, MI, The University of Michigan.

Reading B
Political transition and youth violence in post-apartheid South Africa

Andrew Dawes

Source: 'Political transition and youth violence in post-apartheid South Africa: in search of understanding', 2008, in Hart, J. (ed) *Years of Conflict. Adolescence, Political Violence and Displacement*, Oxford, Berghahn, pp. 89–94.

Introduction

It has often been suggested that the violence learnt by youth in a war or political struggle, and the psychological trauma they have experienced are likely to threaten prospects for peace and non-violence in the post-conflict society. In the run-up to the transition from apartheid to democracy, South Africans began to speak of 'lost generations' of young people who would emerge from the conflict as 'unsocialised' and with a propensity for violence that would threaten the social order of the post conflict period (Chikane, 1986; Dawes, 1994; Reynolds, 1995). Similar concerns have been expressed in other theatres of political struggle, including Northern Ireland, Palestine and Israel (Cairns, 1996).

It was true that generations of young South Africans had made enormous sacrifices in terms of lost years of education. There were many appalling acts of violence (and celebrations of violent acts) by the young. Many young people, both white and black were psychologically traumatised by what they had done and what had been done to them, as the Truth and Reconciliation Commission reports and other accounts have recorded (Straker and the Sanctuaries Treatment Team, 1987; Reynolds, 1995; Foster et al., 2005). At the same time many showed remarkable resilience and political understanding beyond that expected for their years.

During the closing years of the apartheid period, the lost generation discourse was fuelled by (frequently) racist images of rampaging violent and uneducated (black) youth in the media. Black as well as white commentators expressed deep concern that South Africa would reap the whirlwind when democracy finally arrived (Straker, 1989). The fear was that the new democracy would be undermined by the violent criminality of the cohort of young adults who would inherit the peace (Chikane, 1986). Were these concerns valid? Can one attribute criminal and interpersonal violence in a 'post political conflict' society to the psychological damage caused to the young during the conflict? ...

South Africa: A 'Post-conflict' Society?

As is well known, in 1994 a negotiated political settlement led to a democratic order and the cessation of what was, in effect, a low-intensity civil war. In that sense, South Africa is at peace. Hostilities have ended, there are no armed groups contesting power, and three multiparty elections have been held.

However, the fact South Africa is formally at peace does not mean that the post-apartheid political and economic order is uncontested. For example, since the late 1990s, there has been significant tension within the ruling alliance of the African National Congress (ANC), the Communist Party and the Congress of South African Trade Unions (COSATU). As I write, a national one-day strike is under way against the ANC's neoliberal economic policy. Many youth are on the street.

Notwithstanding the efforts of the Truth and Reconciliation Commission (TRC) to 'heal the nation' as the slogans of the day put it, racial tension and racism are not dead. Legislation to restore land to (or provide compensation for) those dispossessed under apartheid was passed in 1996. This Act, designed to benefit blacks, has produced new racial conflicts as white farmers, whose land once belonged to blacks, resist redistribution by refusing to sell their farms to the state.

Despite enormous gains in housing provision since the mid-1990s, millions live in simple shacks without basic services. Many have been on housing waiting lists for years. Recently, street demonstrations calling for more housing have turned violent as barricades have burnt in the streets, police have been stoned by protestors (young and old) and protestors have been shot.

These actions feel like a flashback to the bad old days. While popular uprisings were previously focused on the structural violence of apartheid, today they are a response to contemporary structural inequalities that are a function of the prevailing economic order, itself a legacy of the apartheid system. The structure of South African society remains fundamentally stratified on economic lines, with persons of colour – black Africans in particular – constituting the vast majority of the urban and rural poor. As under apartheid, race and class remain largely intertwined (Seekings and Natrass, 2005; Natrass and Seekings, 2001).

According to Galtung (1990), a society is structurally violent when institutionalised economic, cultural or political practices lead to inequality of opportunity and social exclusion. Thus a free market system in a democratic society that has high levels of inequality (as is the case in South Africa), and that contains few protections for the poor and socially excluded, may be considered structurally violent. Such societies create structurally unequal opportunities for survival, development and access to material resources as well as social capital.

Contemporary South Africa, despite its democratic institutions, remains structurally violent and one of the most unequal societies in the world (Seekings and Natrasss, 2005). ... Beyond the numbers, an earlier UNDP report on South Africa captured the essence of the experience of the sentiments shared by many of the poor: 'The dull ache of desperation, the acute tensions generated by violence and insecurity, the intricacies of survival and all its emotions – despair, hope resentment, apathy, futility and fury' (UNDP, 2000).

While there have been enormous advances in all spheres of life, South Africa is not free of conflict. However, it is correctly described as 'post-conflict' in the sense that the political conflict that marked the country for decades and which was associated with ongoing political violence and repression has ended. ...

The 'Lost Generation': A Racist Narrative?

I always find it of interest that the concern about violence in the post-apartheid South Africa is a concern about the experience of blacks. I raise this because of the silence about the socialisation of white male youth into violence. From the late 1960s, every white male was conscripted into the South African Defence Force (SADF) on leaving school (at seventeen or eighteen years of age). Hundreds of thousands participated (willingly and otherwise) in the violent repression of blacks inside the country, as well as serving in the Namibian and Angolan theatres of war (Korber, 1992). There is minimal research on these issues in South Africa. However, Korber's study powerfully demonstrates the lasting traumatic impact on a young conscript of his involvement in atrocities. For many, the experience must have been similar to that of American conscripts in the closing chapters of the Vietnam war.

Given the fact that far more young whites than blacks were exposed to military violence through conscription and soldiering in the years subsequent to 1976[1] (a new cohort was enrolled each year), it is of interest that they were not constructed as part of the 'lost generation'. This was a term reserved for the young who were black, undereducated, poor and supposedly prone to political and other forms of violence. One must also consider a couple of key differences in the discourse that separated young blacks from whites. The political violence of the former was framed as 'illegitimate' – it aimed to undermine the state. Also, perhaps most frightening, the violence seemed to be out of the control of a command structure of elders – it was being orchestrated by youth who had abandoned education to participate in political struggle.

In contrast, the young white men were well educated, defending their country and under the control of a formal military command structure – in essence they were constructed as carrying out legitimate military business of the (illegitimate) regime. They were supposedly contained by a traditional military structure. How could they be 'lost'? The matter did not arise. The 'lost generation' was therefore, by definition, 'black and dangerous' (Straker, 1988).

References

Cairns, E. (1996) *Children and Political Violence*, Oxford, Blackwell.

Chikane, F. (1986) 'Children in turmoil: the effects of township unrest on children', in Burman, S. and Reynolds, P. (eds) *Growing Up in a Divided Society. The Contexts of Childhood in South Africa*, Johannesburg, Ravan Press.

Dawes, A. (1994) 'The emotional impact of political violence', in Dawes, A. and Donald, D. (eds) *Childhood and Adversity: Psychological Perspectives from South African Research*, Cape Town, David Philip.

Foster, D., Haupt, P. and de Beer, M. (2005) *Theatre of Violence. Narratives of the Protagonists in the South African Conflict*, Cape Town, HSRC Press.

Galtung, J. (1990) 'Violence and peace', in Smoker, P., Davies, R. and Munske, B. (eds) *A Reader in Peace Studies*, New York, Pergamon.

---

[1] The year of the Soweto uprisings, a series of clashes between adolescent school children and youth and the South African authorities. 23 people were killed on the first day including several black teenagers. It was one of the first and most famous organised protests by the young in South Africa against apartheid.

Korber, I. (1992) 'Positioned to kill: a new approach to the question of military violence', *Psychology in Society*, vol. 16, pp. 32–48.

Natrass, N. and Seekings, J. (2001) 'Democracy and distribution in highly unequal economies: the case of South Africa', *Journal of Modern African Studies*, vol. 39, pp. 471–98.

Reynolds, P. (1995) *The Ground of All Making: State Violence, the Family and Political Activists. Co-operative Research Programme on Marriage and Family Life*, Pretoria, Human Sciences Research Council.

Seekings, J. and Natrass, N. (2005) *Class, Race, and Inequality in South Africa,* New Haven, CT, Yale University Press.

Straker, G. (1988) 'From victim to villain: a "slight" of speech? Media representations of township youth', *South African Journal of Psychology*, vol. 19, pp. 20–7.

Straker, G. and the Sanctuaries Treatment Team (1987) 'The continuous traumatic stress syndrome: the single therapeutic interview', *Psychology in Society*, vol. 8, pp. 48–78.

UNDP (2000) *South Africa: Transformation for Human Development*, Pretoria, UNDP.

Reading C
A long way gone

Ishmael Beah

Source: *A Long Way Gone: Memoirs of a Boy Soldier*, 2007, London, Fourth Estate, pp. 105–9.

That morning didn't come just with sunrise; it brought with it soldiers, the few who were able to make it back to the village. Their well-polished boots were drenched in dirt and they sat away from each other, clinging tightly to their guns, as if those were the only things that comforted them. One soldier, who sat on a cement brick underneath the kitchen, bowed his head in his hands and rocked his body. He got up and walked around the village and returned to sit on the brick again. He did this over and over throughout the day. Lieutenant Jabati was on the radio, and at some point he threw it against the wall and walked into his room. We civilians didn't speak among ourselves during that day. We only watched the madness unfold in some of the soldiers.

At midday a group of over twenty soldiers arrived in the village. The lieutenant was surprised and delighted when he saw them, but he quickly hid his emotions. The soldiers prepared themselves and left for war. There was nothing to hide anymore; we knew the war was near. Soon after the soldiers left, we began hearing gunshots closer to the village. The soldiers who guarded the village ordered everyone inside. The gunfight went on into the evening, interrupting the songs of birds and the chants of crickets. At night soldiers came running to the village for ammunition and a quick respite. Wounded soldiers were brought back only to die by lamplit surgery. The soldiers never brought back their dead colleagues. Prisoners were lined up and shot in the head.

These things went on for many days, and each time the soldiers went to the front lines, few returned. Those left behind became restless and started shooting civilians who were on their way to latrines at night. The lieutenant asked his men to gather everyone at the square.

'In the forest there are men waiting to destroy all of our lives. We have fought them as best we can, but there are too many of them. They are all around the village.' The lieutenant made a circle in the air with his hands. 'They won't give up until they capture this village. They want our food and ammunition.' He paused, and slowly continued: 'Some of you are here because they have killed your parents or families, others because this is a safe place to be. Well, it is not that safe anymore. That is why we need strong men and boys to help us fight these guys, so that we can keep this village safe. If you do not want to fight or help, that is fine. But you will not have rations and will not stay in this village. You are free to leave, because we only want people here who can help cook, prepare ammunition, and fight. There are enough women to run the kitchen, so we need the help of able boys and men to fight these rebels. This is your time to revenge the deaths of your families and to make sure more children do not lose their families.' He took a deep breath. 'Tomorrow morning you must all line up here, and we will select people for various tasks that have to be carried out.' He left the square, followed by his men.

We stood in silence for a while and slowly started walking to our respective sleeping places, as the curfew was approaching. Inside, Jumah, Alhaji, Kanei, Moriba, Musa, and I quietly discussed what we were going to do.

'The rebels will kill anyone from this village because they will consider us their enemy, spies, or that we have sided with the other side of the war. That is what the staff sergeant said,' Alhaji said, explaining the dilemma we faced. The rest of the boys, who were lying on their mats, got up and joined us as Alhaji continued: 'It is better to stay here for now.' He sighed. We had no choice. Leaving the village was as good as being dead.

'Attention. This is an order from the lieutenant. Everyone must gather at the square immediately.' A soldier spoke into a megaphone. Before he had finished his last word, the square was filled. Everyone had waited for this moment that would determine what we were going to do for our safety. Before the announcement, I sat with my friends near the window in the kitchen. Their faces were blank; they showed no emotion, but their eyes looked pale with sorrow. I tried to make eye contact with each of them, but they all looked away. I tried to eat my breakfast, but fear had taken away my appetitive.

As we found spots in the back of the crowd, gunshots filled the air, then faded to a silence even more unbearable than the reports.

The lieutenant stood on several bricks so that he could be high enough to be seen by all. He let silence settle in our bones, then waved his hands to some soldiers who brought before us two bodies—a man and a young boy who had lived in the village. The blood that soaked their clothes was still fresh and their eyes were open. People turned their heads away, and little children and babies began to cry. The lieutenant cleared his throat and started speaking in the midst of the cries, which eventually ceased as he went on.

'I am sorry to show you these gruesome bodies, especially with your children present. But then again, all of us here have seen death or even shaken hands with it.' He turned to the bodies and continued softly: 'This man and this child decided to leave this morning even though I had told them it was dangerous. The man insisted that he didn't want to be a part of our war, so I gave him his wish and let him go. Look at what happened. The rebels shot them in the clearing. My men brought them back, and I decided to show you, so that you can fully understand the situation we are in.' The lieutenant went on for almost an hour, describing how rebels had cut off the heads of some people's family members and made them watch, burned entire villages along with their inhabitants, forced sons to have intercourse with their mothers, hacked newly born babies in half because they cried too much, cut open pregnant women's stomachs, took the babies out, and killed them … The lieutenant spat on the ground and continued on, until he was sure that he had mentioned all the ways the rebels had hurt every person in the gathering.

'They have lost everything that makes them human. They do not deserve to live. That is why we must kill every single one of them. Think of it as destroying a great evil. It is the highest service you can perform for your country.' The lieutenant pulled out his pistol and fired two shots into the air. People began shouting, 'We must kill them all. We must make sure they never walk this earth again.' All of us hated the rebels, and we were more than determined to stop them from capturing the village. Everyone's face had begun to sadden and grow tense. The aura in the village rapidly changed after the speech. The morning sun had disappeared and the day became gloomy. It seemed as if the sky were going to break and fall on the earth. I was furious and afraid, and so were my friends. Jumah looked toward the forest with his hands behind his back, Moriba was holding his head, Kanei stared at the ground, Musa wrapped his hands around himself, Alhaji covered his eyes with his left hand, and I stood akimbo to stop my legs from shaking. All women and girls were asked to report to the kitchen; men and boys to the ammunition depot, where the soldiers watched their movies and smoked marijuana.

As we walked toward the building, a soldier who carried a G3 weapon came out and stood at the doorway. He smiled at us, lifted his gun, and fired several rounds toward the sky. We dropped to the ground, and he laughed at us as he went back inside. We walked through the door and came upon the tents inside the building. The building was roofless except for the tarpaulin that covered the boxes of ammunition and guns stacked against the wall; and in the only common space, a huge television screen sat on top of a dilapidated drum. A few meters away from the television stood a generator, along with gallons of gasoline. The soldiers came out of their tents as the staff sergeant led us to the back of the house, where none of us had been before. There were more than thirty boys there, two of whom, Sheku and Josiah, were seven and eleven years old. The rest of us were between the ages of thirteen and sixteen, except Kanei, who was now seventeen.

A soldier wearing civilian clothes, with a whistle around his neck, stepped up to a rack of AK-47s and handed one to each of us. When the soldier stood in front of me, I avoided eye contact, so he straightened my head until my eyes met his. He gave me the gun. I held it in my trembling hand. He then added the magazine, and I shook even more.

'It seems that all of you have two things in common,' the soldier said after he had finished testing all of us. 'You are afraid of looking a man in the eye and afraid of holding a gun. Your hands tremble as if the gun is pointed at your head.' He walked up and down the line for a bit and continued: 'This gun'—he held the AK-47 high up—'will soon belong to you, so you better learn not to be afraid of it. That is all for today.'

Chapter 5

Resilience and well-being

Samantha Punch

Contents

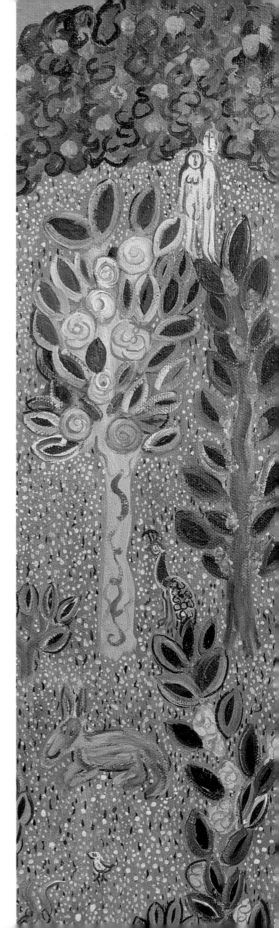

In this chapter, you will:

- consider how to define key concepts in the study of resilience
- discuss what factors can increase children's resilience and which risks can increase their vulnerability
- consider the significance of cultural context for studies of resilience and well-being
- assess the significance of well-being and discuss why it is a contested concept
- examine the importance of inter-generational relationships in children's lives.

1 Introduction

This chapter explores children's resilience and well-being. It looks at why these concepts have come to prominence in recent years and how they are defined. As the various chapters in this book have suggested, children in both the minority and majority world face a number of adversities and risks, and adults have come up with a variety of interventions which attempt to ameliorate the negative impacts of some of these risks. The previous three chapters have looked at the specific adversities of poverty, ill-health and violence, while this chapter looks at children's own reactions to these adversities. In particular, it will focus on the concept of resilience. Children are not always vulnerable or passive victims – even when faced with the most difficult circumstances – and sometimes they seem to thrive despite all the odds being stacked against them. This chapter will explore what resilience means and how the concept might be used to protect children. The second half of the chapter focuses on the related concept of well-being – a holistic term designed to describe and promote a better quality of life for children. Both these terms are contested and somewhat slippery, however, and this chapter will explore their meanings in various contexts as well as asking questions about how useful they really are in practice.

2 What is resilience?

Resilience can be defined as the ways in which children cope with, and even respond positively to, adversity – 'positive development, or thriving, under stress' (Liebenberg and Ungar, 2009, p. 5). As Ungar elaborates elsewhere:

> In the context of exposure to significant adversity, whether psychological, environmental, or both, resilience is both the capacity of individuals to navigate their way to health-sustaining resources, including opportunities to experience feelings of well-being, and a condition of the individual's family, community and culture to provide these health resources and experiences in culturally meaningful ways.
>
> (Ungar, 2008, p. 225)

Much of the research into resilience looks at why different children respond differently to events and situations – why some children appear to do well and even thrive in difficult circumstances, while other children are overwhelmed by them. Resilience research therefore looks at the influence of children's temperament on their social adjustment, as well as the role of social support in protecting children from adversities. More recent scholarship also looks at the role of cultural factors.

Increasingly, the concept of resilience is being used as an underpinning principle for policy and practice relating to vulnerable children. It is seen as part of 'more positive approaches to practice that counteract the preoccupation with risk and problems that can characterise child protection and safeguarding bureaucratic systems' (cited in Daniel et al., 2009, p. 18). As Robbie Gilligan has argued:

> A resilience-led perspective tends to be optimistic and pragmatic. It believes that change is often possible, even in unpromising conditions, and that change may start in simple ways: one thinks the glass is half full rather than half empty.
>
> (Gilligan, 2009, p. 9)

Figure 1   A refugee in Macedonia being comforted by her child

Gilligan argues that change may come through supportive relationships, may emerge from the ordinary and every day, may grow from a single opportunity or positive turning point, and may come through new ways of thinking about issues. Like others, he notes that a resilience approach can encourage people to look first for strengths and possibilities, and appreciate that children themselves can be agents of change. It also encourages any interventions to be holistic and multidisciplinary, although in practice this can be difficult to achieve. As Daniel (2010) argues, research into resilience poses key challenges for a system of state 'protection' that is based upon the assumption of damage and focuses on risk assessment because many findings show that there are considerable differences in the ways that children respond to adversity, which means that negative outcomes cannot always be assumed. She also warns that over-focusing on protecting children from harm may lead to unintended consequences of limiting opportunities for children to develop coping strategies and build resilience.

The first reading associated with this chapter looks at children's resilience in practice in a refugee camp in Nepal. Despite the poverty, inadequate housing and social insecurity here, children not only show resilience but also support their parents and other adults in the community.

Figure 2   Photo taken by a Bhutanese child living in a refugee camp in Nepal

Activity 1   Reading A
Allow about 30 minutes

This reading, 'Seen but not heard: refugee children and models for intervention', focuses on ethnically Nepalese children and families who have been forced to flee their homes in Bhutan. These children have experienced many dimensions of adversity. They are poor. They have been persecuted on the grounds of their ethnicity and sometimes witnessed the brutality of Bhutanese soldiers. They have lost their homes and familiar surroundings, been forced to travel with their families and to make a new life in a refugee camp. We might expect these children to be suffering badly. However, the author of this reading, anthropologist Rachel Hinton, offers a very different account of children's lives.

As you read through this extract make a note of the ways in which children show resilience in the face of adversity, and ask yourself why they might, in some cases, be able to cope better than adults.

Comment

By almost any criteria, these children are living in adversity and might be expected to be doing very badly – suffering the effects of homelessness, insecurity and possibly poor mental health. Certainly some of the children appear to miss the familiar landmarks and security of home. However, their reaction to these adverse circumstances is less predictable. Many children show not only resilience but also very active strategies for coping and for supporting their parents. Children appear to adapt much faster than adults to their new surroundings, possibly because they have fewer memories of home in Bhutan and are not as nostalgic about the past as their parents. They also show great resilience in adapting to the changes and difficulties they face; they acknowledge that there are aspects of their previous lives they miss – such as apple trees – but they do not dwell on it and Hinton claims that they have incorporated their old lives into their new ones much better than adults. Perhaps most surprising is the way in which children respond to the realisation that they need to support their parents as well as be supported by them. They are clearly attuned to the needs of others and this too can be a form of resilience, eliciting emotional support from their parents while also promoting their parents' emotional well-being.

Summary of Section 2

Resilience can be defined as the ways in which children cope with, and even respond positively to, adversity.

Resilience is an important concept in contemporary research and policy work with children, because it is seen as promoting a more positive and holistic understanding of children's lives, which acknowledges their strengths as well as their vulnerabilities.

3   What makes children resilient?

In situations of adversity, identifying the factors that make children vulnerable or resilient is extremely complex. For example, Lynn Beardsall and Judy Dunn (1992) studied pairs of siblings in the UK, where one sibling was six years old and the other was older. They observed the impact of a traumatic event on each of the siblings, such as the death or illness of a family member, unemployment of the primary breadwinner, parents divorcing, and so on. They judged that the negative effect of the events on these siblings was the same in only 31 per cent of cases:

The following example illustrates the differing impact of 'shared' events on two siblings: in one family the father had to leave home for 3 months because of his job; this had far more impact on the first-born son than on his sister; the family was then involved in a car accident in which there was a fire, the father was injured and the driver of the other car killed. The first-born son was considerably disturbed by the events, his sister only temporarily upset. In another family, there was a rift between the parents and a close family friend—a supportive 'granny' figure, who then stopped visiting the family: this had a severe impact on one child, who had been especially close to the friend, and only a mild effect on the sibling.

(Beardsall and Dunn, 1992, p. 353)

There are many reasons why these children might react differently to the same events. We could ask about their age, gender, birth order, or the temperament and personalities of the particular children involved. We could consider the intensity and quality of their relationships with other family members, the availability of emotional support from friends, teachers or others outside the family, and so on. We could also ask about the long-term effects of this – while the boy in the first example was more upset than his sister in the short term, would that still be true later on in life? In order to try to untangle these issues, researchers into resilience have tried to identify the factors that they believe promote resilience, examine the interplay between them and then study children's lives over a long time frame.

3.1   Reacting to economic hardship

Around 1930, research teams in California began two of the very first major longitudinal studies to look at how different forms of adversity affect children in the long term. The Oakland Growth Study followed up a sample of children born in 1920–21. Children in the Berkeley Guidance Study were around eight years younger, born in 1928–29. What neither research team could have known as they began their work was that the 1930s would turn out to be a time of acute economic hardship for many American families, with inevitable impacts on the children in these studies. Their childhoods were dominated by the Great Depression. A decade later, the USA would become involved in World War II, creating new challenges and opportunities for the children in the studies, some of whom were young adults by this time.

Figure 3   A migrant agricultural family in Nipomo, California, during the Great Depression (1929–34)

Many years later, Glen Elder and his colleagues reviewed the impact of these events on the children in both studies, comparing children in families most badly hit by financial hardship (the 'deprived' group) with children in families who had been less seriously affected. Children in the deprived group were adversely affected by the reduction in family income, as well as by the consequent shift in family roles and responsibilities, notably the greater reliance on mothers and older children to earn money to support the family. They experienced changes in the relationships with their parents, with unemployed and frequently demoralised fathers tending to withdraw, while their wives took on greater power and emotional significance for the children. Frequently, the stress induced by economic hardship and role changes led to greater marital conflict, exacerbated parental irritability and increased arbitrary and inconsistent discipline, which was sometimes linked to their fathers' heavy drinking (Elder, 1974).

One especially significant feature of these studies is what they tell us about the way children were differently affected by economic hardship according to their age as well as their gender. Recall that the two cohorts were born eight years apart. So the 167 children in the Oakland Growth Study were already around ten years old at the onset of the Great Depression:

> Thus, they entered the Great Depression after a relatively secure phase of early development. Later, they avoided the scars of joblessness after high school by virtue of wartime mobilization. By contrast, the 214 members of the Berkeley cohort experienced the vulnerable years of early childhood during hard times and the pressures of adolescence during the unsettled though prosperous years of World War II.
>
> (Elder et al., 1993, p. 15)

In fact the effects were even more subtle, especially in relation to gender. Many of the boys in the Oakland study looked for part-time work to supplement family income during their early teen years. They gained relative independence much earlier than would otherwise have been the case, spending more time away from home with their peers. Girls in the Oakland study also took on more responsibilities, but their work tended to be within the home, especially where their mothers were the main breadwinners and younger siblings needed care. They did not earn money, so did not gain the independence enjoyed by their brothers or have as much opportunity to spend time with their peers. Overall then, the childhood and teenage years of the Oakland cohort were strongly affected by economic hardship, but these young people made different adaptations to their changed circumstances, especially according to their gender.

Gender also shaped the impact of hardship for the younger children in the Berkeley study but in this case it was the boys who appeared more vulnerable. They were more likely to develop behavioural problems, which in some cases lasted into adolescence, and their school achievement was frequently poorer than that of the girls in the study. They also tended to have lower self-confidence and poor motivation. Elder et al. linked the greater vulnerability of boys to their fathers' demoralisation and irritability, their inability to offer their sons a positive role model, and their tendency to use more punitive forms of discipline.

These studies of the children of the Great Depression demonstrate the effects of economic adversity in children's lives, as well as the different patterns of effect according to children's age and gender. Another lesson from this research is that many of the adverse effects on children are not so much about economic hardship as about the social and emotional consequences of hardship for parents. This in turn has serious repercussions for children's feelings of security, as well as for the quality of parent–child relationships.

3.2   Coping under stress

While the Oakland and Berkeley studies looked at the long-term impacts of early poverty on children, another longitudinal study looked at why not all children were affected by adversity in the same way, and why some children coped and even thrived in adverse circumstances. This study was carried out by Emmy Werner and Ruth Smith and looked at 700 babies born in 1955 on the Hawaiian island of Kauai. It followed, at intervals throughout their childhood, the progress of the babies into their adult lives, providing a rich resource of research data about the way adversities affected individual children, as well as the factors that helped many to cope. At the start of the study the total population of Kauai was about 32,000, of mixed ethnic descent, living mainly in small towns scattered around the 30-mile wide island. The economy was based predominantly on sugar and pineapples, but it underwent significant change during the course of the study – notably through the growth of tourism, and scientific and military installations because of the strategic importance of Hawaii as a US State located in the Pacific Ocean. One of the remarkable features of this longitudinal study was the success in keeping track of children and families, with 88 per cent of the babies followed through to the age of 18.

About half the children were growing up in poverty, with many compounding risk factors such as perinatal complications, poor living conditions, family instability and low parental education. Not surprisingly, many of these high-risk children did indeed go on to suffer at school, get into trouble with the law, or suffer from mental or physical health problems. However, Werner and Smith report:

> there were others, also *vulnerable*, exposed to poverty, perinatal stress and family instability, reared by parents with little education or serious mental health problems, who remained invincible, and

developed into competent and autonomous young adults, who
worked well, played well, loved well, and expected well.

(Werner and Smith, 1982, p. xv)

Werner and Smith set out to investigate what factors protected some
children from risk or what made some children 'vulnerable but
invincible'.

Activity 2   Reading B
Allow about 30 minutes

Turn to Reading B, 'Vulnerable but invincible', at the end of the chapter.
This extract is taken from the concluding chapter of Werner and Smith's
report in which they sum up the main findings of their study. They begin by
setting out some brief details of the children's backgrounds and of the
social changes during their childhood. They go on to explain the adversities
which made these children part of a high-risk group.

As you read through the extract, make a list of the factors that distinguish
'resilient high-risk' children from 'vulnerable high-risk' children. For both
groups, note 'internal' qualities of the children (e.g. temperament, social
responsiveness), as well as 'external' qualities of their social environment
(e.g. close, supportive relationships in family and community).

Comment

Out of a cohort group of 700, only 204 children 'developed serious
learning and behavior problems in childhood or adolescence'. As Werner
and Smith explain, they became particularly interested in the children
who developed into competent and autonomous individuals, despite the
high risks. They identified a specific group of high-risk children, who were
resilient, called their 'index group'. They found that these children
possessed internal attributes which made them resilient, for example,
they were physically robust, as well as securely attached to their
caregivers. They also had particular external factors which supported
their resilience, such as a variety of adults in their lives whom they loved
and trusted, and who cared for them. Werner and Smith also point out
interesting gender differences, confirming the findings of Elder et al.
(1993), suggesting that girls and boys may be differently vulnerable at
different points in their lives.

Werner and Smith's pioneering research into risk and protective factors
associated with children's long-term resilience has been very influential in
providing a theoretical framework for studying childhood resilience. Their

work emphasises children's own role in the processes that shape their resilience, and they present children as active agents who respond and react to adversity. Even though in one sense these children are victims – since they have no control over the quality of the environment into which they are born, especially the care they receive during their earliest months and years – they play an active part in determining the outcomes of adversity in other ways, through the qualities they bring to each difficult situation they meet.

Figure 4   Two Hawaiian girls in the 1960s – the era when Werner and Smith were carrying out their longitudinal study

Boyden and Mann summarise the 'internal' (i.e. psychological or emotional) qualities that make children resilient:

> Some children are better able to manage stress because of disposition or temperament. Thus, protective factors such as resourcefulness, curiosity, a goal for which to live, and a need and ability to help others are largely matters of temperament and coping style. Generally, children who are able to remain hopeful about the future, are flexible and adaptable, possess problem-

solving skills, and actively try to assume control over their lives are likely to be less vulnerable than those who passively accept the adversity they face (Punamaki, 1987). ... The capacity to engage in critical thinking can also help to shield a child from simplistic interpretations of experience that are self-defeating (Garbarino, Kostelny, & Dubrow, 1991). Personal history also influences coping (Garbarino, 1999). Children who have experienced approval, acceptance, and opportunities for mastery are far more likely to be resilient than those who have been subjected to humiliation, rejection, or failure.

(Boyden and Mann, 2005, p. 7)

Stories of children surviving situations of extreme adversity illustrate how a child's own resourcefulness can enable them to form mutually beneficial relationships with adults. Apfel and Simon (1996) cite two cases: a 12-year-old Cambodian girl in a refugee camp, whose acting talents attracted the attention of a North American woman who subsequently adopted her; and an Israeli writer, Elie Wiesel, who as a 13-year-old boy in Auschwitz survived partly through receiving an extra bowl of soup from other camp inmates in return for his stories about his home life before the war.

While such stories are revealing, and even inspiring, they also reveal one of the key criticisms of research on resilience – especially that focusing on internal factors – which is an inherent tendency to blame the individual for their failure to thrive in the face of adversity (Este et al., 2009). Even if more children in Auschwitz had been able to tell stories, they would not all have been fed as Elie Wiesel was, and it is absurd to suggest that other children suffered because they were not resilient enough, or did not have the 'right' internal qualities to elicit support. It is not always the case that children need to change their attitude or learn to put up with adversity because it will make them stronger. A very real danger of focusing only on children's resilience in the narrow sense of individual temperament is that absolves adults from the responsibility of looking after vulnerable children. While some children may undergo hardship and thrive, it should not mean that others should receive no external help and support, and children should never be blamed for not having the 'right' attitude.

There are other problems with the concept of resilience in that it can sometimes fail to take into account the internal dynamics of interpersonal relationships. While close relationships are seen as necessary to making a child resilient, it is also important to remember that close relationships are not always positive. Peer and sibling relationships play a powerful role in children's social, emotional and cultural lives (Punch, 2008) and while supportive friends can help buffer difficult experiences at home, rejection or bullying can do the opposite. It is also worth bearing in mind that some caution needs to be exercised when using the term 'resilience', because 'some young people who appear to be resilient may in fact be internalising their symptoms' (Daniel et al., 2010, p. 70) and, thus, by being labelled or assumed to be 'resilient' they may be denied much-needed support.

Another concern has been that most research on the topic has been carried out from a minority-world perspective, over-relying perhaps on minority-world assumptions and theories (Ungar, 2005). Whilst it is now recognised that rather than focus on the individual, studies should consider multiple levels and be culturally sensitive, this in turn has resulted in layers of complexity, and made the term 'resilience' so broad and vague as to be meaningless. As Glantz and Sloboda (1999, p. 110) point out: 'Unfortunately, the concept of resilience is heavily laden with subjective often unarticulated assumptions and it is fraught with major logical, measurement, and pragmatic problems.' Many have critiqued resilience because of its lack of practical usefulness and the fact it is such a broad term with multiple definitions that lead to rather arbitrary decisions about what to measure and which variables to focus on (Ungar, 2005). The lack of clarity around the meaning of resilience leads to much ambiguity and complexity when striving to understand it in different cultural contexts.

Activity 3   The qualities that make children resilient

Allow about 15 minutes

Having read through both the Hinton and the Werner and Smith readings, based on your own knowledge and understanding come up with a list of qualities that you think are most likely to make children resilient. Fill in a three-column table to group these into internal (or individual) characteristics, familial or community characteristics, and cultural ones.

Comment

The following are some of the factors identified from the readings which could promote children's resilience and coping strategies.

Individual	Family and community	Cultural
Positive attitude	Support and acceptance from family	Religious beliefs
Hopes or goals for the future	Strong attachments in early childhood	Cultural expectations about the role of children and the extent to which they should be protected
Creativity	Loving relationships with peers and siblings	Cultural expectations about the expression of grief and trauma
Problem-solving skills and ingenuity	Inter-generational relationships with grandparents or other adults	How education is valued

This is just a brief list and there may be many other factors that you can come up with. Breaking them down in this way is helpful in that it shows the different levels at which children's resilience can be supported. What is much less easy to do is to know what weight to give to each of these factors. As an intervention strategy, the promotion of resilience is fraught with difficulty because it is so difficult to know with each individual child, which factor or combination of factors is most likely to promote their resilience.

3.3 Children's resilience in diverse contexts

Different children show different levels of resilience in different situations and there are many variables which must be taken into account. A further level to consider is the extent to which expectations of children, and the ways in which they are treated, are culturally defined. Arguably these cultural expectations will powerfully modify whether a particular type of coping strategy is encouraged or discouraged. For example, take the issue of how far children's age affects their vulnerability or resilience. Minority-world research suggests that, as a general rule, younger children are more vulnerable than older children – although the sensitivity of the early years should not be exaggerated (Schaffer, 2000). However, research carried out in Ethiopia has indicated that in some situations it is not chronological age itself that affects resilience so much as cultural expectations of the behaviour and activities at certain ages (Boyden and de Berry, 2000). In Ethiopia many boys were conscripted into the army in the 1980s and 1990s to fight in the war with Eritrea. Agencies involved in reintegrating these boys back into their communities after the war noticed a distinct difference in their ability to cope with civilian life and to come to terms with what they had done as combatants, which depended on whether or not they had been initiated. Their initiation ceremony emphasised that these boys had made a transition to manhood and sanctioned warfare as a manly activity. The younger boys had not been initiated and therefore viewed themselves as still children, despite their experiences at war. They found it much harder to come to terms with what they had done and to reconcile the brutality they had experienced, and indeed inflicted, with their status as children. In this context, undergoing an initiation ritual was a key protective factor which improved these young men's resilience by sanctioning their experiences of adversity.

Figure 5 Former child soldiers walking away from guns as part of a demobilisation ceremony

Catherine Panter-Brick and Mark Eggerman's (2012) study of child mental health in Afghanistan found that while one in five schoolchildren were at risk of a mental health disorder, four out of five Afghan children appeared quite resilient. The research also showed that 'everyday violence' such as domestic beatings and violence in the neighbourhood was just as significant as the 'militarized violence'. Despite the most obvious violence involved in the military conflict, this study suggested that war-related violence should not be the only focus, and that there is a 'need to understand how military, structural, and domestic violence are intertwined' (Panter-Brick and Eggerman, 2012, p. 379). The authors also found (in a separate study) that family connectedness was central to better outcomes and building resilience, as were religious faith and an emphasis on social respectability. Yet, a complex picture emerged in which the same cultural factors that promoted resilience in some children and young people, could be, at the same time, a source of entrapment and frustration for others because of the structural constraints which would prevent their realisation: poverty, poor governance, social injustice and military conflict:

> In this sense, culture is not just an anchor of resilience, but also an anvil of pain. On one hand, the profession and maintenance of cultural values is central to the construction of social identity, order, and hope. On the other, inability to conform to cultural dictates is source of great psychosocial distress. Failure or frustration in attaining social and cultural milestones lies at the root of social suffering and mental ill-health ...

> (Eggerman and Panter-Brick, 2010, p. 81)

Figure 6 Living and playing among soldiers is an everyday part of life for many children in Afghanistan

Summary of Section 3

Certain individual traits related to temperament – such as a flexible and adaptable outlook, an ability to solve problems, a sense of purpose, and a belief in a better future – promote children's resilience.

External factors, such as an adult or peer who loves and supports the child, may also promote resilience.

By looking at resilience only in terms of individual characteristics there is a danger of blaming the victim for not coping appropriately with the situation. Therefore, it is always important to look at a child's social and cultural environment.

The concept of resilience has been criticised as too broad and unpractical to be truly useful in policy and practice.

4 What is well-being and why is it important?

Resilience remains an important concept in research and policy with children, and has led to a shift in thinking about interventions in children's lives from a narrower focus on child welfare to the more holistic approach of child well-being. While research on resilience focuses on children's response to adversity, work on well-being looks at what interventions try to achieve – a good quality of life for all children. Well-being has therefore come to be understood in the broadest way, which incorporates three key dimensions: material well-being, subjective well-being and relational well-being. This three-dimensional approach to well-being means that people's own perceptions of their lives are important, as well as their relationships and material standards of living. McGregor sums up the interplay of factors and the various elements that combine to produce well-being:

[Well-being arises] from the combination of:

1   what a person has

2   what a person can do with what they have, and

3   how they think about what they have and can do. ...

[It involves] the interplay between:

1 the resources that a person is able to command;

2 what they are able to achieve with those resources, and in particular what needs and goals they are able to meet; and

3 the meaning that they give to the goals they achieve and the processes in which they engage.

(McGregor, 2007, p. 317)

Figure 7 Promoting children's well-being is now an important part of the mandate of organisations such as UNICEF and Save the Children

---

Activity 4 What is children's well-being?

Allow about 15 minutes

Think about, and make a list of, things you think count as leading to children's well-being. After you have done this, reflect on what problems you had in making this list.

Comment

There are many possible responses to this activity. Listed below are just some of the things that might lead to, or promote, children's well-being.

1 Good physical health.

2   Happiness, including good mental health, life satisfaction, positive emotions.

3   Financial and material resources (e.g. having enough to eat, adequate living accommodation, access to a roughly similar standard of living or quantity of material goods as others in their society).

4   Positive relationships and social networks (e.g. family relationships, friendships, pets).

5   Safety and security (e.g. not being at risk from violence in the home or in the community, not being bullied, not living in a situation of war).

6   Leisure opportunities (e.g. time, space and access to leisure and play facilities).

7   Sense of identity and self-worth (e.g. a sense of belonging within the community, feeling valued).

8   Good education (e.g. positive school experience, diverse learning opportunities, good relations with peers and teachers).

9   Participation in decision making (e.g. opportunities to influence their daily lives).

10 Living in a safe and clean environment (e.g. not at risk from pollution or street crime, access to outdoor space).

Child well-being encompasses a broad range of domains which means that it can be defined and interpreted in a number of ways. You may have come up with other suggestions or you may disagree with some of the suggestions in the list above. For example, work might be seen as harmful to children's well-being in some circumstances but, in others, working can provide children with an opportunity to contribute to the well-being of their family, which may give them a sense of pride and self-worth. Also, while most would agree that emotional security is important for children's well-being, it is hard to specify what constitutes 'happiness'. Similarly, having 'enough' food can contribute to children's well-being but if this is the 'wrong' sort of food – too fatty or with too much salt or sugar – then it may cause harm. This was explored in Chapter 3.

Definitions of well-being are also closely dependent on social and cultural background both within and between countries. While some opportunities and resources for well-being are available to whole countries or regions, many others are only accessible to particular groups in a society. Living in an affluent country may protect many children from certain kinds of adversity, but even wealthy children may experience ill-health, physical, emotional or sexual abuse, or an acrimonious parental divorce. Hence, well-being is a fluid, holistic and ambiguous notion which is difficult to define.

Figure 8 UNICEF publishes regular reports on children's well-being across Europe. Swedish children have some of the highest levels of well-being

'Well-being' is a term that is now used regularly by policymakers, practitioners and academics (McAuley and Rose, 2010; Bradshaw, 2011). Over the last decade, indicators of children's well-being have been developed to explore children's quality of life, moving from a focus on basic needs and what children lack to a more constructive emphasis on the strengths and positive aspects of their present lives. The benefits of this approach are highlighted by Jones and Sumner:

> The relevance to children of using a well-being lens is that it:
>
> - focuses on what children feel about what they can do and be;
> - respects children's feelings about what they can do and be;
> - expands the focus to include children's physiology and psychology;
> - is based on children's current experiences;
> - emphasises the importance of the local cultural context and specificity in construction of childhood well-being;

- addresses 'new' areas of well-being particularly important to children—autonomy, enjoyment/fun, relatedness and status.

(Jones and Sumner, 2009, p. 34)

Recent research from Australia, which explored children's own perspectives of well-being, found that positive feelings such as happiness, excitement and peacefulness were important to them (Fattore et al., 2007). Other central issues included the importance of feeling and being safe, being able to make choices and exert influence in their daily lives, feeling valued and having a positive sense of self. Unlike adults, who tended to dwell more on the past or the future, children usually prioritised the present. So while adults emphasised the importance of a good education to children's well-being – thinking ahead to the future – children emphasised the importance of their present lives, and feeling safe and secure were most important to their current well-being (McAuley et al., 2010). Fattore et al. claimed that:

> when children contribute to concepts of well-being they talk about positives of well-being in their 'presents'. The contrast of this finding with traditional adultcentric findings which have focused on negative aspects of children's well-being for their futures, sums up the way in which attention to children's standpoint(s) has the potential to challenge, complement and overall enrich existing adult-child social relations.

(Fattore et al., 2007, p. 26)

Other studies have found that the quality and strength of interpersonal relationships are crucial for children's sense of well-being. A key intergenerational relationship which can enhance children's well-being is that between grandparents and grandchildren. Whilst geographical distance and the quality of the parents' relationships with the grandparents can shape families' experiences, many grandparents provide emotional, financial and practical support for their grandchildren. Mason et al. (2007) identify the two cultural norms of grandparenting in the UK as 'being there' and 'not interfering'. Nevertheless, in Ross et al.'s 2005 British study, both adults and children described how grandparents often played a key role in 'listening' to grandchildren, sometimes acting as useful mediators between children and their parents. Many young people said they could share problems and concerns with their grandparents, thereby contributing to their emotional well-being. As children got older, the direction of care and support often altered, as some teenagers took on greater responsibility for their grandparents, whereas others spent more time with friends. Yet for these young people, despite contact decreasing, the closeness and sense of connectedness with grandparents continued. Thus, supportive family relations and inter-generational practices can increase children's resilience and well-being.

Figure 9 Having a close relationship with a grandparent can boost a child's resilience

Not all children live within families, however, and children living in residential care have to build relations with a range of adults, such as care workers and social workers. Recent research has found that everyday food practices can be used to promote children's social and emotional well-being as well as their physical well-being. Punch et al. (2009) illustrated the ways in which food played an important role in the lives of looked-after children in Scotland. Through food, they argued, children could experience a sense of consistency and nurture, as well as learning how to develop autonomy and a sense of control. Food practices can be used as a powerful, although often subtle and symbolic, way of demonstrating trust, care and predictability; hence they can be central to the building and sustaining of relationships, which are often complex, in residential care.

Summary of Section 4

Well-being is a holistic concept which recognises the importance of understanding, and supporting, children's physical and emotional needs.

Researchers who look at children's well-being explore children's quality of life, placing an emphasis on the strengths and positive aspects of their present lives.

Research on well-being looks at children's own perceptions of what promotes their well-being and how children perceive this in the present.

Adults and children may prioritise different types of well-being.

Strong inter-generational relationships can promote children's well-being.

5 What's wrong with well-being?

While well-being has proved a useful concept for many researchers and policymakers, for others it is more problematic. Virginia Morrow and Berry Mayall have claimed that it is a benign umbrella term which is 'conceptually muddy, but has become pervasive' (Morrow and Mayall, 2009, p. 221). For some it is problematic as it describes both a state of being and an outcome of intervention. However, the view that it is too conceptually vague is the most common criticism:

> wellbeing is a socially contingent, culturally-anchored construct that changes over time, both in terms of individual life course changes as well as changes in socio-cultural context. Imposing concepts and measures based on what it means for a 2-year-old boy in Los Angeles to be 'doing well' on a 12-year-old girl growing up in rural Ethiopia would be a weak starting point for analysing child wellbeing, as even if both children are growing up in poverty, differences of cultural and historical context and individual life phase are highly significant.
>
> (Crivello et al., 2009, p. 53)

Activity 5   Criticisms of 'well-being'

Allow about 15 minutes

Having read the chapter so far, what criticisms might you level at the term 'well-being'?

Comment

One obvious criticism of the term 'well-being' is that it is too vague. A threat to children's well-being can encompass any adversity, from the death of a pet to losing their entire family in a war. While the concept of well-being was developed to allow for subjective definitions and variability, if there are too many ways of defining and describing it, it loses any usefulness it once had and it becomes impossible to draw out broader conclusions.

You could also criticise the idea of well-being for focusing exclusively on the positive. The sections on resilience suggested that children can cope positively in adversity and that their well-being could be enhanced by meeting and overcoming challenges. While extreme adversity is highly likely to damage children, a childhood without difficulties, or some threats to well-being, may not be beneficial in the long term. It can be argued that parental overprotection may deny children opportunities to develop their strengths and competencies, which in turn may constrain the building of their resilience or the development of their coping strategies. For example, partly because of adult concerns around road safety and fears of 'stranger danger', very few children in the UK now walk to school by themselves. In 1971, 80 per cent of seven to eight year olds walked to school on their own in Britain, but by 1990 this had dropped to nine per cent (Hillman et al., 1990). In not walking to school, children are at risk from a lack of physical exercise, but they are also denied the opportunity of becoming independent and learning problem-solving skills. Children's leisure time tends to be spent indoors or in organised activities which parents chaperone their children to by car. Thus, much of children's time is structured and under adult supervision, and some argue that 'paranoid parenting' may mean too much control and surveillance of children by adults.

You might also argue that it is impossible to ensure happiness. While international legislation such as the UNCRC discusses the best interests of the child and asserts children's rights to a certain level of care and provision, it does not, and cannot, legislate for happiness.

Finally, it can be hard to distinguish the right levels of provision in supporting children's well-being. As discussed in Chapter 3, too much food can be as harmful as too little. It is equally possible to argue that while it is good that children have choices and opportunities as consumers, too many material goods can also be damaging to children.

Figure 10 In 2011, Save the Children said it is 'a national embarrassment' that the UK lags so far behind other nations in terms of the well-being of its children

Activity 6   Reading C

Allow about 30 minutes

Turn to Reading C, 'What is wrong with children's well-being in the UK?', where some of the negative implications of using well-being as a way of understanding contemporary children's lives are discussed. The reading is a response to UNICEF's Innocenti Report Card 7, entitled *Child Poverty in Perspective: An Overview of Child Well-being in Rich Countries* (UNICEF, 2007). This received a great deal of publicity in the British news media because it placed the UK's children at the bottom of the league table of rich nations in relation to emotional well-being and 'happiness'. Ever since its publication it has become a truism that British children are the unhappiest, most stressed and most emotionally deprived children in Europe, and this report has become central to contemporary debates around 'childhood in crisis' (Kehily, 2010). It is this report, perhaps more than any other, that provoked a debate about what well-being means and how it can be best promoted. As Morrow and

Mayall point out in their response, however, this report is far from definitive and, while it did set the agenda about well-being, it has numerous flaws.

As you read the extract from Morrow and Mayall's thought-provoking paper, consider the following questions:

- What are the key issues involved in measuring and interpreting findings about children's well-being?
- To what extent is well-being a useful concept? What are the advantages and disadvantages of using this term?

Comment

Morrow and Mayall's article illustrates that the multiple definitions of well-being can lead to problems when attempting to measure it. It is difficult to measure child well-being because, as well as depending on the definition used, it also depends on how the information is obtained and interpreted. How can we define and measure something which is intangible and subjective? How can we compare various research studies that have used different definitions and indicators of well-being? Difficulties with definitions and measurement may thus lead to different conclusions about the implications arising from the results. On the basis of this account, it could be argued that the situation of children in the UK is not as bad as it is portrayed and that British children are not as unhappy as has been suggested.

Nevertheless the focus on children's well-being raises important questions about how childhood is conceptualised and what constitutes a good childhood. While no one wants children to suffer, there are important questions which need to be asked about whether – in an imperfect world – a life without any form of failure, disappointment, grief or pain really is a good one, and whether this truly enhances children's well-being, adding to a good quality of life, either for children in the present or for their future selves.

Summary of Section 5

Well-being has been criticised as too vague a concept to be useful.

Concerns over children's well-being have added to the sense that childhood is in crisis, even though these fears may have been overplayed.

> Questions need to be asked about whether a life without any sort of difficulty is conducive to children's well-being and whether children will ever learn to be resilient if they are overprotected.

6 Conclusion

Resilience and well-being are two recent concepts that researchers and policymakers have tried to define and use when discussing children's lives. They represent a shift in understanding childhood by starting with children's strengths instead of concentrating on what they lack. Rather than assuming that children are vulnerable and weak, a more positive focus on children's agency, and their potential for resourcefulness and social competence, can point to interventions that build on their capabilities. At best, both resilience and well-being acknowledge children's strengths as well as their vulnerabilities, they are based on children's own perceptions and they look at children's lives holistically, not simply counting how much money or food children have access to, but looking at what makes up a good quality of life – including less tangible things like relationships and psychological health. However, these very qualities also make them open to criticism and their slipperiness has been much critiqued. Nor should it be forgotten that in many circumstances children *are* especially vulnerable when confronted with adversity – which affects their physical and psychological well-being, as well as their social adjustment – and that adult interventions are needed to support and protect children in these circumstances. Furthermore, it still remains to be seen how exactly these concepts are operationalised in practice. The terms 'resilience' and 'well-being' are now both used extensively throughout policy and practice in different parts of the world, but how will these help achieve better outcomes for children in the longer term? Whilst both the fields of resilience and well-being research have grown enormously in the last decade, there are still questions which remain to be answered, particularly in relation to bridging the gap between theory and effective interventions.

References

Apfel, R. and Simon, B. (1996) 'Psychosocial interventions for children of war: the value of a model of resiliency', *Medicine & Global Survival*, vol. 3, pp. 1–16.

Beardsall, L. and Dunn, J. (1992) 'Adversities in childhood: siblings' experiences, and their relations to self-esteem', *Journal of Child Psychology and Psychiatry*, vol. 33, no. 2, pp. 349–59.

Boyden, J. and de Berry, J. (2000) 'Children in adversity', *Forced Migration Review*, vol. 9, pp. 33–6.

Boyden, J. and Mann, G. (2005) 'Children's risk, resilience, and coping in extreme situations', in Ungar, M. (ed) *Handbook for Working with Children and Youth: Pathways to Resilience Across Cultures and Contexts*, Thousand Oaks, CA, Sage.

Bradshaw, J. (ed) (2011) *The Well-Being of Children in the UK*, Bristol, The Policy Press.

Crivello, G., Camfield, L. and Woodhead, M. (2009) 'How can children tell us about their wellbeing? Exploring the potential of participatory research approaches within young lives', *Social Indicators Research*, vol. 90, no. 1, pp. 51–72.

Daniel, B. (2010) 'Concepts of adversity, risk, vulnerability and resilience: a discussion in the context of the "child protection system"', *Social Policy and Society*, vol. 9, no. 2, pp. 231–41.

Daniel, B., Vincent, S., Farrall, E. and Arney, F. (2009) 'How is the concept of resilience operationalised in practice with vulnerable children', *International Journal of Child & Family Welfare*, vol. 12, no. 1, pp. 2–21.

Daniel, B., Wassell, S. and Gilligan, R. (2010) *Child Development for Child Care and Protection Workers*, London, Jessica Kingsley Publishers.

Eggerman, M. and Panter-Brick, C. (2010) 'Suffering, hope, and entrapment: resilience and cultural values in Afghanistan', *Social Science & Medicine*, vol. 71, no. 1, pp. 71–83.

Elder, G. H. (1974) *Children of the Great Depression: Social Change in Life Experience*, Chicago, IL, University of Chicago Press.

Elder, G. H., Modell, J. and Parke, R. D. (1993) 'Studying children in a changing world', in Elder, G. H., Modell, J. and Parke, R. D. (eds) *Children in Time and Place*, Cambridge, Cambridge University Press.

Este, D., Sitter, K. and Maclaurin, B. (2009) 'Using mixed methods to understand youth resilience', in Liebenberg, L. and Ungar, M. (eds) *Researching Resilience*, Toronto, University of Toronto Press.

Fattore, T., Mason, J. and Watson, E. (2007) 'Children's conceptualisation(s) of their well-being', *Social Indicators Research*, vol. 80, no. 1, pp. 5–29.

Garbarino, J. (1999) 'What children can tell us about the trauma of forced migration', seminar presented at the *Refugee Studies Programme*, Oxford, University of Oxford.

Garbarino, J., Kostelny, K. and Dubrow, N. (1991) *No Place To Be a Child: Growing Up in a War Zone*, Lexington, MA, Lexington Books.

Gilligan, R. (2009) *Promoting Resilience*, London, British Association for Adoption and Fostering.

Glantz, M. D. and Sloboda, Z. (1999) 'Analysis and reconceptualization of resilience', in Glantz, M. D. and Johnson, J. L. (eds) *Resilience and Development: Positive Life Adaptations*, New York, Kluwer Academic/Plenum Press.

Hillman, M., Adams, J. and Whitelegg, J. (1990) *One False Move: A Study of Children's Independent Mobility*, London, Policy Studies Institute.

Jones, N. and Sumner, A. (2009) 'Does mixed methods research matter to understanding childhood well-being?', *Social Indicators Research*, vol. 90, no. 1, pp. 33–50.

Kehily, M. J. (2010) 'Childhood in crisis? Tracing the contours of "crisis" and its impact upon contemporary parenting practices', *Media, Culture and Society*, vol. 32, no. 2, pp. 171–85.

Liebenberg, L. and Ungar, M. (2009) 'Introduction: the challenges in researching resilience', in Liebenberg, L. and Ungar, M. (eds) *Researching Resilience*, Toronto, University of Toronto Press.

Mason, J., May, V. and Clarke, L. (2007) 'Ambivalence and the paradoxes of grandparenting', *The Sociological Review*, vol. 55, no. 4, pp. 687–706.

McAuley, C. and Rose, W. (eds) (2010) *Child Well-Being: Understanding Children's Lives*, London, Jessica Kingsley Publishers.

McAuley, C., Morgan, R. and Rose, W. (2010) 'Children's views on child well-being', in McAuley, C. and Rose, W. (eds) *Child Well-Being: Understanding Children's Lives*, London, Jessica Kingsley Publishers.

McGregor, J. A. (2007) 'Researching wellbeing: from concepts to methodology', in Gough, I. and McGregor, J. A. (eds) *Wellbeing in*

Developing Countries: From Theory to Research, Cambridge, Cambridge University Press.

Morrow, V. and Mayall, B. (2009) 'What is wrong with children's well-being in the UK? Questions of meaning and measurement', *Journal of Social Welfare and Family Law*, vol. 31, no. 3, pp. 217–29.

Panter-Brick, C. and Eggerman, M. (2012) 'Understanding culture, resilience and mental health: the production of hope', in Ungar, M. (ed) *The Social Ecology of Resilience: A Handbook of Theory and Practice*, New York, Springer.

Punamaki, R. L. (1987) 'Content of and factors affecting coping modes among Palestinian children', *Scandinavian Journal of Development Alternatives*, vol. 6, no. 1, pp. 86–98.

Punch, S. (2008) '"You can do nasty things to your brothers and sisters without a reason": siblings' backstage behaviour', *Children and Society*, vol. 22, no. 5, pp. 333–44.

Punch, S., McIntosh, I., Emond, R. and Dorrer, N. (2009) 'Food and relationships: children's experiences in residential care', in James, A., Kjørholt, A. T. and Tingstad, V. (eds) *Children, Food and Identity in Everyday Life*, Basingstoke, Palgrave Macmillan.

Ross, N., Hill, M., Sweeting, H. and Cunningham-Burley, S. (2005) *Relationships Between Grandparents and Teenage Grandchildren (CRFR Research Briefing 23)*, Edinburgh, Centre for Research on Families and Relationships.

Schaffer, H. R. (2000) 'The early experience assumption: past, present and future', *International Journal of Behavioral Development*, vol. 24, no. 1, pp. 5–14.

Ungar, M. (2005) 'Introduction: resilience across cultures and contexts', in Ungar, M. (ed) *Handbook for Working with Children and Youth: Pathways to Resilience Across Cultures and Contexts*, Thousand Oaks, CA, Sage.

Ungar, M. (2008) 'Resilience across cultures', *British Journal of Social Work*, vol. 38, no. 2, pp. 218–35.

UNICEF (2007) *Child Poverty in Perspective: An Overview of Child Well-Being in Rich Countries,* Innocenti Report Card 7, Florence, UNICEF Innocenti Research Centre.

Werner, E. and Smith, R. (1982) *Vulnerable but Invincible*, New York, McGraw-Hill Book Company.

Reading A
Seen but not heard: refugee children and models for intervention

Rachel Hinton

Source: 'Seen but not heard: refugee children and models for intervention', 2000, in Panter-Brick, C. and Smith, M. (eds) *Abandoned Children*, Cambridge, Cambridge University Press, pp. 199–211.

Since 1990, 87,000 men, women and children have fled from southern Bhutan to the Terai (lowland Nepal). ... For adults who played significant social and economic roles in Bhutan, becoming a refugee has been a marginalizing experience. Their sense of abandonment is acute. In contrast, children's lifeworlds have been transplanted relatively intact into the crowded context of the refugee camp. While adults express feelings of abandonment, many of the children show greater concern with the material aspects of the camp environment.

This chapter discusses some hitherto unexplored social dynamics of camp interaction. It shows that when welfare intervention in the refugee camps focuses primarily on adults and seeks to identify vulnerable individuals or 'victims' for counselling, it overlooks the significant support role played by children, whose perceived position of vulnerability contributes to their being seen but not heard.

Concerned to provide a swift response to the needs of the refugees, policy-makers turned to traditional Western techniques of support. Many of these neglect the significant impact children have on the psychological and emotional worlds of adults. Despite high levels of community participation and involvement in aid programmes, the framework for interventions is rooted in Western notions of individualized and adult-centred counselling. In recent years this approach has been increasingly challenged (Ager 1999). I extend this critique by reversing the focus of attention and flow of intervention from adults to children, highlighting the ways in which children often provide social support. ...

Reversing the focus of attention: children's agency in refugee camps

... The resilience of children and their ability to cope with physical displacement are best understood through an awareness of their lifeworlds, which are distinct from those of adults. Children spoke about losing their homeland in terms of the absence of familiar physical features of home: 'Now, we have no apple garden in the camp, my father doesn't get money from it. I like to eat apples, but we have no money to buy [here in the camp]. I always think of my apple orchard in Bhutan' (Purna, aged twelve). Many children did not block the reality of the present as one might have expected but integrated their new lives with their past ones. Some children described aspects of the changed social environment in positive terms: 'Here [in the camp] we are close to our friends. Here I can play everyday with my older brothers and sisters' (Sumitra, aged eight). The refugee environment brought children new networks of friends and social support.

In contrast to the adults, the refugee children were not always viewed as full social actors, but small events signalled that, far from being passive recipients of support, they were active in promoting cohesion within the social unit. The children I came to know were aware of their care-givers' emotions and used this knowledge to demand and gain attention. They found their own strategies both to provide support and to elicit it from others. These encompassed wider social circles than the nuclear family and included fictive and biological kin. This is not to imply that such strategies were salient in the children's consciousness; they were generally expressed in small gestures and actions such as the following (from my fieldnotes):

> Kaji [my five-year-old neighbour] came to me to ask for a flower for his mother. It was an interesting interaction which fulfilled two purposes: it ensured that I knew and showed approval of his action and his concern for his mother, and additionally it confirmed to him that I was aware of his mother's sadness. It seemed to be his way of taking control and initiating wider social support. Kaji regularly took flowers from my small plot and knew that I was happy for him to do so; he looked upon it as exchange for defending my garden when other children wanted to 'steal' the flowers, as he said, so there was no need for him to ask my permission.
>
> He was alerting my attention to his mother's suffering following his father's elopement with another woman.

The labelling of their parents through involvement in agency counselling also affected children in that it identified their care-givers as 'different' from other community members. ... The children, often without a full awareness of the history of the trauma suffered by adults, tended to internalize problems and to feel personally responsible for their parents' emotional state. Some lacked the tools and vocabulary to discuss the situation or express themselves fully. Coping with their care-givers became a paramount concern and often supplanted their own needs. One example of a child adopting such a role was five-year-old Kamal:

> Kamal regularly elicited caring behaviour. An acutely sensitive, small framed boy, he appeared constantly aware of his mother's psychological state. Frequently in the private forum of his own home he resorted to breastfeeding and behaviour patterns regarded as immature within his culture for a child of his age. In doing so he elicited an earlier maternal preoccupation from his mother which placed her back in a role that provided social value and unique utility. Interestingly this behaviour was infrequent when his mother was less depressed (as defined by self-reports). It appeared that Kamal was highly sensitive to his mother's state of mind.

Kamal's strategy of creating a role as a dependent child resulted from the recognition of the fulfilment this brought his mother. He emphasized and even created dependency and in so doing made salient his parent's value. Simultaneously he was aware of the private nature of this behaviour, and I never observed him playing this role in public space. Not surprisingly, children rarely provided a verbal explanation for this type of behaviour.

Indeed, it was difficult to determine the degree to which such behaviour was a result of conscious decision making. From conversations it was clear that children seldom explicitly considered themselves as supplying social support to their parents. However, on one occasion many months into fieldwork, sitting on the bamboo bunk in the privacy of my hut, thirteen-year-old Susma spoke with an unusual directness and coherence of analysis: 'Sometimes I play at being a child, I am grown up now, but my mother likes to have babies, and it makes her happy when I sit by her and she gives [spoon-feeds] me food.'

Another observed behaviour pattern was of the child's taking on parenting roles. Arati often played a parenting role with regard to her younger siblings that went beyond minding them to include behaviours that her mother usually performed. She was one of the few in the camp who extended such help into school hours: 'Mother is sick, there is no one else to help her; the others are too young. When I go to school she feels alone, so I do not like to attend. It is better that I stay at home; then there is no emptiness and loss.'

Where the children believed they were a cause of their parents' distress they were often less effective at providing support, as Bishnu (aged nine) explained:

> I don't know why mother is angry. Sometimes she sits all day, she doesn't even sit with the others, just inside the hut, without making the tea or cleaning the floors. I try to do the housework, but I think that she is cross with me – perhaps I have done a wrong deed or was bad in Bhutan. These days I stay at school and wait behind in the classroom. ...

Children's roles in community networks of support

Where external support is provided to children, the benefits are usually assumed to be an end in themselves. This narrow focus misses the opportunity to support children as a means of reaching certain vulnerable adults within the community. Children receive particular attention from extended kin and community members, and schooling gives them a valued position within the community.

The refugee children's priority and advantage was their resilience and speed at adapting to the new environment. The social structures and refugee context provided opportunities for building their confidence. Children were able to minimize the negative emotional effects of displacement by engaging in valued activities such as portraying their situation in paintings and playing on sports teams. Such activities and institutional support increased self-esteem, a mechanism for building a positive self-image that was closed to adults. Responsibilities were also given to children by the camp committee members, as Rajman, a health assistant, explained:

> The camp committee discussed this matter [a cholera epidemic] to find a solution. We realized that once one member of a hut had died it would not be long before the next would follow. So we decided to get the help of young boys and to ask them to go around the camp and advise people to go to hospital. After

implementing that policy we found great changes. The people listened, and the numbers dying reduced substantially.

Requests to undertake work valued in the community gave children status and a feeling of self-worth.

In the Bhutanese case, while children's views appear to have been disregarded in public arenas, the young had a significant voice in private spaces, 'behind the plastic sheeting' (in the family hut). The significant influence of children in Bhutanese society had consequences across many domains. From listening to conversations it became clear that children were bringing home messages and ideas into the household that were both listened to and acted upon. …

Conclusion

The perception among outsiders that Bhutanese refugee children in Nepal are abandoned victims is a stereotype reinforced by the international media. Children do not share adults' concepts of abandonment. In fact, many of the supportive relationships which children rely upon are more readily available in refugee camps. Parents, neighbours and teachers live and work close to them and have more time to devote to caring roles. Furthermore, the children themselves display a resilience that has remained largely invisible to policy-makers. … The Bhutanese clearly consider children to have the skills required to take on the roles of community care-givers through both deliberate and unpremeditated actions. Notwithstanding children's critical stage of development and the potential long-term damage that may be produced by stress and trauma, their resilience and role in adding a 'protective' capacity should not be overlooked.

Reference

Ager, A. (1999) *Refugees: Perspectives on the Experience of Forced Migration*, London, Cassell.

Reading B
Vulnerable but invincible

Emmy Werner and Ruth Smith

Source: *Vulnerable but Invincible*, 1982, New York, McGraw-Hill, pp. 152–7.

A BRIEF RÉSUMÉ OF OUR FINDINGS

Our study group consisted of the children and grandchildren of immigrants who left the poverty of their Asian and European homelands to work for the sugar and pineapple plantations on the island of Kauai. Many intermarried with the local Hawaiians, who, oppressed by successive waves of newcomers, lost many lives and most of their land.

The children in our study had few material possessions, and most were raised by mothers who had not graduated from high school and by fathers who were semi- or unskilled laborers. They came of age during two and a half decades of unprecedented social change (1955–1979), which included statehood for Hawaii, the arrival of many newcomers from the U.S. mainland, and a prolonged and ill-fated war in Southeast Asia. During the first decade of their lives the children witnessed the assassination of one U.S. president, and during the second decade, the resignation, in disgrace, of another. In their teens they had access to contraceptive pills and mind-altering drugs, and they saw on television screens the space explorations that put man on the moon and his cameras within the range of other planets. Closer to home, they witnessed the undoing of the delicate balance of the island ecology that had evolved over millions of years by the rapid build-up of the tourist industry.

From an epidemiological point of view, these children were at high risk, since they were born and reared in chronic poverty, exposed to higher than average rates of prematurity and perinatal stress, and reared by mothers with little formal education. A combination of such social and biological variables correctly identified the majority of youth in this birth cohort who developed serious learning and behavior problems in childhood or adolescence.

Yet those in our [resilient high-risk] index group (approximately one of ten in the cohort) managed to develop into competent and autonomous young adults who 'worked well, played well, loved well, and expected well.'

We contrasted their behavior characteristics and the features of their caregiving environment, from the perinatal period to the threshold of adulthood, with other high-risk children of the same age and sex who developed serious coping problems in the first and in the second decades of life.

SEX DIFFERENCES IN VULNERABILITY AND RESILIENCY

At birth, and throughout the first decade of life, more boys than girls were exposed to serious physical defects or illness requiring medical care, and more boys than girls had learning and behavior problems in the classroom and at home.

The physical immaturity of the boys, the more stringent expectations for male sex-role behavior in childhood, and the predominant feminine environment to which the boys were exposed, appeared to contribute both separately and in concert to a higher proportion of disordered behavior in childhood among the males than the females.

Trends were reversed in the second decade of life: The total number of boys with serious learning problems dropped, while the number of girls with serious behavior disorders rose. Boys seemed now more prepared for the demands of school and work, although they were still more often involved in antisocial and delinquent behavior. Girls were now confronted with social pressures and sex-role expectations that produced a higher rate of mental health problems in late adolescence and serious coping problems associated with teenage pregnancies and marriages. ...

Related to this trend was the cumulative number of stressful life events reported by each sex. Boys with serious coping problems experienced more adversities than girls in *childhood*; girls with serious coping problems reported more stressful life events in *adolescence*. In spite of the biological and social pressures, which in this culture appear to make each sex more vulnerable at different times, more high-risk girls than high-risk boys grew into resilient young adults.

COPING PATTERNS AND SOURCES OF SUPPORT AMONG RESILIENT CHILDREN AND YOUTH

The resilient high-risk boys and girls had few serious illnesses in the first two decades of life and tended to recuperate quickly. Their mothers perceived them to be 'very active' and 'socially responsive' when they were infants, and independent observers noted their pronounced autonomy and positive social orientation when they were toddlers. Developmental examinations in the second year of life showed advanced self-help skills and adequate sensorimotor and language development for most of these children. In middle childhood the resilient boys and girls possessed adequate problem-solving and communication skills, and their perceptual-motor development was age-appropriate. Throughout childhood and adolescence they displayed both 'masculine' and 'feminine' interests and skills.

In late adolescence the resilient youth had a more internal locus of control [i.e. a sense of their own agency], a more positive self-concept, and a more nurturant, responsible, and achievement-oriented attitude toward life than peers who had developed serious coping problems. Their activities and interests were less sex-typed as well. At the threshold of adulthood, the resilient men and women had developed a sense of coherence in their lives and were able to draw on a number of informal sources of support. They also expressed a great desire to 'improve themselves,' i.e., toward continued psychological growth.

Among key factors in the caregiving environment that appeared to contribute to the resiliency and stress resistance of these high-risk children were: the age of the opposite-sex parent (younger mothers for resilient males, older fathers for resilient females); the number of children in the family (four or fewer); the spacing between the index child and the next-born sibling (more than 2 years); the number and type of alternate caregivers available to the mother within the household (father, grandparents, older siblings); the workload of the mother (including steady employment outside the household); the amount of attention given to the child by the primary caretaker(s) in infancy; the availability of a sibling as caretaker or confidant in childhood; structure and rules in the household in adolescence; the cohesiveness of the family; the presence of an informal multigenerational network of kin and friends in adolescence; and the cumulative number of chronic stressful life events experienced in childhood and adolescence. ...

THE NEED FOR A CROSS-CULTURAL PERSPECTIVE

... These families were poor by material standards, but a characteristically strong bond was forged between the infant and the primary caregiver during the first year of life. The physical robustness of the resilient children, their high activity level, and their social responsiveness were recognized by the caregivers and elicited a great deal of attention. There was little prolonged separation of the infants from their mothers and no prolonged bond disruption during the first year of life. The strong attachment that resulted appears to have been a secure base for the development of the advanced self-help skills and autonomy noted among these children in their second year of life.

Though many of their mothers worked for extended periods and were major contributors to family subsistence, the children had support from alternate caretakers, such as grandmothers or older sisters, to whom they had become attached.

Many resilient children grew up in multiage households that included members of the grandparent generation. As older siblings departed from the household, the resilient girls took responsibility for the care of younger siblings. The employment of their mothers and the need for sibling caretaking seems to have contributed to a greater autonomy and sense of responsibility in the resilient girls, especially in households where the father was dead or otherwise permanently absent. Their competence was enhanced by a strong bond between the daughter and the other females in the family—sometimes across three generations (mother, grandmother, older sisters, or aunts).

Resilient boys, in turn, were often first-born sons, lived in smaller families, and did not have to share their parents' attention with many additional children during the first decade of life. There were some males in their family who could serve as models for identification (fathers, older brothers, or uncles). There was structure and rules in the household, but space to explore in and less physical crowding. Last, but not least, there was an informal, multiage network of kin, peers, and elders who shared similar values and beliefs, and from whom the resilient youth sought counsel and support in times of crises and major role transitions.

These strong bonds were absent among families whose children had difficulties coping under duress. The lack of this emotional support was most devastating to children with a constitutional tendency toward withdrawal and passivity, with low activity levels, irregular sleeping and feeding habits, and a genetic background (i.e., parental psychoses, especially maternal schizophrenia) that made them more vulnerable to the influences of an adverse environment.

Most of these infants were perceived as retiring, passive, placid, or inactive in infancy by their mothers, and some had feeding and sleeping habits or a temper distressing to their primary caregiver. They experienced more prolonged bond disruptions during the first year of life. Mothers in these families worked sporadically outside the household, but there were few alternative caregivers in the home, such as fathers, grandparents, or older siblings. This lack of dependable substitute care appears to have been especially hard on the boys.

During childhood and adolescence, these youngsters were sick more often, more seriously, and more repeatedly than the resilient children, and they moved and changed schools more often as well. During the same period, they were exposed to more family discord and paternal absence (which took a greater toll among the boys), and to episodes of maternal mental illness (which took a greater toll among the girls).

By age 18 most of these youth had an external locus-of-control orientation and a low estimate of themselves. They felt that events happened to them as a result of luck, fate, or other factors beyond their control. Professional assistance sought from community agencies was considered of 'little help' to them.

Reading C
What is wrong with children's well-being in the UK?

Virginia Morrow and Berry Mayall

Source: 'What is wrong with children's well-being in the UK? Questions of meaning and measurement', 2009, *Journal of Social Welfare and Family Law*, vol. 31, no. 3, pp. 221–5.

Measuring well-being

... the UNICEF Report (2007) focused on six dimensions of well-being [Material well-being, Health and safety, Educational well-being, Family and peer relationships, Behaviours and risks, Subjective well-being]. The authors argue that their report represents an advance on previous reports in the Innocenti series, which had used income poverty as a proxy for child well-being. They argue that comparing child well-being in differing countries is necessary, for, in order 'to improve something, first measure it' (p. 3). Internationally, these measurements and comparisons show what can be achieved and what each country's strengths and weaknesses are. Above all, such reports attempt to show that levels of child well-being are not inevitable, but are policy-susceptible.

However, the authors go on to say that they could use only what data were available. The only data collected with children themselves come from the WHO Health Behaviour in School-aged Children (henceforth HBSC) survey, a cross-national survey that has been running since 1982, and repeated every four years with 11-, 13- and 15-year-olds, which maps trends in children's health risk behaviours (so it has a very specific focus). Furthermore, as the authors note, many of the data are old – and so, we may add, may be unrepresentative of progress made in countries which have introduced policies to improve childhood (such as the UK since 1997). The problem of dealing with necessarily dated data is discussed by Bradshaw elsewhere (Bradshaw 2007). We also identify some problems with the uses that have been made of the HBSC data. Some of the claims made seem to be based on unreflective developmental and cultural assumptions, as we shall demonstrate. Further, some indicators are rather oddly selected.

We now proceed to consider three examples from the six dimensions of well-being, and the indicators used to arrive at them. We note that averaging the indicators means that each is given equal weight

(UNICEF 2007, p. 5) and we are not sure this works well for the data in all cases. We also note that for most dimensions between 18 and 21 countries are being compared. We cannot present here findings for all the dimensions and all countries, but concentrate on the UK, since findings have been so widely reported, as facts.

Example: Dimension 1: material well-being

Indicators used here are: relative income poverty; percentages of children in households without jobs; and reported deprivation (children's reports on low family affluence, numbers of educational resources and fewer than ten books in the home). It is no surprise that the UK is second from the bottom on income poverty and near the bottom on workless households (see UNICEF 2007). But as the authors point out, differences in national wealth need to be taken into account. A poor child in the UK and the USA may be less disadvantaged relatively than a poor child in Hungary or Poland. It is also necessary to take account of the point that some countries have more equal distribution of income (so fewer children will fall below the 50% of the national median). In other words, this is about social exclusion rather than poverty. These points become relevant when we consider 11-, 13- and 15-year-old children's reports on three topics: on household ownership (of cars, own bedroom, holiday with family and computers, where the UK comes eighth in the ranking); on ownership of education-related possessions (UK seventh); and on household ownership of ten or more books (UK seventeenth).

But the averaging of these three sets of reports by children into one component of the dimension, which is then averaged with income poverty and households without jobs, means that the UK's overall score on this dimension is near the bottom, along with the USA, Ireland, Hungary, and Poland. The authors argue that 'children appear to be most deprived of educational and cultural resources in some of the world's most economically developed countries' (UNICEF 2007, p. 11). Perhaps we should note, however, that a wider encompassing of social factors might provide a (somewhat) differing picture; thus, for instance, in more affluent nations, books and computers and space to work are freely available in schools and libraries. We suggest that there is a need to combine quantitative and qualitative data in order to interpret findings more systematically and accurately when attempting to make international comparisons.

Example: Dimension 3: educational well-being

The indicators used here are: school achievement at age 15 (including achievement in literacy, numeracy and science); percentage of young people aged 15–19 in full- or part-time education; and the transition to employment (including percentage not in education, training or employment, and percentage of 15-year-olds expecting to find low-skilled work). Again, the authors deplore that adequate, comparable data were not available on the quantity and quality of early years provision (UNICEF 2007, p. 21).

This dimension includes indicators that are so disparate as to defy averaging, which may account for the unusual group of those who top the ranking: Belgium, Canada, Poland and Finland; and those at the bottom: France, Austria, Italy and Portugal. Overall the UK ranks at seventeenth place on this dimension; but does better on the first one: achievement at age 15 (ranked ninth). We have some difficulties with these indicators. Whilst it is the case, as the authors argue, that we need to know how well the education system serves our children, it does not follow, we submit, that a long period in school is necessarily a good thing. There seem to be some cultural pre-conceptions here. And/or it may be that the economic welfare of the country, rather than children's 'educational well-being', determined the choice of these indicators. Many people, including children, would argue that we learn more out of school than in school; and an indicator under material well-being – possession of educational resources at home, puts the UK near the top (in seventh place).

Example: Dimension 4: family and peer relationships

> … The report presents a sad picture of relationships with friends, which are so important to children. Not much more than 40% of the UK's 11-, 13- and 15-year-olds find their peers 'kind and helpful', which is the worst score of all the developed countries' (Guardian 14.02.07).

Oddly, other sections of the HBSC survey did have questions specifically about friends; perhaps these could have been used in this dimension.

Comments on these dimensions

We agree with the authors that a start has been made towards using a range of indicators on children's well-being. Child poverty may indeed underlie many of the findings, and may account for the UK's poor showing on some dimensions, although the precise relationships are not clear. It was also useful to maintain a focus on children's well-being as a multi-dimensional issue, requiring a range of policy responses. Somehow a balance had to be struck between retaining each facet of the problem in separate tables and combining them through averaging. In some cases we think averaging did a disservice to the data, as we have indicated. However, commentators have a duty to read such reports carefully before referring to them. Our consideration is motivated more by our concerns about the relatively low status of children in the UK and the deplorable way that the report has been so misrepresented in the media. These misrepresentations affect adults' perceptions. In the Primary Review (an independent review of primary education in England conducted at the University of Cambridge, funded by Esmée Fairbairn Foundation [see http://www.primaryreview.org.uk]), parents, teachers, local authority staff and children's organisations presented a gloomy vision of today's childhood; and this long-established vision has been bolstered by the media representation of the UNICEF Report (Alexander and Hargreaves 2007).

The UNICEF Report focused, in many of the indicators, on deficits – what children do not have, negatives, rather than positives, particularly in relation to 'risky health behaviours'. We know from our own research (Mayall 2002, Morrow 2000) that children feel subordinated to adults; they are not able to make their own decisions (not often consulted), they do not have to take major responsibility for decisions – and they accept their status on these points; they regard good personal relations as key to their happiness (but these do not have to be with two parents, but can include a range of people). For example, children aged 8–12 years say playing out is their preferred activity, but is often circumscribed by anxious parents. So what matters to children differs from what concerns adults (Mayall 2002, Morrow 1998). Recent research has explored children's understanding of well-being. For example, in Australia, Fattore *et al.* (2007) undertook qualitative research with 8 to 15 year olds and found that well-being includes feelings:

> in particular happiness, but integrating sadness is also relevant. Well-being is about feeling secure, particularly in social relations …

also as being a moral actor in relation to oneself (when making decisions in one's best interest) and when one behaves well towards others ... well-being is the capacity to act freely and to make choices and exert influence in everyday situations. This was not necessarily being independent from others. (Fattore *et al.* 2007, p. 18)

They also found that children articulated clear ideas about the importance of having a positive sense of themselves, material resources, physical environment and home. Sixsmith *et al.* (2007) in Ireland undertook research with 8 to 12-year-olds, using qualitative methods (photography) to explore children's, parents' and teachers' views of child well-being. They found marked differences between these three groups about what constitutes children's well-being. These qualitative studies show great potential for complementing, or expanding upon, larger scale survey research by providing deeper insights into children's everyday lives and what matters to them from their point of view (Morrow 2000).

In the specific case of the UK, adults tend to construct children and childhood as a social problem. This construction links in to social class divides. It is entirely possible that media, teachers and even parental concern about childhood affects children's self-image and may partially account for low scores. If childhood is (objectively) bad and children think so too, could this be because children have internalised their risky and at risk status? What is the impact on children themselves of societal denigration of children and childhood?

References

Alexander, R. and Hargreaves, L. (2007) *Community Soundings. Primary Review Briefings*, Cambridge, University of Cambridge.

Bradshaw, J. (2007) 'Some problems in the international comparison of child income poverty', in Wintersberger, H., Alanen, L., Olk, T. and Qvortrup, J. (eds) *Childhood, Generational Order and the Welfare State: Exploring Children's Social and Economic Welfare*, Odense, University Press of Southern Denmark.

Fattore, T., Mason, J. and Watson, E. (2007) 'Children's conceptualisation(s) of their well-being', *Social Indicators Research*, vol. 80, pp. 5–29.

Mayall, B. (2002) *Towards a Sociology for Childhood. Thinking from Children's Lives*, London, Open University Press.

Morrow, V. (1998) *Understanding Families: Children's Perspective*, London, National Children's Bureau/Joseph Rowntree Foundation.

Morrow, V. (2000) '"Dirty looks" and "trampy places" in young people's accounts of community and neighbourhood: implications for health inequalities', *Critical Public Health*, vol. 10, no. 2, pp. 141–52.

Sixsmith, J., Nic Gabhainn, S., Fleming, C. and O'Higgins, S. (2007) 'Children's, parents' and teachers' perceptions of child wellbeing', *Health Education,* vol. 107, no. 6, pp. 511–23.

UNICEF (2007) *Child Poverty in Perspective: An Overview of Child Well-Being in Rich Countries,* Innocenti Report Card, vol. 7, Florence, Italy, UNICEF Innocenti Research Centre.

Chapter 6

Research on childhood issues as social problems

Martyn Hammersley

Contents

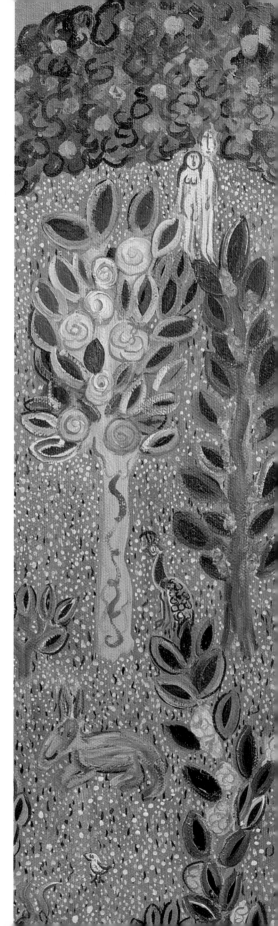

In this chapter, you will:

- consider the socio-political processes involved in some childhood issues becoming recognised as social problems that require policy intervention

- examine the complexities involved in identifying and diagnosing problems like poverty, ill-health and violence as they affect children and young people

- reflect on how social research can contribute to, or become implicated in, the identification of childhood problems and the development of policies to deal with them

- examine some of the considerations that must be taken into account in evaluating research findings, and their implications for the construction of social problems and policy interventions

- explore the arguments surrounding the distinctions between research 'on', 'with' and 'by' children.

1 Introduction

Much social research concerned with the lives of children and young people addresses topics that are widely taken to be major social problems, such as poverty, violence and ill-health. Furthermore, most researchers hope that, in studying such topics, their work will lead to practical interventions that improve children's lives. However, the relationship between research, social problems, policymaking and practice is not a simple one. What is, and what is not, treated as a high priority social problem depends on social, cultural and political processes in which research can play a variety of roles. Much the same is true about the development of policies to deal with such problems. Moreover, in this context we can ask fundamental questions about the function and character of research. For example, does it provide 'objective facts' about social problems, or should it be aimed at 'giving voice' to those affected by these problems? This opens up the issue of what the relationship should be between researcher and researched: is it justified to do research 'on' people or should researchers always carry out research 'with' them? Indeed, should the aim be to enable people, including children, to do research on their own lives? And should the aim of research be limited to producing knowledge, or is the goal to bring about change of some kind? In this chapter we will examine these issues.

2 The social construction of childhood problems

We all tend, much of the time, to accept current definitions of social problems as given, moving straight to thinking about who is to blame or who is responsible, and what should be done. Yet, doing this, we are likely to overlook the complex processes that determine whether, and how, particular social issues come to be publicly formulated as problems requiring remedy. We will also tend to neglect the assumptions built into these processes regarding what is good and bad, what is of greater and lesser importance, what causes what, what is and is not remediable, who can be blamed or held responsible for what, and so on. In short, we need to give attention to 'the social construction of social problems' (Holstein and Miller, 1993). Moreover, as we shall see, research can play an important role in this process.

Earlier chapters, especially Chapter 1, have shown that political processes are involved in how problems become public issues, and come to be formulated in particular ways. While events – such as a dramatic case of child cruelty or neglect, a famine, a war, an unusual accident, or even the publication of research findings – may trigger attention, it is politicians, interest groups, charities, government agencies, the mass media and others who play the key role in publicising and perhaps also dramatising problems. They frame issues as social problems requiring action, identify causes, allocate blame and responsibility, and propose remedies. In doing this they often appeal to research findings to establish the validity of their arguments.

So, in thinking about social problems relating to children and young people, policy interventions directed at these, and the role of research, we need to consider, continually, how each issue got defined as a problem, and how it came to be framed the way that it is. Moreover, we need to be aware of our own inclinations to see some issues as problems while treating others as of lesser importance. These inclinations will have been shaped by currents of opinion within the society and the local communities to which we belong, and within the various other cultural groupings in which we participate.

If we look at the history of minority-world societies over the past 200 years we will, of course, find a considerable range of childhood issues that have been treated as social problems requiring policy intervention. Many of these, such as 'childhood poverty' and 'youth violence', are perennial ones, recurrently on the public agenda, moving up and down in the priority they are given at different times. Other problems disappear off the policy agenda for one reason or another, for example because a particular practice has been largely abandoned (such as sending children up chimneys to clean them). Equally important new problems also emerge, often associated with emergent technologies. For instance, when television became commonplace in homes in minority-world societies many argued that it had damaging effects on children, not least in diverting them from healthier and better activities, such as active hobbies or outdoor games. Much later, similar claims arose with the arrival of home computers, video games and mobile phones – all were seen as having damaging effects on children's health, moral values, social lives, education or general well-being.

Earlier chapters have also provided some sense of the varying ways in which 'the same' problem has been viewed at different times within the same society, and of cross-cultural variation in what is treated as a problem. Such comparisons provide perspective on what we take to be social problems associated with children and young people in our own societies today.

Activity 1   Childhood poverty as a social problem
Allow about 20 minutes

Poverty – and especially its effects on children – is a social problem that continually reappears in one form or another on the public agenda in the UK, and one that is recognised across many societies. However, there are significantly different ways of thinking about its character and causes, and about remedies for it.

- Read through the first section of Chapter 2 again (the part that deals with the definition of 'poverty'), using your notes as a guide. There are two main approaches to this discussed there – one focusing on 'absolute', the other on 'relative', poverty. What would you say are the key assumptions underlying each of these?

- Now look back at Chapter 1. How would child poverty be defined by the three ideologies discussed there?

Comment

Assumptions underpinning the notion of absolute poverty probably include: that the physical survival of any human being is a good thing in itself; that all children have a right to life; and/or that children are essential for the continuance of human communities.

Another set of assumptions concerns the minimal levels of food, water, shelter, care, etc. that are required for the physical survival or health of children. There is scope for variation in judgement here, and this is perhaps even more true if we think in terms of well-being rather than poverty, as Chapter 5 makes clear. In fact, even attempts to specify an absolute poverty threshold almost always come to be influenced by ideas about what is an acceptable quality of life and what are the requirements for children to achieve this.

The idea of 'relative poverty' is concerned with what would be a minimum level of resources required to participate as a member in the society concerned. Clearly, one set of assumptions involved here is about what counts as being able to participate and what resources are needed for this. There is also a background assumption that all members of a society, and perhaps especially children, have a *right* to participate in their own society. In addition, there could be issues about who does and does not 'belong' to, or in, a society.

In Chapter 1 we saw that there was considerable concern, on the part of philanthropists and others, about child poverty among the working class in the new urban areas created by the Industrial Revolution. Several rather different ideological positions seem to have played a role in this. From some religious viewpoints, child poverty exposed children to upbringings that would lead them into a life of sin. A more secular version of this theme derived from Romantic ideas about the need for children to be insulated from the adult world. From this perspective, it was believed that many working-class children were being deprived of a childhood. There were also many commentators who were concerned that what Friedrich Engels (1845) called 'the condition of the working class in England' would lead to revolts of the kind that had happened on the European continent. In all these cases, poverty was not being viewed primarily, or at least not solely, in terms of lack of material resources, but in broader terms that related to particular ideas about what is a good life for children, and what the consequences were likely to be if the conditions for this were not met.

A rather different conception of the good life was associated with the notion of relative poverty, this time very much defined in material terms, as regards what standard of living is expected in a society and also what resources are required for people to grow up in a manner that enables them to fulfil their role as citizens. This notion depended upon the welfarist perspective that emerged in the twentieth century.

Finally, under the heading of 'children's rights', poverty seems to be defined as an absence of the resources required for children to flourish, and/or as a denial of rights to children that are commonly assigned to adults. There is some overlap with the previous notions, but a slightly different emphasis – in particular these are seen as *universal* rights rather than being tied to membership of a particular political community. Once again, there are assumptions involved here about what is a good life for a child, and for an adult, perhaps with a particular emphasis on the importance of autonomy or freedom. Of course, these can vary across societies, as well as within them, with the result that there can be clashes between attempts to promote universal rights for children and local cultures.

Built into how social problems are constructed are ideas about how they have arisen, who is to blame and what should be done. In Chapter 1, philanthropists, concerned with 'saving' working-class children, tended to see parents as being to blame for their children's poverty, and for the moral danger they faced as a result. As Shurlee Swain argues in Reading A of Chapter 1, a key focus was on the absence of parents, or their deleterious effects on their children, so that the children tended to be viewed as orphans, as for example in the archetype of Oliver Twist. Here, the remedy proposed was to take children away from their parents and to bring them up in institutions where they would be properly socialised.

However, there were other nineteenth-century commentators who gave more attention to the social causes of the impoverished conditions in which working-class families lived; though they had different views about these causes, and about what should be done. There were those who looked back to pre-industrial types of community and work, and proposed to re-establish these to overcome what they saw as the dehumanising conditions of modern factories and urban living conditions. Others identified the problem of poverty as a direct product of a capitalist system in which economic power was concentrated in the hands of a few – and served profit rather than human need – whose overthrow could lead to a new, better kind of society. For them, what was required was political action to transform the current patterns of economic and social organisation into one that 'serves need rather than profit'. There were also less radical, and often more influential, positions. For example, welfarist views in Britain in the first half of the twentieth century treated capitalism as essential for generating wealth but also insisted that its operation must be controlled, and its unacceptable side effects remedied, through state intervention. In some versions, the focus shifted from poverty defined in relative terms to inequality, with arguments, as we saw in Chapter 2, to the effect that a high level of inequality generates a wide range of problems within societies, from high levels of infant mortality to a lower average level of school achievement.

The case of poverty is by no means unique in being open to different definitions, ideas about its causes and proposed remedies. We saw in Chapter 4 that while everyone would probably regard violence as a problem, what counts as violence in particular situations is by no means simple or uncontroversial, nor is who is to blame for it. Similar problems surround issues like child abuse and bullying. While perhaps less obviously problematic, there are also uncertainties about what counts as health and illness, as outlined in Chapter 3. One of the central issues I want to address in this chapter concerns the role that research can play in constructing social problems, explaining them and evaluating remedies.

> ## Summary of Section 2
>
> Childhood issues come to be recognised as social problems requiring policy interventions through socio-political processes.
>
> This social construction of social problems involves assumptions of various kinds and part of the task of research is to address these.
>
> Different ideological perspectives lead to very different understandings of 'the same' problem.

3 The role of research

Research sometimes triggers concern for a problem, or shapes how it is formulated. For example, in Britain the public and political attention given to poverty in the 1970s derived to a significant extent from research on this topic, notably that carried out by Peter Townsend (1971, 1979). Immediately prior to this it had been widely believed that the problem of poverty had been solved by the welfare state and by the general economic prosperity of the late 1950s and early 1960s. Townsend formulated the distinction between absolute and relative poverty, and documented the surprising extent of the problem in the UK, at a time when many commentators were more focused on the problems of what they called 'the affluent society' (Galbraith, 1958). Here, then, we have a case of research playing a key role in moving an issue up the public policy agenda, and at the same time reshaping the way it is understood.

In many societies in the 1990s it came to be widely argued that policy and practice in the public sector – whether in relation to health, education or other fields – should be 'evidence-based'. In other words, that it should be guided by research evidence about which interventions are and are not effective. Such ideas became particularly influential in relation to the treatment of children and young people in schools, and in the context of social work interventions. There was also pressure on researchers to adopt a rather narrow focus on identifying 'what works'.

However, there are important questions to be addressed about researchers' orientations towards how their work might shape policymaking and practice. Is the sole task of the researcher to produce knowledge which documents the existence and scale of a problem, the conditions that lead to it or to any reaction against it, and the effects of interventions; and then to make this knowledge publicly available and perhaps correct any misinterpretations? Or should researchers go beyond this to present views about what are more and less serious problems, how they should be framed, who is responsible for them, and what should be done? Do researchers also have a responsibility to work with policymakers or practitioners so as to ensure social scientific knowledge is used effectively, and for desirable purposes (Gewirtz and Cribb, 2006)?

There has long been considerable variation in attitudes among social researchers about what their role should be. While the general trend in recent decades has been towards adoption of a broader definition of their role, there remain those who oppose this, on the grounds that this tends to increase the danger of biased conclusions and to lead to misuse of the authority of research for political purposes (Hammersley, 2008). So, there is considerable disagreement about the function of social research, and about what is required of researchers if their work is to be of practical value.

It is important to recognise in this context that there are different types of social research. Some researchers work in universities where still, albeit to a decreasing extent, they can identify research topics, seek funds to investigate them, and publish findings in a relatively autonomous fashion. Others work for particular agencies – governments, political parties or interest groups, commercial organisations, charities, etc. – where research topics are often effectively assigned, and researchers may be constrained in what methods they can use and in what results they can publish. In practice, rather different expectations will be placed upon researchers in these various contexts. And the relationship of their work to policymaking and practice will vary as well. We also need to recognise that the 'reception' of research findings by audiences, and their 'impact', is dependent upon the multiple ideologies and interests at stake, as well as contingent events such scandals, wars or elections.

Activity 2   The case of 'crack babies'
Allow about 45 minutes

Look back at your notes on the reading by Ortiz and Briggs on 'crack babies' in Chapter 1. Then answer the following questions:

- What was the problem of 'crack babies', as initially formulated?
- Who was involved in identifying and dramatising this social problem?
- What role did research play?
- What evidence do Ortiz and Briggs use in challenging the idea that this was a significant social problem?

Comment

Here are my responses, adding in some additional information from beyond the reading in a couple of places:

'Crack' is a solid, smokable form of cocaine that came to be widely used illegally in the United States and elsewhere from the early 1980s onwards. In the last few years of that decade, the fact that some impoverished African American women were smoking crack during pregnancy became a major social issue. It was claimed that crack had a range of damaging effects on babies, from premature birth, through death in the first few months, to physical defects, retarded intellectual development and behavioural problems.

The key people involved in the construction of this as a social problem, according to Ortiz and Briggs, were the media, commentators belonging to neo-conservative think-tanks, and right-wing politicians; though they note that a much wider range of influential people expressed concern, including liberal African American commentators. They also suggest that medical researchers and others 'jumped on the crack babies bandwagon' (p. 41).

Official statistics about increasing usage of crack amongst mothers, and about rising infant mortality, certainly played a role. It is also the case that early medical research on the topic, as well as doctors' assessments, suggested that cocaine caused damage to babies.

For evidence, Ortiz and Briggs appeal to the corrections that were made to the relevant official statistics, which suggested that there had, in fact, been no significant increase either in usage of crack or in infant mortality. However, their main source of evidence is the medical study by Frank et al. (2001) on the effects of prenatal exposure to cocaine on babies.

It is worth looking carefully at this evidence by Deborah Frank and her colleagues. We might ask: 'Why do Ortiz and Briggs believe, and why should we believe, that the findings of this study are correct, by contrast with those of earlier studies, many of which had suggested that smoking crack during pregnancy was dangerous?' In fact, Frank et al. were not the first to argue that this early claim was not reliable; after initial findings suggesting a link with infant mortality and birth defects, medical researchers increasingly raised doubts about it.

Frank et al.'s article was published in the *Journal of the American Medical Association* in 2001, and the authors are described as belonging to the School of Medicine and the School of Public Health at Boston University. For those of us who are not medical researchers, and are not fully competent to assess their research, this is important information: the article will have been peer reviewed, and furthermore we can assume that positions in schools of medicine and public health are not given to people who have no relevant expertise. At the same time, we must remember that what was involved initially was a dispute *within* medical research: those who produced the early research which suggested that crack had damaging effects probably also worked in medical schools and had their work published in refereed journals. So, while looking at authors' credentials may help, it does not resolve the problem; we have to make the best assessment we can of their arguments and the evidence they offer.

Frank and her colleagues describe their article as a 'systematic review'. What this means is that it is not a product of new research but rather a synthesis of previous studies. They attempt to determine what reasonable conclusions can be drawn from all of the currently available relevant research on the topic. Other things being equal, the findings of a systematic review should be more reliable than those of any single study.

A key feature of this particular type of review is that an exhaustive search is carried out for relevant articles, and these are then subjected to an explicit selection process to try to ensure that the information they provide is reliable.

The criteria that Frank and her colleagues used in selecting studies for inclusion were the following:

- The reports must be published in a peer-reviewed English-language journal.

- The research must have included a comparison group.

- The researchers must have recruited samples prospectively in the perinatal period (i.e. in the time immediately before or after birth).

- Masked assessment must have been used; in other words those carrying out the assessment should not have been aware of the hypothesis being tested.

- The study must not have included a substantial proportion of babies exposed *in utero* to opiates, amphetamines, phencyclidine or maternal human immunodeficiency virus (HIV) infection.

The authors reported that these criteria had two purposes. The first four are designed to ensure that the level of likely validity of the findings is above an acceptable threshold. The final criterion was intended to eliminate studies where severe confounding variables were present, in other words factors which might obscure any effect of cocaine or might give the false appearance of an effect when none exists, such as smoking and excessive use of alcohol.

Frank et al. were interested in determining the effect of prenatal cocaine exposure on a *range* of outcome variables: physical growth of babies, cognitive development, language skills, motor skills, behaviour, attention and emotion. They report that they found 74 research reports on the topic of prenatal exposure to cocaine, but that only 36 met the criteria they had laid down. They then synthesised the findings from these by comparing studies that provided information about each outcome variable they were interested in, trying to take account of how effectively potentially confounding variables (such as use of other drugs) had been controlled, and how well the variables had been measured.

Their main conclusion is that studies which reported damaging effects of prenatal cocaine exposure did not control for other factors likely to cause such effects, notably alcohol and marijuana use. By contrast, studies that *had* controlled for these factors generally reported no effect. We should note, though, that Frank et al. report their findings in a rather more cautious fashion than did Ortiz and Briggs. Where the latter declare that 'Crack has very little, if any, effect on pregnancies or fetuses' (p. 40) and that 'crack was a correlate, not a cause' (p. 41), Frank et al. write that 'there is no convincing evidence that prenatal cocaine exposure is associated with developmental toxic effects that are different in severity, scope, or kind from the sequelae of multiple other risk factors' (Frank et al., 2001, p. 1613).

In terms of broad methodological philosophy this systematic review, and the various studies on which it draws, fall into the category of what is frequently called positivist research. It is modelled on natural science, and is concerned with testing a hypothesis about a causal relationship through measuring and controlling relevant variables. As we saw, Frank et al. were especially concerned to ensure that confounding variables were controlled: this is a major issue in investigations of this kind. Not surprisingly, none of the studies the authors reviewed employed experimental method; in other words, none of them randomly assigned pregnant women to treatment and control groups, administered cocaine to those in the treatment group, and then compared the children of mothers in the two groups for damaging effects! Instead, the studies relied upon comparative method: comparing samples of babies who had and had not been exposed to cocaine, trying to ensure as far as possible that they were similar on all other relevant variables. It is important to recognise, however, that there are often serious obstacles to ensuring similarity. Much depends upon the accuracy of judgements about what would be relevant variables having an effect on the outcome (if some are omitted then the results may be misleading), whether these can be measured accurately, and whether sufficient cases can be found to serve as a control group for each of the potentially confounding variables. Since these requirements can be very difficult to achieve, results will always be subject to potential error. This partly explains why medical research on this and other topics frequently produces conflicting findings.

We also need to remember that there may be problems in measuring the wide range of outcome or effect variables with which Frank et al. were concerned. For example, variation in the physical growth of babies is probably relatively easy to measure, whereas differences in cognitive development, and (even more) in 'affective expression' or in the 'normality' of children's behaviour at school, etc., are much more difficult to assess accurately. There is also the question of how long-lasting any effects might be, and whether some of them may only appear after a delay. This might suggest the need for longitudinal studies that follow children over a period of several years, monitoring key areas of development, along the lines of the study by Werner and Smith in Hawaii, mentioned in Chapter 5 (Werner and Smith, 1982).

Summary of Section 3

There are different views about the role that research should play in relation to policymaking and practice.

In looking at research findings we need to give careful attention to how they were produced, and the implications of this for their likely validity.

There will always be some threats to validity that need to be assessed.

4 Explaining a moral panic

The research that we examined in the previous section was medical, though it was clearly very closely related to what became a social issue. Most social research is concerned with describing and explaining social processes of one kind or another, and indeed sometimes the processes through which a social problem comes to be framed and policies developed to deal with it, as in the case of Ortiz and Briggs's reading. Here, too, we need to pay close attention to the nature of the research and the evidence on which it is based.

Activity 3   Evaluating an explanation

Allow about 20 minutes

Briefly answer the following questions:

- What explanation do Ortiz and Briggs offer for why the use of crack cocaine during pregnancy by some African American mothers became identified as a major social problem?
- What evidence do they provide in support of their explanation?
- Is their article a product of research, and if so of what kind?

Comment

Ortiz and Briggs argue that the whole formulation of the problem of 'crack babies' was spurious. The explanation they present is that the idea that poor African American women were damaging their babies by taking crack fitted influential ideological discourses, particularly those associated with neoconservatism. Such views claim that poverty is caused by the behaviour or personal characteristics of the poor themselves, rather than being a product of socio-economic conditions. The authors argue that the symbol of the crack baby also fed into racial ideologies, so that even though at the time the typical user of crack cocaine was a young white male, the focus of the moral panic was upon use of this drug by lower-class African American women.

Ortiz and Briggs go on to claim that this set of ideological discourses, and their role in constructing 'crack babies' as a social problem, served political functions. They report that it 'explained away a multitude of things caused by Reagan-era economic policies, such as homelessness and increasing infant mortality rates, especially among African Americans' (pp. 42–3). They also argue that it distracted attention from the economic factors that caused lower-class African Americans to be involved in the drug trade, and obscured the failure of government policies in this area as well.

Having established that there is little evidence that mothers taking crack cocaine during pregnancy has a major effect on their babies, Ortiz and Briggs argue that the genuine problems these mothers and their children have arise from the fact that they are poor and subject to discrimination. While the authors do not cite much evidence to support this claim, there is a large body of work that reveals deep levels of poverty amongst some African American urban communities in the United States, and its effects, along with the role of racial discrimination in this. Ortiz and Briggs also do not offer much evidence about the prevalence of the discourses they identify as underpinning the moral panic that surrounded 'crack babies', though they do refer to a book by Humphries (1999) which contains evidence about this.

Ortiz and Briggs's work is qualitative in character, offering an interpretation of how 'crack babies' came to be seen as a major social problem. The reading by them in this book is an extract from an article that was originally published in the journal *Social Text*, and in trying to get a more detailed sense of the character of their work it is useful to look at a description of this journal. The following information is provided by Duke University Press:

> *Social Text* covers a broad spectrum of social and cultural phenomena, applying the latest interpretive methods to the world at large. A daring and controversial leader in the field of cultural studies, the journal consistently focuses attention on questions of gender, sexuality, race, and the environment, publishing key works by the most influential social and cultural theorists. As a journal at the forefront of cultural theory, *Social Text* seeks provocative interviews and challenging articles from

emerging critical voices. Each issue breaks new ground in the debates about postcolonialism, postmodernism, and popular culture.

(Duke University Press Online, 2012)

Further research on the internet reveals that this journal was involved in a controversy a few years ago, often referred to as the Sokal hoax. A physics professor, Alan Sokal, submitted an article to test whether influential journals in cultural studies would 'publish an article liberally salted with nonsense if (a) it sounded good and (b) it flattered the editors' ideological preconceptions' (Sokal, 1996, p. 62). The article was published, and Sokal announced the hoax on the day of its publication.

This controversy took place at the height of intellectual debates about the effects of 'postmodernism' on the humanities and the social sciences. This label refers to an influential set of ideas that were developed in France in the 1960s and 1970s. These raised questions about modernist assumptions influential in the minority world since the time of the Enlightenment, relating to the intellectual authority of science, the prospects for social and political progress, and the universal validity of minority-world ideals. 'Postmodernism' contributed to what was referred to as 'the science wars' in the 1980s and early 1990s in the United States, and Sokal's hoax was a central part of this (see Ross, 1996). To some extent, what was involved here was infighting between different disciplines: Sokal demonstrated that the editors and referees of the journal had not properly scrutinised the validity of the claims derived from physics in his article. However, he and others used the hoax as a basis for more general criticisms of work in cultural studies, to the effect that the theoretical ideas deployed in this journal and other similar ones are 'nonsense', even though the hoax did not demonstrate this.

Putting this scandal aside, what we can infer from the publication of Ortiz and Briggs's article in *Social Text* is that they were writing from a cultural studies perspective. While there are disputes about whether or not this approach adopts a scientific orientation (and about what this means), we can certainly take their article to be a product of research. At the same time, the *kind* of research involved is clearly very different in character from the work of Franks and her colleagues (and from the studies that they synthesised). There is no sign, for example, of Ortiz and Briggs engaging in a systematic synthesis of evidence about the moral panic they describe. Their orientation is, in some respects, closer to that of intellectual traditions in humanities, or even journalism, than it is to medical research; and much the same can be said of a great deal of qualitative work in social science generally. However, this does not mean that we cannot assess the likely validity of the claims made, for example, by examining how well supported by evidence they seem to be.

Let us look briefly at the likely validity of Ortiz and Briggs's claim that there was a moral panic over 'crack babies'. To start with we need to understand the nature of this claim. 'Moral panic' is a widely used concept, and a series of moral panics have been identified relating to children and young people (Krinsky, 2008; Goode and Ben-Yehuda, 2009). However, it is by no means unproblematic (Waddington, 1986). So what exactly does the term mean? 'Panic' here refers to an overreaction to some issue on the part of the mass media, politicians and the general public. Use of this term, then, immediately implies a judgement by the commentator that the problem concerned was much less serious than claimed, or might even be entirely spurious. As we saw, this was certainly the view of Ortiz and Briggs. The word 'moral' in this context is intended to indicate that the societal reaction was moralistic. Thus, a *moral* panic identifies some category of person or group of people as disreputable, blameworthy, etc. Indeed, often, as in the case we are considering here, the people at the centre of a moral panic are presented as symbolising what is wrong with a whole society, and may thereby come to be blamed for many of its ills. Implicit in usage of the term 'moral panic', then, is criticism of the process by which some issue has come to be treated as a major social problem, the assumptions underlying this, and the way some group has been singled out for criticism and blame.

In this respect, we can see that in their work Ortiz and Briggs aim to play a role in the reconstruction of 'crack babies' as a social problem, in effect redefining it as a problem resulting from poverty that is caused by social conditions and government policies. Or, equally, we might see them as characterising the real problem as an ideological intervention by powerful forces within US society, one which had damaging consequences for the mothers and children concerned, in that some of the children were taken away to be placed with 'better' parents. Thus, the authors are adopting quite a broad definition of the role of the researcher, in terms of the dimension or contrast introduced earlier, one which goes beyond simply providing factual information.

While the account provided by Ortiz and Briggs is convincing in many respects, there are questions that can be asked about it. For example, we saw that they turned Frank et al.'s finding of 'no convincing evidence of effects greater than other risk factors' into the conclusion that smoking crack during pregnancy has no damaging consequences. And, from a common-sense point of view, we might reasonably suspect that if alcohol and tobacco can have damaging effects in pregnancy, then so too can smoking crack cocaine. On this basis it might be suggested that there were, and perhaps still are, at least some grounds for concern about the exposure of babies to cocaine; in other words, that the problem is not *entirely* spurious. Also, while Ortiz and Briggs use the fact that cocaine has no damaging effects to support the claim that what was involved here was a panic, we must remember that initial medical opinion and research *had* suggested that crack had damaging effects. For this reason, there were even more grounds for people *at the time* than there are now to think that there was a genuine problem, thereby explaining why it was given such attention by the media, commentators, politicians and others. It is important to point out, however, that this does *not* mean that the factors that Ortiz and Briggs identified played no role. Indeed, we might still reasonably judge that the societal response to the problem was an exaggerated one, and those factors may well explain why this was the case. Furthermore, the authors' reference to researchers 'jumping on the bandwagon' makes the important point that researchers are not immune to the effects of moral panics. The general point, though, is that what is involved in the construction of social problems is not usually a simple contrast between the genuine and the spurious, but rather a dimension of judgement about the relative seriousness and significance of a problem, with scope for considerable disagreement about these matters.

It is also worth pointing out that, in explaining the overreaction to the problem that took place, we are faced, at least in some respects, with a similar sort of analytical problem to that of medical researchers seeking to find out whether cocaine damages babies. In both cases we are concerned with what caused what: was the outcome (moral panic/ perinatal mortality) the result of this factor (neoconservative ideology/ exposure to cocaine) or of something else? Yet it is striking that, while Ortiz and Briggs rely upon Frank et al.'s carefully documented attempt – on the basis of multiple previous studies and taking account of confounding factors – to come to sound causal conclusions, they do not employ the same sort of approach in putting forward their own conclusions about why the moral panic occurred. On the contrary, the way they write seems to imply that identifying the factors involved in generating this moral panic is a matter of observing what happened and having the appropriate theoretical framework to make sense of it. Yet, it could be argued that, in fact, it is at least as difficult to determine what causes a social phenomenon like a moral panic as it is to determine what causes variations in the level of perinatal mortality, and that candidate explanations are even *more* open to reasonable disagreement than in the case of determining any effects of cocaine on babies.

Ortiz and Briggs would probably argue that while the method that Frank and her colleagues used was appropriate in studying the physical effects of cocaine, it is not appropriate in studying social processes. Indeed, they might well deny that causal processes are involved in this case, at least of the kind that operate on physical phenomena. Many qualitative researchers would agree with them, and this is one of the fundamental theoretical and methodological disagreements to be found within social science today. Earlier, I described the approach of Frank et al. as 'positivist', a label that has acquired a strong negative connotation in most parts of social science, but one that is not too misleading if we treat it simply as a label for an approach concerned with testing hypotheses through measuring and controlling variables. It is harder to characterise Ortiz and Briggs's position, since there is not one single anti-positivist orientation amongst social scientists, but many. We mentioned one possible label, 'postmodernism', earlier, but this is just as controversial and even less specific in meaning than 'positivism'. Perhaps the best we can do here is to say that the authors aimed to provide a convincing cultural interpretation of the events they describe. Indeed, in the article from which the reading comes they treat this case, along with two others, as a means of diagnosing the ideological forces that have operated, and that still operate, in US society; forces to which they are, of course, themselves strongly opposed.

As I have already suggested, such cultural interpretations are, by their nature, rather more likely to be questioned and rejected than conclusions about the physical effects of crack, especially by those who do not share the same political position. For example, if we were to ask neoconservative commentators about why they thought that 'crack babies' were a serious problem, they would no doubt offer a rather different account from Ortiz and Briggs. They might even insist that it *was* a genuine problem, perhaps even refusing to accept the conclusions of Frank et al. This would indicate not just the power of their ideological convictions, but also the fact that even the kind of careful causal analysis in which Frank et al. engage is open to a sceptical response. There is always some scope for questioning the validity of scientific findings. Moreover, in the political processes surrounding the social construction of social problems this will often be exploited to the full, or be taken to quite unreasonable lengths, in order to advance or protect particular political positions.

In short, the fact that research of all kinds never produces conclusions whose validity is *absolutely certain* means that there is always room for those on different sides of an argument to deploy scepticism. Of course, this is generally done selectively, with commentators challenging the evidence that does not fit their own preconceptions and prejudices, while adopting a more lax methodological standard when it comes to those claims with which they agree. Researchers themselves are not immune from these tendencies.

In this section, and the previous one, we have examined how research findings, of various kinds, can be involved in the processes by which some issues come to be identified and treated as social problems, and also in subsequent revisionist accounts of the nature and extent of the problem. What also became clear is that the effects of research findings on public opinion and policymaking are likely to be highly mediated, being simplified and perhaps even distorted in the process. Up to now, though, we have been concerned with how the publication of research findings might influence these processes. Yet research also has effects on the social world through the ways in which it is carried out, and researchers take different views about what the proper relationship should be between researcher and researched.

Summary of Section 4

Research relevant to childhood issues as social problems can take a variety of forms, and we need to take account of this when we assess its findings.

When claims are made about 'moral panics' we need to recognise that these imply an overreaction to a problem, or even that the problem is spurious, and so we need to pay close attention to the evidence that is taken to support this interpretation.

We must also look at the evidence offered in support of the explanation for why the moral panic occurred.

Research findings are fallible, and are therefore open to divergent interpretations, especially by those who are committed to particular political positions.

5 Relations between researcher and researched

The research that we have mentioned or discussed up to now in this chapter – that by Townsend, Ortiz and Briggs, and Frank et al. – was primarily concerned with documenting facts about the world: about the extent and causes of poverty, whether cocaine use by pregnant women damages their babies, or why the moral panic about this issue arose and what its consequences were. In effect, in carrying out their work these researchers treated the people they were studying, including the children, as *objects* of investigation. It is striking, for example, that in neither of the articles on 'crack babies' (that of Ortiz and Briggs or that by Frank et al.) do we hear the voices of the children whose development might have been affected, or even those of their mothers.

Over the past decade or so, there have been increasing calls for research dealing with childhood issues to be carried out *with* children, rather than *on* them; or indeed to be carried out *by* children (Alderson, 2000; Woodhead and Faulkner, 2000; Kellett, 2010). A number of arguments have been used to support this. Some of these are methodological, to do with the likely validity of the knowledge produced by these different approaches. Others are ethical or political in character, being concerned with how children ought to be treated by researchers and what the aim of research should be.

One methodological argument insists that only by researching *with* children, or through their carrying out research themselves, will genuine understanding of their lives be produced. For example, Kellett (2005, p. 4) claims that 'children are party to the subculture of childhood which gives them a unique "insider" perspective that is critical to our understanding of children's worlds'. Advocates of this position point out that there is a tendency for researchers, as there is for policymakers and many others dealing with children, to assume that they already know what is wrong with children's lives, and what needs to be done. Yet, sometimes, those seen as the victims of a problem do not view their situation in the way generally assumed. Indeed, in the case of adults seeking to interpret the perspectives of children, there are clearly significant barriers that can distort understanding, deriving from developmental differences, the distinctive locations that children occupy in societies, and/or the peer cultures they develop.

There is a range of ways in which the experience and views of children can be accessed and included in the research process (see Clark, 2005). An obvious one is to interview them, and a great deal of research with children has involved this. Another approach is ethnographic studies that combine listening to what they say with participant observation in some of the settings that are central to their lives (see, for example, Corsaro, 2003). The history of work of these kinds predates the methodological arguments about researching 'on or with'; furthermore, it may still be criticised as 'adult-led, adult-designed and conceived from an adult perspective' (Kellett, 2005, p. 4). The significance of this is that what children say in such interviews will be determined by their being interviewed by an adult, as well as by the particular sorts of question that adults are likely to ask. Thus, Thomson (2008) argues that:

> Being able to say what you think, in the ways that you want, is highly dependent on what you are asked, by whom, about what, and what is expected of you. ... Power relations of class, gender, race, ethnicity, dis-ability, sexuality and age all constrain social relations and may profoundly limit what can be said ...
>
> (Thomson, 2008, p. 6)

She recommends participatory inquiry to overcome these restrictions, thereby allowing much more scope for children to express their views. Other lines of argument underpinning the idea that research should be carried out 'with' or 'by' children are ethical or political in character, often appealing to their rights. This parallels similar arguments that have been put forward in relation to research on women, on people with disabilities and on indigenous communities (Zarb, 1992; Denzin et al., 2008). It is claimed that doing research *on* people infringes their autonomy, treats them as less than human, or at least as less knowledgeable than the researcher, and thereby simply reinforces the inequalities to which they are subjected.

There is some force in these methodological, ethical and political arguments, but there are also serious questions that can be raised about them. For example, is there a tendency here to exaggerate the degree to which researchers shape the data they produce? Who the researcher is, and what he or she asks, may shape but surely never completely determines what is said. It is also worth noting that this methodological argument seems to assume that the experiential world of children is completely separate and different from that of adults, and, perhaps even more importantly, that all children share much the same experiential world, irrespective of differences in cultural background, gender, or in the segments of a society from which they come (defined, for example, by social class or ethnicity). Once we take account of these other factors, it is no longer quite so obvious that children are best able to understand one another, interview one another or to report on what life is like for children generally.

Activity 4   A child's eye view?
Allow about 20 minutes

Look again at Reading A in Chapter 2, which was entitled 'A child's eye view of poverty'. Then answer the following questions:

- On what sorts of evidence does this article draw?
- Try to identify which decisions about the research were made by the researcher and which were made by the children.
- In broad terms, what are the differences between this evidence and that which Ortiz and Briggs relied upon in concluding that exposure to cocaine has no damaging effects on babies?

Comment

Sutton describes her research as 'participatory'. She reports that 'The aim was to enable children to have input into what issues to research and how best to research them. [Inquiry] therefore focused on exploring the topics that children themselves deemed important from their own perspectives' (Sutton, 2007, p. 9). Her research involved 42 children aged 8–13 from two contrasting socio-economic backgrounds in the UK. Within each socio-economic category, the children were allocated to groups of between four and six members on the basis of age and gender. Each group was asked what they thought was most important in their lives, constructing a list, and they were encouraged to engage in open discussion about these things, deciding for themselves how best to do this.

The researcher initiated this piece of research, decided on the overall design, including the selection of the children to be involved, and how they were to be allocated to groups. Nevertheless, beyond providing an initial stimulus, about what is most important in their lives, the children were allowed to carry out their discussions freely. It seems, however, that it was the researcher who transcribed and analysed the data, and who wrote the research report.

As we saw, Ortiz and Briggs relied upon Frank et al.'s review, which in turn depended upon studies producing primarily quantitative data about the physical condition, intellectual and emotional development, etc. of the children concerned. By contrast, Sutton aimed to access the subjective experience of children. She collects data from children's discussions for this purpose and employs qualitative analysis. In some respects her analysis is similar to that of Ortiz and Briggs, in that it is concerned with identifying key themes. At the same time, her attitude towards these themes is very different from the way Frank et al. treated the ideological discourses they identified. It is also worth noting that Sutton sets up her research in such a way as to allow a comparison between children from rather different socio-economic circumstances. There is, perhaps, a parallel here with the way in which Frank et al. seek to control for confounding variables in their work, although Sutton's research is, in other respects, very far in design and focus from the positivist model.

One of the ways in which the case for participatory research with children is often formulated is the argument that it is important to 'give voice' to children or to 'respect their voices' (see Fielding and Bragg, 2003). This parallels a similar emphasis in other areas where research is done on subordinated or marginalised groups, and also a broad trend in public sector organisations to take account of clients' perspectives on the services they use – of course, in many cases these clients will include children. There has also been increased attention to understanding the experiences and preferences of children in legal processes, and here too this may be formulated in terms of 'children's voice'. Furthermore, the right of children to be consulted about matters that concern them has been enshrined in the United Nations Convention on the Rights of the Child – Article 12 of which requires 'respect for the views of the child' – and in legislation based upon this in many countries (see Kellett, 2005, 2010).

It is worth giving some attention to the notion of voice that is involved here. One way of thinking about it is in terms of democracy, where a common principle is that everyone should have a 'say' about what is happening, and perhaps also that the views of everyone should count equally, as they do in voting. However, in the case of clients' voices being heard in public sector organisations, the model is a rather different one: that of the market. It is assumed that giving clients voice will encourage service providers to be responsive to them in the way that, it is assumed, private sector operators must be responsive to consumers if they are to build or retain their market share. Here, having a voice is treated as equivalent to expressing one's preferences through selecting from the goods available; though, in practice, what may be involved is a form of social control in which they are being socialised as 'consumers' (Bragg, 2007).

Whether interpreted in democratic or in market terms, there is a tendency to presuppose that the origin of each person's 'voice' lies within them and represents something genuine about them, while recognising that it may sometimes be distorted by external conditions. But serious questions can be raised about this idea. Rather than thinking of interviews with children as either allowing or preventing them expressing their genuine experiences and views, we might argue that (as with people generally) what they say on any particular occasion is always, in some sense, a response to what others have said or done. It is also usually designed for an audience, whether clearly identified or more general and vague. Furthermore, what is said will draw on a variety of discourses, or voices, that are available in the cultural settings in which children participate. Influential psychological theories, such as those of G. H. Mead and Lev Vygotsky, have emphasised that our 'internal' thought processes derive from the 'external' processes of social interaction in which we engage. Others have pointed out how, in speaking, children employ a variety of voices modelled on those of others (see Maybin, 2006).

So, what people say never comes from some inner, socioculturally untainted source. Nor can we assume that children's voices simply display their unique perceptions and feelings, or represent their best interests, or even express their preferences in an unmediated fashion. To think of genuineness of voice as requiring that what is said comes from some uniquely personal inner core that is untouched by the outside world is misleading. But this is not to suggest that what a child, or anyone else, says cannot be genuine. The point is that reaching this conclusion involves evaluation, which relies upon assumptions about what would, and would not, count as an autonomous judgement, and what would amount to distortion.

In the case of Sutton's work the aim was to involve the children in the research process in order to try to ensure that what they said would be as little influenced by the researcher and the research process as possible. However, as we saw, this was not an example of participatory research in the full sense, since the researcher played a major role in initiating and designing the research, as well as in processing and analysing the data. This is not uncommon in research that is given this label – other examples would include, for instance, a primary school head teacher engaging students in 'visual research' as part of their schooling (Johnson, 2008). But there are those who have argued that children can and should be involved in all aspects of the research process, including analysis and writing up (see, for example, Kellett, 2005, 2010; Nind, 2011).

Activity 5   Children as researchers?

Allow about 20 minutes

Think about the following issues:

- If adults plan and carry out research into childhood issues, will this distort the accounts that children present about their world?
- Do children have, or can they learn, the knowledge and skills required to carry out research?

Comment

It is certainly true that the personal and social characteristics of researchers shape the kinds of data produced and the analytic conclusions reached. Furthermore, there are clearly significant differences between adults and children in their perspectives on the world, which means that it may sometimes be difficult for adult researchers to engage with children in ways that generate productive data, and to understand their perspectives and practices. However, we must remember that, as noted earlier, age and generation are not the only social categories that will shape the research process, and that children and young people can differ from one another in many ways (gender, social class, ethnicity, etc.) that may involve barriers to relations and to understanding. At the same time, we should not assume that differences between researcher and researched are *always* barriers. Sometimes they can facilitate the research process, for example by leading to those being studied trying to explain what they would not need to explain to peers.

What is required for carrying out research varies somewhat, depending upon its character. Where its aim is to contribute to a body of academic knowledge, for example, children may find it impossible to read and understand the literature. What is required also varies across the different tasks involved in the research process. At one end of the spectrum, children may well be able to carry out audio-recorded interviews on the basis of relatively little training. They may also be able to participate, with adult researchers, in planning research and in doing analysis. It seems unlikely, however, that they could carry out a whole research project alone – or even be able to serve as the main decision maker – in an effective way, or analyse data in the manner required; even if much depends not just upon age but also relevant abilities. After all, many adults do not have the skills and knowledge necessary to carry out research.

It is important to note that, very often, the argument that children should be in control of research is associated with the idea that research projects must be designed to bring about change in children's circumstances. For example, Thomson argues that 'In working *with* [participants], researchers aim to transform not only the power relations embedded in their research, but also those in the context in which the research is being conducted' (Thomson, 2008, p. 7). Thus, she suggests that research *with* children *in schools* should have the following features. It must:

- address issues of importance to students and be in their collective interests;
- work with students' subjugated knowledges about the way in which the school works;
- allow marginalised perspectives and voices to come school centre-stage;
- use students' subjectivities and experiences to develop approaches, tools, representations and validities;
- interrupt the power relations in schools including, but not confined to, those which are age related; and
- be geared to making a difference.

(Adapted from Thomson and Gunter, 2007, p. 331)

In the terms outlined earlier, this involves a very broad conception of the role of the researcher (whether adult or child), and locates it within a particular political orientation – one that is geared to challenging 'power relations' and bringing about 'change'. As indicated earlier, not everyone agrees with this view about the proper task of research. A very sharply contrasting position is captured by the title of a book by Stanley Fish (2008) addressed to his colleagues in cultural studies: *Save the World on Your Own Time*. He insists that the task of academic work is not to pursue political goals, but to explore intellectual issues. However, even aside from this sort of fundamental disagreement, questions could be asked about the political perspective involved in advocating participatory research, as outlined by Thomson and Gunter: Is it true that all power relations should be challenged? Is bringing about just any 'difference' a worthwhile goal, and if not how do we decide what is and is not worthwhile? Are there even times when the status quo needs to be protected? There are implicit value assumptions involved in what is proposed by the authors, which require attention and justification.

Summary of Section 5

Research can affect the social world through how it is carried out as well as through the impact of its findings.

Some have argued – on methodological, ethical and political grounds – that research should not be carried out *on* children but only *with* and *by* them.

These arguments sometimes depend upon the notion of giving voice to children, but the concept of 'voice' is quite complex, and it is not easy to determine what would amount to 'genuine voice'.

Participatory research can take a variety of forms, with children playing different roles in the research process.

The viability and value of these kinds of research are a matter of debate.

---

6 Conclusion

In this chapter we have examined some of the issues surrounding the relationship between social research and the construction of childhood issues as social problems requiring intervention, and other issues concerned with the proper relations between researchers and researched.

It was noted that issues get on to the agenda of public discussion and policymaking through the activities of various agents, including interest groups of various kinds, politicians, commentators, journalists and others. Moreover, there are important, and often controversial, assumptions built into the way they get formulated as problems, ideas about their causes and what must be done about them. We examined the role that research can play in this process, focusing particularly on the case of the moral panic about 'crack babies' in the United States in the late 1980s. One point that came out from this is the highly mediated character of the role that research plays in the social construction of childhood problems; in other words, many other factors are always involved. Not only are other sources of ideas and evidence besides research usually deployed, but there is a host of organisations – from think tanks to lobbying groups – who publish what they claim are research findings and who are often very successful in getting these reported in the media, and in influencing policymakers.

It is also necessary to remember that research findings are almost always processed before they shape policymaking and practice; they are summarised and interpreted by various agents. In fact, there is even considerable mediation of this kind when we as readers are influenced by research findings. For example, the reading by Ortiz and Briggs included in this book is a section extracted from an article published in a cultural studies journal, the final version of which may have been shaped by comments from journal referees. Furthermore, this article cites a systematic review published in a medical journal, this review itself referring to a substantial number of research reports published in refereed journals in the health and psychology fields. In other words, the findings from each of those original research reports will have been filtered, assessed and interpreted several times over from different angles by the time you came to read the account of the findings provided by Ortiz and Briggs in this book.

Significant differences in how researchers define their task and go about their work were also noted, along with the fact that there is always scope for questioning the validity of any research findings, and for alternative interpretations of them. This interpretive leeway will often be exploited in the political processes associated with the social construction of childhood problems.

The final section of the chapter looked at different ideas about the proper relationship between researchers and those they research, especially in the case of children. We examined some of the arguments for doing research *with* rather than *on* them, and for children carrying out research themselves. To a large extent, these hinge on the notion of 'voice', but we found that this is more complex and uncertain than is sometimes recognised. We also noted that research that is given the label 'participatory' can vary considerably in what role children played within it. Finally, we raised some questions about the methodological, ethical and political rationales for this kind of research.

References

Alderson, P. (2000) 'Children as researchers: the effects of participation rights on research methodology', in Christensen, P. and James, A. (eds) *Research with Children: Perspectives and Practices*, London, Falmer.

Bragg, S. (2007) '"Student voice" and governmentality: the production of enterprising subjects?', *Discourse: Studies in the Cultural Politics of Education*, vol. 28, no. 3, pp. 343–58.

Clark, A. (2005) 'Listening to and involving young children: a review of research and practice', *Early Child Development and Care*, vol. 175, no. 6, pp. 489–505.

Corsaro, W. (2003) *We're Friends, Right?*, Washington, DC, Joseph Henry Press.

Denzin, N., Lincoln, Y. and Smith, L. T. (eds) (2008) *Handbook of Critical and Indigenous Methodologies*, Los Angeles, CA, Sage.

Duke University Press Online (2012) *Books and Journals by Title:* Social Text, http://www.dukeupress.edu/Catalog/ViewProduct.php?productid=45631 (Accessed 26 July 2012).

Engels, F. (1845) *The Condition of the Working Class in England in 1844*, Leipzig, Otto Wigand.

Fielding, M. and Bragg, S. (2003) *Students as Researchers: Making a Difference*, Cambridge, Pearson.

Fish, S. (2008) *Save the World on Your Own Time*, New York, Oxford University Press.

Frank, D. A., Augustyn, M., Knight, W. G., Pell, T. and Zuckerman, B. (2001) 'Growth, development, and behavior in early childhood following prenatal cocaine exposure: a systematic review', *Journal of the American Medical Association*, vol. 285, no. 12, pp. 1613–25.

Galbraith, J. K. (1958) *The Affluent Society*, Boston, MA, Houghton Mifflin Company.

Gewirtz, S. and Cribb, A. (2006) 'What to do about values in social research: the case for ethical reflexivity in the sociology of education', *British Journal of Sociology of Education*, vol. 27, no. 2, pp. 141–55.

Goode, E. and Ben-Yehuda, N. (2009) *Moral Panics: The Social Construction of Deviance*, 2nd edn, Oxford, Wiley-Blackwell.

Hammersley, M. (2008) 'Reflexivity for what? A response to Gewirtz and Cribb on the role of values in the sociology of education', *British Journal of Sociology of Education*, vol. 29, no. 5, pp. 549–58.

Holstein, J. and Miller, G. (eds) (1993) *Reconsidering Social Constructionism: Debates in Social Problems Theory*, New York, Aldine.

Humphries, D. (1999) *Crack Mothers: Pregnancy, Drugs and the Media*, Columbus, OH, Ohio State University Press.

Johnson, K. (2008) 'Teaching children to use visual research methods', in Thomson, P. (ed) *Doing Visual Research with Children and Young People*, London, Routledge.

Kellett, M. (2005) 'Children as active researchers: a new research paradigm for the 21st century?', *NCRM Methods Review Papers 3*, Southampton, ESRC National Centre for Research Methods.

Kellett, M. (2010) *Rethinking Children and Research: Attitudes in Contemporary Society*, London, Continuum.

Krinsky, C. (ed) (2008) *Moral Panics over Contemporary Children and Youth*, Farnham, Ashgate.

Maybin, J. (2006) *Children's Voices: Talk, Knowledge and Identity*, Basingstoke, Palgrave Macmillan.

Murdoch, L. (2006) *Imagined Orphans: Poor Families, Child Welfare, and Contested Citizenship in London*, New Brunswick, NJ, Rutgers University Press.

Nind, M. (2011) 'Participatory data analysis: a step too far?', *Qualitative Research*, vol. 11, no. 4, pp. 349–63.

Ross, A. (ed) (1996) *Science Wars*, Durham, NC, Duke University Press.

Sokal, A. (1996) 'A physicist experiments with cultural studies', *Lingua Franca*, May/June, pp. 62–4.

Sutton, L. (2007) 'A child's eye view', *Poverty*, vol. 126, pp. 8–11.

Thomson, P. (ed) (2008) *Doing Visual Research with Children and Young People*, London, Routledge.

Thomson P. and Gunter, H. (2007) 'The methodology of students-as-researchers: valuing and using experience and expertise to develop methods', *Discourse: Studies in the Cultural Politics of Education*, vol. 28, no. 3, pp. 327–42.

Townsend, P. (1971) *The Concept of Poverty: Working Papers on Methods of Investigation and Life-styles of the Poor in Different Countries*, London, Heinemann.

Townsend, P. (1979) *Poverty in the United Kingdom*, London, Allen Lane.

Waddington, P. (1986) 'Mugging as a moral panic: a question of proportion', *The British Journal of Sociology*, vol. 37, no. 2, pp. 245–59.

Werner, E. and Smith, R. (1982) *Vulnerable but Invincible*, New York, McGraw-Hill.

Woodhead, M. and Faulkner, D. (2000) 'Subjects, objects or participants? Dilemmas of psychological research with children', in Christensen, P. and James, A. (eds) *Research with Children: Perspectives and Practices*, London, Falmer.

Zarb, G. (1992) 'On the road to Damascus: first steps towards changing the relations of disability research production', *Disability, Handicap and Society*, vol. 7, no. 2, pp. 125–38.

Acknowledgements

Every effort has been made to contact copyright holders. If any have been inadvertently overlooked the publishers will be pleased to make the necessary arrangements at the first opportunity.

Grateful acknowledgement is made to the following sources:

Figures

Cover image: Little Girl with Roses, 2000 (oil on canvas), © Holzhandler, Dora (Contemporary Artist)/Private Collection/The Bridgeman Art Library ; page 5: © UNICEF/NYHQ2005-2124/Pirozzi Children play with cognitive-development toys at an early childhood development centre in the town of Kisantu, some 150 km east of Kinshasa, the capital. UNICEF provides the centre with furniture and supplies, toys and teacher training; page 7: © Fox Photos/Getty Images; page 14: Eglantyne Jebb (1876–1928) Founder of Save the Children Fund, Reproduced with kind permission from Save the Children; page 15: Two Starving Austrian Children, Reproduced with kind permission from Save the Children;page 19: © Popperfoto/Getty images; page 21: © Popperfoto/Getty Images; page 24: © International Labour Organization/M, Crozet; page 27: UN Photo; page 28: © UNICEF/INDA2009-00087/Khemka India, 2009; Note this image must be used in the following context Arfa Khatun (2nd from right in front row) and Sunita Mahato (1st on right in 2nd row), both 13 years old at the Bagandih special school under National Child Labor Project (NCLP), Purulia. Besides providing basic education, the NCLP runs a Child Activist Initiative in Purulia, which teach girls leadership qualities, problem solving skills, communication skills and about Child Rights. Bagandih Ward, JhaldaMunicipality, District Purulia, West Bengal; page 59: AFP/Getty Images;page 61: Christopher Furlong/Getty Images; page 63: Jeff J Mitchell/Getty Images; page 66: Courtesy of GreenPeace; page 68: © Young Lives/Sebastian Castañeda Vita, www.younglives.org.uk; page 72: © Heather Montgomery; page 74: © Photofusion Picture Library/Alamy; page 76: © SCPhotos/Alamy; page 78: © Rupert Rivett/Alamy; page 80: Max Trujillo/Stringer/Getty; page 106: World Health Statistics 2011, WHO; page 107: Image UNI2125: © UNICEF/NYHQ2007-2533/Bell In 2007 in Panama, an Embera girl smiles, in the remote indigenous community of Playon Chico in DariénProvince, on the border with

Colombia. The Embera, who are among Panama's seven indigenous groups, inhabit one of three largely autonomous 'comarcas' (provincial-level indigenous territories) established by the Government. Playon Chico is accessible only by boat or by helicopter. Darién is the country's largest and least-developed province; page 108: © UNICEF/NYHQ2005-2337/Mun An unassembled auto-disable syringe – consisting of a detachable needle (with a 0.5ml pre-set volume limit), a syringe barrel with a tamper resistant plunger rod, and a needle shield – is displayed with an unopened syringe package at UNICEF's central supply warehouse in Copenhagen, the capital. Auto-disable syringes are rendered inoperable after a one injection, thereby reducing the risk posed to health staff and the general public by the misuse or unsafe handling of contaminated needles and syringes during immunization activities. Some 900 distinct UNICEF supply items are stocked at the warehouse; page 109: © UNICEF/NYHQ2005-0155/Grusovin A girl drinks safe water at a tap / in the village of Islamabad in Kalmunai District, AmparaProvince. The village is among several on a 5–6 kilometre coastal stretch where 8,000 people were killed by the tsunami and thousands more were left homeless. UNICEF is providing water purification tablets and supporting the repair of pipes and the installation of safe water points and latrines in the village; page 110: © UNICEF/NYHQ2008-0130/Pirozzi Two children look at a map in a book in the library at EdithDurhamCompulsorySchool in Tirana, the capital. The school is one of the best in the country although its library, as in other schools, is inadequate. With support from IKEA, UNICEF has donated new books to the school through the 'Albania Reads' initiative; page 112: Isabella Tree/Hutchinson Library; page 114: © Robert Harding; page 116: Jean-Leo Dugast/Panos Pictures; page 118: Donna Day/Getty Images; page 119: Dermot Tatlow/Panos Pictures; page 122: Martin Woodhead; page 126: Catherine Panter-Brick; page 131: © Khamidulin/Dreamstime.com; page 132: © Irene Abdou/Alamy; page 156: Courtesy of Children 1st; page 157: Courtesy of Children 1st; page 159: © Imagestate Media Partners Limited-Impact Photos/Alamy; page 160: © The Kobal Collections; page 162: © Bubbles Photolibrary/Alamy; page 168: © Kuttig - People/Alamy; page 173: © John Callan; page 174: PhotoAlto sas/Alamy; page 177: Julio Etchart/Alamy; page 182: Scott Nelson/Getty Images; page 184: Giacomo Pirozz/Panos Pictures; page 209: Andrew Testa/Panos Pictures; page 210: Copyright © PhotoVoice; page 217: Mike Teruya/Free Spirit Photography; page 221: © UNICEF/NYHQ2001-0093/Mann Adolescent boys wearing civilian clothes walk away from the weapons they once carried as child soldiers, during a demobilization ceremony in a transit camp near the town of Rumbek, capital of the province of Lakes in southern Sudan, after being evacuated by UNICEF from a combat zone in a nearby province. They have discarded their weapons and their uniforms to symbolize the end of their military service and the beginning of their civilian lives; page 222: Miguel Villagran/Getty Images; page 224: © UNICEF/NYHQ2011-1485/Friedman-Rudovsky Children laugh, sitting in the back of a flat-bed truck in a cane field where their parents are working, near their home village of San Juan del Carmen. The truck is used to take villagers and their children to and from the fields. The children spend most of their day playing, but sometimes help their parents work. Although children in the village no longer have to work in the fields, many help their parents plant cane or clear the fields to supplement the family income; page 226: © Anatoliy Samara; page 228: © Carme Balcells/Shutterstock; page 231: PA Wire/Press Association Images.

Text

Page 34: Swain, Shurlee. 'Sweet childhood lost: idealized images of childhood in the British child rescue literature', *Journal of History of Childhood and Youth*, vol. 2, no. 2 (2009), 199–204, 206–209. © 2009 The JohnsHopkinsUniversity Press. Reprinted with permission of The Johns Hopkins University Press; page 40: Ana Teresa Ortiz, Laura Briggs, 'The culture of poverty, crack babies, and welfare cheats: the making of the "healthy white baby crisis"', in *Social Text*, vol. 21, no. 3, pp. 39–57. Copyright, Duke University Press. All rights reserved. Reprinted by permission of the publisher. www.dukeupress.edu; page 46: Khlinovskaya Rockhill, Elena, 'Social orphans and the *neblagopoluchnaia* family: the cycle of child displacement in the Russian north', from *Sibirica*, vol. 4, no. 2, 2004, Reproduced by permission of Berghahn Books Inc; page 56: *A Sheet of Paper for Bed*, 2001, BBC News, http://news.bbc.co.uk/1/hi/world/africa/1186527.stm; page 86: Adapted from 'A child's eye view', vol. 126, pp. 8–11 of *Poverty*, 2007, by Liz Sutton, CPAG, London; page 94: Adapted from Goldstein, Donna, 'Nothing bad intended: child discipline, punishment, and survival in a shantytown in Rio de Janeiro, Brazil' (1995) in Nancy Scheper-Hughes and Carolyn Sargent (eds.) *Small Wars: The Cultural Politics of Childhood*, Berkeley, University of California Press, pp. 389–395; page 98: Adapted from 'Suffering child: an embodiment of war and its aftermath in post-Sandinista Nicaragua, 1998 by James Quesada; page 138: Adapted from

Fadiman, A., *The Spirit Catches You and You Fall Down*, 1997, Farrar, Straus and Giroux, New York; page 142: de Vries, J. 'The obesity epidemic: medical and ethical considerations', in *Science and Engineering Ethics* (2007), vol. 13, no. 3, pp. 55–67, With kind permission from Springer Science +Business Media B.V; page 147: Adapted from 'Mortal ills, fated deaths', *Death Without Weeping: The Violence of Everyday Life in Brazil*, 1993, Nancy Scheper-Hughes, University of California Press; page 190: Herr, K., Anderson, G., 'Violent youth or violent schools?', *International Journal of Leadership in Education*, 2003, Routledge, Abingdon, Reprinted by permission of Routledge (Taylor & Francis Ltd, www.tandfonline.com); page 195: Adapted from Dawes, A., Hart, H., 'Political transition and youth violence' from *Years of Conflict: Adolescence, Political Violence and Displacement*, 2008, Pg 89–110, Berghahn Books Inc, United States, Reproduced by permission of Berghahn Books Inc; page 200: Reprinted by permission Harper Collins Publishers Ltd © 2007, Ishmael Beah, *A Long Way Gone: Memoirs of a Boy Soldier*. Also Farrar, Straus and Giroux, LLC; page 237: Adapted from Rachel Hinton, 'Seen but not heard: refugee children and models for intervention', pp. 199–212, in Catherine Panter-Brick, Malcolm T. Smith (eds), *Abandoned Children*, (2000); page 242: Adapted from Werner, E. E., Smith, R. S., 'Summing up', Chapter 14, pp.153–157, *Vulnerable but Invincible*, 1982, McGraw Hill, New York; page 247: Morrow, V. and Mayall, B. (2009) 'What is wrong with children's well-being in the UK? Questions of meaning and measurement', *Journal of Social Welfare and Family Law*, vol. 31, no. 3, pp. 217–229, Routledge. Reprinted by permission of the publisher (Taylor & Francis Ltd, http://www.tandfonline.com).

Index

Mali
Bozo people and concepts of health 113
malnutrition 112, 114, 129
deaths from 107, 133, 148–9, 150
effects on future development 108
inequalities 125, 126
and obesity 117, 118–19
Maputo Declaration on Child Soldiers 179
markets
and the giving of voice 276–7
Mason, J. 227
material well-being 223, 225, 248
maternal health 128
Mayhew, E. 67
Mead, G. H. 277
measles 107, 129–30
Memmi, Albert 96
mental health
cross-cultural differences in concepts of 115
and resilience 221–2
and well-being 225
military spending
by national governments 77
Millennium Development Goals (MDGs) 127–9
Mills, Martin 173–4
minority-world countries ix
age distribution of population viii
health and medicines 113, 117, 132–3
poverty in 55
children's experiences of 57, 58
relative poverty 60–4, 86–93
and resilience research 219, 220
welfare states 22–3
MMR vaccination 129–31
moral panics 266–72
and crack babies 16–17, 40–4, 269–72
defining 269
Morrow, Virginia and Mayall, Berry
'What is wrong with children's well-being in the UK?'
229, 231–2, 247–51
mortality see child and infant mortality
mothers
African Americans and crack babies 16–17, 40–4,
262–5, 266–72
health beliefs
and child mortality in Brazil 123–4, 147–51
and diarrhoeal disease 113–14, 131–4

national differences
health inequalities 124–5
obesity 145

poverty and social inequality 76–9
National Health Service (NHS) 19, 21
National Society for the Prevention of Cruelty to
Children 34
national sovereignty
and children's rights 26
Nepal
Bhutanese refugees in 209–11, 237–41
children in rural 126
NGOs (non-governmental organisations)
and interventions in children's lives 3
early childhood development programmes 5–6
Nicaragua
social inequality and poverty 78–9, 98–102
Nigeria
child mortality 122
health beliefs 113–14
Northern Ireland
poverty 60
violence
in the home 162
and young men 176–7

Oakland Growth Study
on resilience to economic hardship 212–15
obesity 117–20, 142–6
and fears about children 163
intervention measures to combat 120, 145–6
and malnutrition 117, 118–19
and social inequality 73, 145
Ofsted statistics on child violence 162
Olweus, Dan 172
oral rehydration salts (ORS) 131–4
Ortiz, Ana Teresa and Briggs, Laura
'Crack babies' 16–17, 40–4
and social research 262–5, 266–72, 273, 275, 276, 281

Pakistan
age and experiences of poverty in 82
child mortality in 122
Palestinian children
induction into violence 181–3
Panter-Brick, Catherine 221–2
Papua New Guinea
Huli people and health
concept of 111–12
and ORS treatment programmes 132–3
Parentline in Scotland 156–7
parents
and child displacement in the Russian north 24–5,
46–7, 49–51